HOW TO SQUEEZE

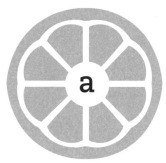

a

LEMON

HOW TO SQUEEZE

a

LEMON

1,023 KITCHEN TIPS, FOOD FIXES, and HANDY TECHNIQUES

{ EDITORS, CONTRIBUTORS & READERS OF **Fine Cooking** }

The Taunton Press

ACKNOWLEDGMENTS

Special thanks to the readers, authors, editors, copy editors, and other staff members of *Fine Cooking* who contributed to the making of this book.

Text © 2010 by The Taunton Press, Inc.
Cover photograph © Ocean Photography/Veer

The Taunton Press, Inc., 63 South Main Street, PO Box 5506, Newtown, CT 06470-5506
e-mail: tp@taunton.com

Editor: Erica Sanders-Foege
Copy editor: Valerie J. Cimino
Indexer: Heidi Blough
Cover and interior design: Laura Palese
Layout: Laura Palese

Fine Cooking® is a trademark of The Taunton Press, Inc., registered in the U.S. Patent and Trademark Office.

The following names/manufacturers appearing in *How to Squeeze a Lemon* are trademarks:
Bon Ami®, Bar Keepers Friend®, Cuisinart®, Eden Foods®, Knox®, Kraft®, Masonite®, Microplane®, Minute® Tapioca, Nutella®, Oxo®, Popsicle®, Pyrex®, Scanpan®, Silpat®, Styrofoam®. Toll House®.

Library of Congress Cataloging-in-Publication Data
How to squeeze a lemon : 1,023 kitchen tips, food fixes, and handy techniques / editors, contributors, and readers of Fine Cooking.
    p. cm.
 Includes index.
 ISBN 978-1-60085-326-5
 1. Cooking. I. Fine cooking.
 TX643.H69 2010
 641.6'4334--dc22
                          2010031141

Printed in the United States of America
10 9 8 7 6 5 4 3 2

INTRODUCTION

It's not unusual to hear the word *geek* used in the halls or around the table at *Fine Cooking:* It's a term of endearment. We like the science behind cooking—the more we know about why things work the way they do, the more we have to share with you, from why a batch of whipped cream will go from light and fluffy to grainy and unusable in seconds (see page 119 for the solution to that one) to how to actually squeeze a lemon so that it won't squirt you in the eye in the process (find the answer to that one on page 47)—the more you'll learn.

Becoming a good cook is really just a long, delicious learning process, and that's where this book comes in. It's a chance for the crack cooks in our Test Kitchen to share some "Aha!" secrets they've learned in the process of triple-testing every recipe that runs in *Fine Cooking*. We've also included dozens of handy tips, any one of which may change the way you prepare something from this moment forward. But we didn't stop there. We invited our contributors (who include cookbook authors and chefs) and some of the best cooking teachers we know to contribute too, along with our smart, savvy readers (recognize your advice in here?). All in all, there are more than 1,000 great tips and techniques in the pages that follow, each one culled from the collective wisdom of hundreds of amazing cooks.

This companion volume to *Fine Cooking's* first book of tips, the award-winning *How to Break an Egg*, begins where that handy reference left off five years ago. So it's high time for a new collection of creative shortcuts, kitchen-tested techniques, and smart substitutions. Since then, we've added 30 issues of *Fine Cooking* to our archives and created finecooking.com, a total resource for home cooks that features more than 4,000 recipes, how-to videos, and a community of passionate cooks just like you. Here's to becoming an ever-smarter, better cook.

—Laurie Buckle
Editor, *Fine Cooking*

TABLE OF
CONTENTS

1

EQUIPMENT

PANS

Play it safe with nonstick

—MARYELLEN DRISCOLL,
Fine Cooking contributor

Nonstick tops cookware sales, yet there remain concerns about its safety. Although nonstick coatings begin to break down and release potentially toxic fumes when heated above 500°F, experts confirm that cooking with nonstick is safe, provided it's used properly. To be safe:

- Don't heat nonstick cookware when it's empty.
- Don't use heat hotter than medium-high.
- Replace pans that begin to flake.

Also of concern is the toxic effect of the manufacturing process on the environment. Some manufacturers, including Cuisinart® and Scanpan®, have introduced pans made from PFOA-free technologies. (Perfluorooctanoic acid, or PFOA, is a man-made chemical identified by the Environmental Protection Agency as a likely carcinogen.) PFOA isn't used to make nonstick cookware but to make materials that are then used to create most nonstick surfaces. Even though there's no indication that people are exposed to PFOA through the use of nonstick cookware, more companies are expected to follow suit in introducing PFOA-free cookware.

How to add height to a pan

—Fine Cooking Test Kitchen

The recipe calls for a cake pan that's 3 inches deep; yours is only 2. Don't despair. You can make a paper collar to support the cake as it rises. Here's how: Cut two 16 by 6-inch strips of parchment. Fold the two strips lengthwise to get two 16 by 3-inch strips. Butter one side of each strip. Line the inside edge of the pan with the strips, nestling them into each other, with the folded edge on the top and the buttered side facing in.

Bubble wrap protects nonstick cookware

—RENEE TATE, via email

I recycle the bubble wrap that comes in parcels to use as a protective lining between my expensive nonstick pans when stacking them in drawers or cabinets. This prevents the nonstick surface from getting scratched by the bottom of other pans.

Cleaning broiler pans

—KAREN HERBST, Chicago, Illinois

After you remove cooked meat from the broiler pan, lay heavy-duty paper towels over the surface of the pan, dampen thoroughly with hot water, and let sit. When it's time for cleanup, you'll find that nearly all the cooked-on residue comes right off with the paper towels.

Ramekins rarely have their capacity inscribed on them. To measure a ramekin, fill it with water, and then pour the water into a measuring cup. You may find that few measure up to exactly a round number. For example, you may end up with ¼ to ½ inch of space left at the top once you have determined a ramekin's liquid capacity. You can use china markers to note the capacities on the bottoms of the ramekins. If your ramekin doesn't match the size called for in a recipe, you may need to adjust cooking times accordingly.

Stainless-steel saucepans can sometimes develop white, cloudy spots on the surface. These are mineral deposits left after boiling water, particularly hard tap water. Clean the pan with a little vinegar and warm water and the spots will easily wash away.

· CAST IRON 101 ·

Season it right. Cast iron is porous, so new pans need to be "seasoned" with oil to keep foods from sticking. For the initial seasoning, most manufacturers recommend coating the pan with a bit of shortening and baking for an hour or more. Here's how:

1. Heat the oven to 350°F. Meanwhile, heat your pan on the stovetop until hot. With a thick wad of paper towels, spread 1 to 2 teaspoons of lard, bacon grease, or solid vegetable shortening all over the inside and outside of the pan. Apply a very thin coating of fat—too much grease and you'll end up with a gummy residue in your pan.

2. Put the pan upside down on the center rack of the oven for 1½ hours. (Slide a baking sheet or piece of aluminum foil onto the rack beneath the pan to catch any drips.) Turn off the heat and let the pan sit in the oven until cool. The pan won't be deep black right away but will develop a dark patina with regular use.

Preserve the patina. Once the pan is seasoned, it's quite simple to maintain. Some say that washing cast iron destroys the seasoning; these folks prefer to just wipe the pan clean, using coarse salt as an abrasive for cooked-on residue. From our experience, though, that's often not enough. So in the *Fine Cooking* test kitchen, we wash our cast iron with soap and water and immediately towel it dry. Next, we set it on a burner on medium heat until the pan is hot and completely dry. While the pan is still hot, we use a paper towel to spread a thin coating of vegetable oil on the interior. With this extra attention, our cast iron stays perfectly seasoned.

—JENNIFER ARMENTROUT,
Fine Cooking contributor

What shape is best?

—MOLLY STEVENS,
Fine Cooking contributor

The most versatile Dutch ovens are round and wide with sides more straight than sloped. These give you the largest area for searing or browning, a critical first step in many braises and stews. Dutch ovens should also be at least 4 inches deep to accommodate pot roasts and other large braising cuts.

Oval pots are appealing, but when sautéing or searing on the stovetop, the ends of the oval tend to cook unevenly. The oval shape, however, is ideal for elongated pot roasts and whole poultry.

Keeping foil flat on baking sheets

—RETSU TAKAHASHI, Brooklyn, New York

I've found that lining a baking sheet with foil is easier said than done. Lay one end flat, and the other always lifts off. The sheet never sits perfectly flat and snug in the pan. I've discovered that if I lightly wet the underside of the foil, that little bit of moisture acts like glue between the foil and the pan.

A better technique for scrubbing pans

—MARYELLEN DRISCOLL,
Fine Cooking contributor

I just got a new pan and am trying to ward off any burned-on stains. In my experience, using a damp sponge to apply a cleanser like Bon Ami® or Bar Keepers Friend® doesn't work well. I've found that making a paste with the cleanser and scrubbing it on the pan with my finger is a more effective method. I think sponges absorb too much of the cleanser and don't create enough friction.

When all else fails, clean with baking soda

—MARY JANE FELGENHAUER,
Carrboro, North Carolina

After repeated soakings and scrubbings failed to clean a pan with a layer of scorched milk firmly encrusted on the bottom, I sprinkled on a layer of baking soda, added enough water to cover, and waited a couple of hours. The baking soda lifted the burnt milk, making cleanup easy. I've since tried this with other stuck-on foods, and it always works.

Preventing rust in baking pans

—MARIA OLAGUERA, Overland Park, Kansas

A source of frustration for me is finding spots of rust in my baking pans, even after carefully washing and drying them. I have found a good way to prevent this. Right after I remove baked goods from the pans, I wash the pans and dry them with a dishtowel. Then I put them in the oven, which has been turned off. The residual heat is just enough to thoroughly dry the pans and remove any moisture left behind in hard-to-reach spots. This is especially effective for muffin tins, air-insulated pans, and any baking sheets or pans with rolled edges or rims. A few minutes in the still-warm oven does the trick.

Dry out clay baker with baking soda

—ANNE TUFTS,
Agassiz, British Columbia, Canada

I use my clay baker quite often but find that when I pull it out of the cupboard it often has mold in it, because the porous clay holds moisture. I solved this problem by sprinkling the inside of the baker with baking soda before putting it away and storing it with the lid off. When I'm ready to cook, I quickly rinse it out and I'm all set to go.

KITCHEN
APPLIANCES

BLENDER

A better blender utensil: celery
—J.D. MCDONALD, Berkeley, California

➤ When making pesto, chimichurri, or other savory sauces in my blender, I was always nicking rubber spatulas while attempting to push all the herbs and other ingredients down into the blades. One day, I stumbled on the idea of using a stalk of celery, which lets me safely push everything toward the blades (when the blender is not running) without scratching my utensil.

A safer way to clean your blender
—DABNEY GOUGH, *Fine Cooking* contributor

➤ Cleaning a blender jar can be an annoying and tricky task. Taking it apart is easy, but then suddenly you have four pointy blades in your hand, and then there's the gasket, which is easy to lose.

Fortunately, there's a better and safer way. Without taking the jar apart, fill it about one-third full with warm water and add a squirt of dishwashing soap. Put the lid on, return it to its base, and turn it on for a few seconds—it'll practically clean itself. Pour out the water, sponge off any residue from the jar and lid, and rinse.

Replacement beaker for immersion blender
—ERIKA SZYMANSKI, Rochester, New York

➤ I love my immersion blender, but the beaker that came with it cracked almost immediately. I've found that 16-ounce plastic ricotta and sour cream containers make perfect substitutes. They are just the right width for the blade and tall enough to prevent splatter when mixing liquids.

Tips for the hand blender
—JOANNE BOUKNIGHT, *Fine Cooking* contributor

➤ These hand-held electronic gizmos are great for mixing mainly liquid ingredients in limited quantities. Follow these tips to make the most of yours.

- To prevent splashing, immerse the blender into the food as far as possible before turning it on, and keep it fully immersed while the blade is spinning. This is the key to avoiding major splatters.
- To minimize suction, which can pull the blender to the bottom of the container, tilt the shaft slightly while blending and use low speed whenever practical. Always keep one hand on the container of food, unless you're blending in a heavy soup pot.

- If food gets stuck between the blade and the guard, unplug the blender before attempting to clear it. A chopstick or a wooden skewer is handy for dislodging food safely.
- Don't leave a hand blender standing up in its beaker or any container, even if it looks stable, as they are top-heavy by construction.
- If you need to pause midtask, set the blender down on its side, or detach the motor and leave the shaft standing.

What a hand blender ▶ can do for you

—JOANNE BOUKNIGHT,
Fine Cooking contributor

SAUCES

Make lump-free gravy quickly, and purée fresh or canned tomatoes into sauce in seconds. Emulsified sauces like mayonnaise and vinaigrettes are a snap with a hand blender.

PURÉED SOUPS

Any vegetable or bean soup is a prime candidate for a hand blender since you can use it right in the pot (beware—a few blenders aren't intended for hot liquids).

GAZPACHO

Puréeing raw vegetables can be a challenge, but good hand blenders can handle it.

DRINKS

Smoothies, milk shakes, mixed drinks, frothed milk for cappuccino or hot chocolate—they're all easy with a hand blender.

APPLESAUCE

For ultrasmooth applesauce, the hand blender beats the food mill. The top models can even pulverize apple skin.

PESTO

Blend half the herbs with all the other ingredients except the cheese, and then blend in the other half. Stir in the cheese by hand.

PURÉED BERRIES

For a simple coulis, purée perfectly ripe raspberries with fresh lemon juice and sugar, and then strain out the seeds.

What hand blenders cannot do (well) for you

—JOANNE BOUKNIGHT,
Fine Cooking contributor

➤
- Make mashed potatoes
- Whip cream
- Mix cookie and cake batters
- Make compound butters
- Mix ground meat
- Grind nuts

CONVECTION OVEN

Tips for getting more out of convection

—Fine Cooking Test Kitchen

➤ **Follow the rule of 25.** When following a recipe written for a conventional oven, lower the temperature by about 25°F. And even with the temperature reduction, expect the food to be done about 25% faster than the recipe suggests.

Use low-sided baking pans for best air circulation.

Watch for doneness. Start checking early and often until you get used to cooking the convection way.

FOOD PROCESSOR

Hard cheese cleans your food processor

—ANA WEERTS, Brookfield, Wisconsin

➤ Whenever I shred carrots in my food processor, I'm left with an orange tinge on the plastic bowl that won't wash out easily. Pulsing a few small pieces of hard cheese like Parmesan instantly removes the orange hue. And you have freshly chopped cheese for your salad.

Minimize food processor cleanup

—MIKE WEIDERHOLD, Springfield, Virginia

➤ I love the speed and consistency of a food processor, but washing all the parts afterward can be a chore. To greatly reduce the cleanup, I stretch plastic wrap over the top of the work bowl before attaching the cover and feed tube and pressing the start button. When I'm done, the only parts that need to be washed are the bowl and blade. Of course, I do this only when I'm not adding ingredients through the feed tube.

Wash a food processor blade safely

—MARYELLEN DRISCOLL,
Fine Cooking contributor

➤ Washing a metal food processor blade by hand can be tricky. Instead of trying to hold the blade with one hand while sponging it off with the other, I wedge the handle of a wooden spoon into the cavity on the underside of the spindle and hold the spoon, keeping my fingers (at least on the hand that's not holding the sponge) a safe distance from the sharp blades.

Cleaning a food processor blade

—GEORGENE HAWKINS-KUNZ,
Fircrest, Washington

➤ Here's how to get the last sticky remnants off a food processor blade without endangering your fingers or fussing with a rubber scraper. First, empty the contents of the work bowl, but don't worry about getting everything. Reassemble the processor (with the blade) and pulse several times. The remainder of the ingredients will now be up against the side of the bowl—not on the blade—so you won't have to scrape it. Take the blade out to make it easy to scrape down the sides of the work bowl.

GRINDER

Cleaning a spice grinder

—MARYELLEN DRISCOLL,
Fine Cooking contributor

➤ I've come across all sorts of tips for cleaning spice grinders, but I prefer kosher salt. Before "cleaning" with salt, thoroughly sweep out the bowl and under the blade with a pastry or small basting brush, preferably a round one. After grinding the salt, sweep again with the brush, and then unplug the machine and swipe it with a damp cloth or sponge.

Clean an electric grinder with bread

—DAN MYERS, Franklin, Michigan

➤ In an ideal world, I'd have two grinders: one for coffee and the other for spices. But I only have one, and I always had trouble cleaning it when switching from coffee beans to dried spices and vice versa. Now, I tear half a slice of stale white bread into a few pieces and grind it up in the mill. This removes most of the spice or coffee residue and minimizes the "contamination" of whatever I grind next.

ICE CREAM MAKER

Keep it cold for best results
—MARYELLEN DRISCOLL,
Fine Cooking contributor

➤ The key to excellent homemade ice cream is to keep things cold at every step.

- Freeze the canister (or disk) overnight in the back of the freezer, where it tends to be the coldest. If you hear liquid sloshing inside the canister when you shake it, it needs more freezer time.
- Refrigerate the ice cream mixture until it's completely chilled (ideally 38°F) before freezing in the machine. The colder your mixture, the slower the canister will lose its chill and the better the ice cream will freeze.
- Don't remove the canister from the freezer until you're about to pour in the ice cream mixture.
- Unless you like your ice cream the slumping consistency of soft serve, plan on hardening it in the freezer for at least a few hours or overnight. Transfer to shallow containers for faster freezing.

Make a swirl
—DAVID LEBOVITZ,
Fine Cooking contributor

➤ To swirl an ingredient like jam or Nutella® into ice cream, let the swirling ingredient come to room temperature first. With a spoon, drop it in small dollops between layers of just-churned ice cream as you remove it from the machine. Gently drag a spatula to swirl the ingredient as best you can; to keep the swirls distinct, avoid vigorous stirring.

Ice cream sandwiches at the ready
—COREEN FRANKE, Saskatoon,
Saskatchewan, Canada

➤ My family loves ice cream sandwiches, so when I make homemade ice cream, I transfer it to zip-top freezer bags and lay them flat in the freezer. Once the ice cream freezes, I peel off the bag and use a biscuit cutter to cut out rounds of ice cream to sandwich between two cookies. You can do this with store-bought ice cream, too.

2 scoops on scooping
—MARYELLEN DRISCOLL,
Fine Cooking contributor

➤ - The more continuous and smooth the movement of the scoop, the easier it is to form an evenly shaped ball. It helps to drag the scoop around the edge of the container rather than back and forth.

- To save time and trouble when serving ice cream to a crowd, scoop it ahead and store it in the freezer on a chilled baking sheet or in individual bowls. Cover the ice cream well with plastic wrap.

**Microwave oven ➤
demystified**

—Fine Cooking Test Kitchen

HOW IT WORKS

In a microwave oven, an electronic device generates a form of electromagnetic radiation called microwaves, which are very similar to radio waves but with a shorter wavelength and higher energy. When you put food in a microwave oven, water molecules in the food absorb the microwaves and start flip-flopping around and getting hot. This hot water and steam, in turn, heat the rest of the food.

WHY IT COOKS FOOD SO FAST

A regular oven heats the air inside the oven, and this hot air gradually transfers its heat energy to the food. This type of heat transfer is a slow, inefficient process. Microwaves, on the other hand, efficiently deposit their energy directly into the food, agitating the molecules and quickly creating widespread heat within the food.

HOW MICROWAVES HEAT

Microwaves penetrate food to a depth of about $\frac{1}{2}$ inch. This outer region heats up rapidly, creating a layer of very hot food that surrounds a cool interior. Heat energy transfers from this hot outer region to the container, making it very hot. Heat also transfers to adjacent food molecules in the cooler center. But as in a regular oven, it takes time for heat from the hot exterior of the food to work its way deep into the food. In a microwave, you can speed things along by stopping and stirring the food, which distributes the heat and moves cool food out toward the walls of the container, where the microwaves can reach it when you continue the heating.

Why microwave ovens are safe

—Fine Cooking Test Kitchen

➤ • The microwaves bounce back and forth off the walls of their steel-box enclosure and remain imprisoned. (If, however, your oven is beat up and the door doesn't close tightly, you'd be wise to replace it.)

• Microwaves have a wavelength of an inch or two and simply can't fit through the holes in that perforated metal screen in the door.

• The device that generates the microwaves turns off instantly when the door opens.

Watch out for superheated liquid

—Fine Cooking Test Kitchen

➤ When heating a mug of water for tea or coffee, be careful. Even before the water appears to boil vigorously, pockets of water in the cup may actually become "superheated" (that is, hotter than water's boiling point, 212°F). Then, if you disturb the water by grabbing the cup, the water may boil explosively and scald you. To prevent this, put a fork in the cup to "defuse" any superheated water before removing the cup from the oven.

Microwave dos and don'ts

—ROBERT L. WOLKE,
Fine Cooking contributor

➤ Do use containers that are designed for use in the microwave and are labeled microwave-safe.

Do vent the lid.

Do prevent splatters by covering food with waxed paper, parchment, or white paper towels.

Don't put metal in a microwave; it will overheat and may actually spark.

Don't use plastic containers that are designed for cold storage, such as margarine tubs, yogurt containers, or water bottles.

Don't let plastic wrap touch the food that's being heated.

Don't put plastic bags from the grocery store or Styrofoam® plates in the microwave. They will melt.

4 steps to perfect waffles

—NICOLE REES, *Fine Cooking* contributor

During one period in my life, I ate a homemade Belgian waffle every day. For a while, I kept batter ready in the fridge and dutifully warmed the waffle iron every morning. Things went faster once I realized I could freeze a whole batch of waffles and toast them in the oven. Once you discover how easy it is to make waffles, I think you'll be a convert too. Here are a few tips for waffle success.

- Always let your waffle iron heat up until a few drops of water flicked on the surface sizzle.
- Grease the waffle iron between waffles by applying a light coating of nonstick cooking spray or brushing on a light coating of vegetable oil.
- Give the waffle iron a minute to heat the oil after you apply it.
- If the "ready" light or alarm on your waffle maker corresponds to a level of doneness you like, great. If not, don't be afraid to peek under the lid after a couple minutes. You can always leave the waffle in longer if it's too pale, or you can crisp it further in the oven.

The right amount of batter and a little patience

—JOANNE SMART, *Fine Cooking* contributor

- Start with about ½ cup batter for the smallest irons and ⅔ cup for bigger ones; increase as necessary to fill out waffles.
- The very first waffle is usually a throwaway, so adjust the amount of batter and the iron's settings until you get the results you like.

Skewer that waffle

—GEORGANNA ULARY, Red Hook, New York

To remove an obstinate waffle from the waffle iron, I insert two bamboo skewers horizontally through opposite sides of the waffle and gently pull them away from the iron. The waffle comes away more neatly than when I use a fork or spatula.

Alternative use for a waffle maker

—JUDY WONG, Oakland, California

Pressed sandwiches are one of my favorite things for lunch, and you don't need a panini press to make them. I fire up my waffle iron and cook the sandwiches that way. The bread comes out toasty and crisp, and the heated weight of the lid presses the sandwich to gooey perfection.

KNIVES,
CUTTING BOARDS

&

KITCHEN
TOOLS

**How to evaluate a ➤
chef's knife**

—MARYELLEN DRISCOLL,
Fine Cooking contributor

A chef's knife should feel comfortable when you hold it, like a natural extension of your hand. It should inspire confidence, not instill fear. If it feels wrong, move on. If it feels pretty good, start chopping (or mock chopping), noting how you respond to the knife's physical characteristics.

WEIGHT

You'll need to try several knives to find your ideal knife weight. One school of thought is that a hefty chef's knife cuts through foods more easily because it "falls" with more force. Another is that a lighter chef's knife flows more freely and lets you maneuver the knife more skillfully. Bottom line: Choose the style that feels right to you.

BALANCE

"Perfect balance" is in the palm of the beholder. Judge balance by gripping the knife by its handle. If it feels uncomfortably weighted toward the back of the handle or toward the blade, then it probably isn't for you. An unbalanced knife will make you work harder. Side-to-side balance is also important. When you come down on the blade, the knife shouldn't feel unstable, like it wants to teeter toward one side or the other.

SIZE

An 8-inch chef's knife is the most popular among home cooks because of its versatility. A 10-inch knife's longer blade can cut more volume but may feel intimidating. A 6-inch knife can offer an element of agility, like that of a paring knife, but falls short when working with volume or when slicing through something large, like a watermelon.

**The anatomy of a ➤
chef's knife**

—MARYELLEN DRISCOLL,
Fine Cooking contributor

THE HANDLE

A good handle is one that feels comfortable and secure to you. You shouldn't have to strain to hold onto it, and it shouldn't feel slippery when wet. There should be enough clearance on its underside that you don't bang your knuckles as you chop (the height of the blade affects this).

Some knives' handles have molds or indentations to facilitate grip. These work for some people. For others they force an unnatural grip and make the knife hard to hold at awkward angles, such as when butterflying a chicken breast or carving a melon.

THE BOLSTER

Also called the collar, shoulder, or shank, the bolster is the thick portion of metal where the blade and handle meet. The bolster can add strength and stability to a knife as well as act as a finger guard for your gripping hand. Some forged knives have only partial bolsters, which don't extend all the way to the blade's heel, and some knives, especially Japanese-style knives, have no bolster at all. An advantage to partial- or no-bolster knives is that you can sharpen the full length of the blade, right through the heel. As you hold a knife, notice the slope from the bolster to the blade. It may be pronounced or gradual, but neither style should make you feel like you have to tighten your grip.

THE HEEL

Unless it's a Japanese-style forged knife, the heel is the broadest and thickest part of the edge, with the greatest heft. It's meant for tasks that require force, such as chopping through poultry tendons or the hard rind of a winter squash. Watch out for knives that "thunk" at the heel when rocked. The heel shouldn't abruptly stop the rocking motion. Nor should it be so curved that the blade wants to kick backward.

THE SPINE

This is the top portion of the blade, and it typically has squared edges. Note whether the edges feel polished or sharp and rough, which can potentially irritate your gripping hand. The spine should also taper at the tip; a thick tip will be hard to work with.

THE EDGE

A good chef's knife should be sharp right out of the box. To evaluate sharpness, try slicing through a sheet of paper. A really sharp knife will make a clean, swift cut. (Of course, if you have the opportunity, chop some food, too.) Also note the line of the blade. A gentle curve from the tip to the heel can help the knife smoothly rock back and forth during chopping and mincing.

Many professional chefs hone or "steel" their knives before every cooking session. In an ideal world, you would do the same. In reality, though, steeling daily or even weekly can help. So hone whenever it crosses your mind—even the casual use of a steel will extend the life of an edge.

When to sharpen Actually sharpening the knife is another story. How often to sharpen depends on how you care for and use your knives. If you cook a lot, steel less often than you should, and really enjoy a sharp knife, you will probably need to sharpen two or three times a year. You'll know it's time to sharpen when honing doesn't restore the edge as it once did. Keep in mind that while you can hone as often as you'd like, you shouldn't sharpen too often. Eventually, sharpening begins to wear away the blade. As you remove metal, you move up the blade toward the spine, and the blade becomes thicker, making it more difficult to get a good edge.

A steel is not a sharpener. Knife experts may debate the technicalities of sharpening, but there's accord on one point: Regular maintenance of the edge can slow down, though not prevent, dulling. The tool that professionals and home cooks alike use to maintain the edges of their knives is often confusingly referred to as a "sharpening steel." But true sharpening removes metal from the blade to re-create that fine, thin edge. A sharpening steel doesn't technically sharpen; rather, it hones, straightening microscopic serrations along the cutting edge of the blade. Most steels won't remove much, if any, metal.

The surface of a steel may be smooth, finely grooved, or covered with superfine diamond abrasive, but regardless of the finish, steels are meant to do one thing—hone. A steel can also help straighten microscopic curls in the cutting edge, provided they are not too severe. If you have a good sharp knife, steeling it once or twice a week will extend the length of time you can use it. If it is already dull, don't expect a steel to sharpen it.

The unglazed bottom rim of a ceramic or porcelain mug is an ideal surface for honing the edge of your kitchen knives. Use it as you would a knife-honing steel. Hold the knife perpendicular to the rim's surface and then re-angle the blade so it's at a 45-degree angle (half of the previous 90-degree angle). Re-angle it again to half of the 45-degree angle, and start sharpening.

Protect knives with potholders

—PATTY ROWLES,
Pawleys Island, South Carolina

▶ I don't have a knife block in my kitchen, so I use pot-handle holders to protect my knives in the drawer.

- -

Knife care 101

—ADAM RIED, *Fine Cooking* contributor

▶ When it comes to knife use, care, and storage, a modicum of TLC can help prevent damage and preserve sharpness.

- Avoid outright abuse such as hacking through bones or frozen foods.
- Choose a relatively soft cutting board, like wood—preferably end-grain butcher block—or polyethylene plastic.
- Store knives on a magnetic strip or in a block. Avoid knocking the cutting edge against other surfaces.
- Use a bench scraper, not your knife, to scoop up chopped foods from the cutting board.
- Wash knives by hand.

- -

Chopping sticky stuff

—Fine Cooking Test Kitchen

▶ Crystallized ginger and dried fruit such as apricots and figs can be frustrating to chop—as soon as you cut into these sticky-on-the-inside ingredients, they tend to mass together and cling to your knife like glue. Here are a few tips to make the chopping go more smoothly.

Make your knife nonstick. Coat the knife with a light film of vegetable oil or cooking spray.

Chop only small amounts at a time. Things will be less likely to clump together.

Dice rather than chop. Cut the ingredient lengthwise into thin strips, and then cut across the strips into fine dice—you'll get less clumping and sticking than if you chop willy-nilly.

- -

Store electric knife blades in paper towel tubes

—DEBORAH TARENTINO,
Pittsburgh, Pennsylvania

▶ I've hit upon a way to store the blades of my electric knife that keeps them sharp and protects my hands from being cut. I flatten paper towel tubes and store each blade in its own tube. You can even label the outside of the tube with the length and type of blade.

3 tips for picking a cutting board

—LINDA J. HARRIS, PH.D.,
Fine Cooking contributor

➤ When purchasing a cutting board, look for features that will help you use it safely.

Size: The board should be small enough to fit comfortably into your sink or dishwasher.

Color: Having different-colored boards for different tasks can help you avoid cross-contamination.

Channel: A groove around the edge of a board prevents meat juices from spilling onto your countertop.

Plastic vs. wood vs. bacteria

—LINDA J. HARRIS, PH.D.,
Fine Cooking contributor

➤ **Plastic cutting boards** don't absorb moisture, so it's relatively easy to remove surface bacteria from a new, smooth board. But when a board becomes knife-scarred, bacteria can get trapped in the crevices, and it's very difficult to scrub them out. Trapped bacteria can survive for a long time in a dormant state, so when knife cuts become numerous or deep, plastic boards should be replaced or relegated to nonfood use.

Wooden cutting boards need more TLC to maintain than plastic ones. Without regular oiling with food-grade mineral oil, the wood tends to dry out and crack. Frequent exposure to water during cleaning and sanitizing can speed this process, especially if the board isn't properly oiled. All wood is porous, some types more than others. As a result, liquids can soak into the surface, bringing with them any bacteria that happen to be present. For new or well-maintained boards, these bacteria don't seem to pose much risk, as they're likely to remain trapped beneath the surface or die a few hours after the board dries.

Boards that are cracked or knife-scarred are hard to clean. If you don't want to replace an older wooden board after it becomes scarred, you may be able to sand it smooth, reapply oil, and give it a fresh start.

Antimicrobial cutting boards: are they for real?

—LINDA J. HARRIS, PH.D.,
Fine Cooking contributor

In the past few years, hundreds of "antimicrobial" products have come on the market, including antimicrobial cutting boards. From a food safety standpoint, they don't seem to offer any advantage. Bacteria-inhibiting chemicals that are embedded in the boards are considered effective only against slime- and odor-causing organisms, not disease-causing microbes, so these boards need to be cleaned and sanitized just like any other board.

Keep your cutting boards clear of contamination

—Fine Cooking Test Kitchen

Follow these tips to keep your boards clean and free of bacteria.

Separate boards for separate tasks. An easy way to reduce cross-contamination is to have boards for different tasks. You need at least two: one reserved for raw meats, fish, and poultry; another for raw vegetables and fruits and foods that won't be cooked. Cutting boards can be identified by material, color, shape, or design.

Keep them clean. All boards should be cleaned immediately after use. Hot soapy water, elbow grease, and a good rinse under flowing water will remove most bacteria from a board that's in good shape. Most boards, including some wooden ones (check the label), can be cleaned and sanitized in the dishwasher.

Sanitize the surface. After cleaning, sanitize the board with a mild bleach solution (1 teaspoon unscented bleach in 1 quart water) or undiluted white vinegar. Flood the board with the liquid, leave for 5 minutes, rinse with running water, and let it air dry. If you use a board for raw meats and poultry, you might want to sanitize after every use. For boards used exclusively for breads, cooked meats, and cheese, frequent sanitizing isn't necessary, but they still need to be kept clean.

Let it air dry. After cleaning or sanitizing, let the board air dry, or dry it with a clean paper towel or fresh dishtowel. If the dishtowel has been used for other purposes, there's a chance you could contaminate the board again.

Hold the cutting board in place
—JAMES KNODELL, Seattle, Washington

I keep a large maple cutting board on my stone countertop all the time. To prevent the board from sliding around on the smooth surface, I position four inexpensive rubber hose washers (which you can buy at most hardware stores) under the board near the corners. The rubber prevents any movement and keeps the board solidly in place. This works for plastic cutting boards, too.

A silicone mat keeps cutting boards stable
—FELICIA CASOLARY, Sammamish, Washington

I've found another use for my silicone baking mat. I place it under a cutting board before I start chopping. It creates a perfect nonslip surface that keeps my cutting board in place.

Keep cutting boards within reach
—AIMEE HOLCOMB, via email

I've always leaned my cutting boards against the wall, but they had a tendency to slide whenever I picked one up. At a yard sale, I found a letter sorter for 10 cents (you can also find inexpensive ones at office-supply stores). Each cutting board fits perfectly in a slot, and it is no longer a struggle to grab one without creating an avalanche.

Getting the smell of onion or garlic off your board
—TED GRAVENHORST JR., *Fine Cooking* contributor

Lemon or lime juice and a little salt will go a long way toward reducing odor. First, sprinkle your cutting board with either kosher or table salt. Cut a lemon or lime into quarters and use these quarters to rub the salt into the board, squeezing juice onto the board as you go. Let the board sit for 2 to 3 minutes, and then wipe it clean with a damp cloth. That should do the trick.

Power tool gives new life to wooden cutting boards
—CAROLE BEAUCHAMP, Durham, North Carolina

Despite all the new cutting board materials available, I still love using my wooden boards. To keep them smooth and to repair scratches from my knives, I periodically go over them with an electric sander until they are smooth again. I then coat them with mineral oil to keep them from drying out. This simple process has extended the life of my beautiful boards.

Mandoline tricks and tips

—Fine Cooking Test Kitchen

▶ Getting the hang of using a mandoline takes some practice, but these suggestions will give you a good head start.

- Set the mandoline lengthwise in front of you so that you're pushing forward, not sideways.
- Use a sweeping motion from the top to the bottom of the "runway."
- Keep the pressure constant. Don't bear down or let up midway as the food hits the blade.
- For blades that are oriented to hit the food straight on (like Oxo®'s) rather than on an angle, use a gentle back-and-forth sawing motion to slice high-moisture foods that are apt to squish, compress, or collapse under pressure, such as tomatoes, citrus, kiwi, eggplant, and bell peppers.
- For thin or thick julienne, the less mass that has to pass through the blades, the less wedged in (and stuck) the food is likely to get. For example, choose small to medium potatoes for french fries.
- Very dense vegetables, such as winter squash and sweet potatoes, can be difficult to slice, especially into julienne or french-fry cuts. Use your chef's knife on these vegetables instead.
- Lightly grease the runway with cooking spray if it feels sticky.
- For rounded fruits or vegetables, such as potatoes, oranges, or beets, use a knife to cut off a portion to make a flat edge or, if necessary, cut them in half and then slice them cut side down.

6 things to do with a mini torch

—Fine Cooking Test Kitchen

➤ The best-known culinary use for this flame-throwing tool is creating the crunchy caramelized sugar topping on crème brûlée, but we use it for lots more. Mini torches come in petite versions with short nozzles, but we prefer the slightly larger versions, which hold more butane and have longer nozzles that give you more control over the intensity of the flame.

Char the skin of bell peppers or chiles before peeling.

Melt shredded cheese on soups, toasts, or gratins.

Brown meringue.

Toast marshmallows.

Warm up dull chocolate ganache on a cake or tart so it looks shiny.

Light candles or start a charcoal fire.

THERMOMETER

Getting the best results from probe thermometers

—MOLLY STEVENS,
Fine Cooking contributor

➤ • Many probe thermometers come with preset target temperatures for meat. I caution against blindly following these because they're based on conservative USDA recommendations and are not in accordance with many people's tastes. Instead, consult a reliable cookbook for a more realistic listing of meat doneness temperatures.

• When cooking large cuts of meat, set the temperature for 10°F lower than your actual target. When the alarm sounds, try to probe in a few different spots to ensure that you haven't inserted it too near a bone or in a fatty spot. Either of these may throw off the reading.

• Always use a towel or potholder when adjusting the probe. The metal gets extremely hot.

Binder clip holds thermometer in place
—LAURA CONGER, Woodside, California

I love my probe-style digital thermometer but found it would fall into or out of the pot when I was making candy. Now I attach a medium-size metal binder clip onto the side of the pot and slide the probe through the handles. It keeps the probe in the pot but lets it move slightly to allow for stirring.

Calibrate your instant-read thermometer
—Fine Cooking Test Kitchen

An instant-read thermometer is a must-have tool for checking temperatures and gauging the doneness of all sorts of things. Because you rely on your thermometer for accuracy, it's a good idea to check its calibration occasionally and adjust it as necessary.

To check the calibration, bring a small pan of water to a rolling boil and take the water's temperature; it should be 212°F or a few degrees less, depending on your altitude and air pressure. (For the boiling point in your location, visit www.virtualweberbullet.com/boilingpoint.html.)

If the calibration is off, you can adjust a standard (analog) thermometer by turning the hex nut under the thermometer's face with pliers. If the nut resists, use a second set of pliers to grip the sides of the face and turn the pieces in opposite directions. There are only a few models of digital thermometers that can be adjusted. Some calibrate automatically, and others need manual adjustment; follow the manufacturer's instructions for your model.

Keep your instant-read thermometers handy
—NOELLE BOHNENKAMP, Broomfield, Colorado

Whenever I needed a meat thermometer, I used to have to fish around in my utensil drawer to find one. Now, I keep all my instant-read thermometers handy and organized in the hole of my spool of kitchen twine. Not only are they quickly accessible, but I can also make efficient use of the space the roll takes up.

YOU USE THAT TO DO WHAT?

BAKING SHEETS & MUFFIN PANS

Baking sheets go beyond cookies
—DEBI KARAVITES, via email

I keep several heavy-duty rimmed baking sheets in my kitchen and use them for much more than just baking. When I'm defrosting meat, I put the package on a baking sheet to catch any drips. I also use one to hold a cutting board when I'm cutting up chicken or meat; the rimmed sheet catches any juices. Lined with foil, they make roomy trays to transport meat and vegetables to the grill, and they can even serve as platters.

A baking sheet is handy for dredging
—KAREN BRACK, Garland, Texas

When I dredge food for sautéing or frying, I set a bowl of egg wash in the center of a rimmed baking sheet. Then I scoop the flour and bread-crumbs directly onto the baking sheet on either side of the bowl. This leaves me with a clean counter and fewer dishes to wash.

A sheet pan creates countertop space
—ALESSIA BEWSHER, New York, New York

I live in an apartment with no countertop next to the stove, which can be inconvenient. But I've solved the problem: I set an inverted half sheet pan over two burners, reaching front to back, upon which I can place whatever I need to have right nearby. Of course, this only works when I'm using one or two burners at a time.

Alternative use for muffin pans
—LEIGH ABERNATHY, Tumbling Shoals, Arkansas

Silicone muffins pans are a fantastic tool for freezing small amounts of sauce, stock, or pesto. Popping the frozen puck out of the flexible pan is a breeze and far easier than removing it from a traditional metal muffin tin or even an ice cube tray.

COLANDERS

Use a colander to collect waste in the sink
—ALISON MCCORMICK, via email

To save time taking things to the trash can when prepping my ingredients, I put a small colander in the sink and use it as a trash bowl to dispose of peels, eggshells, and other waste. Liquids drip through, but the solids stay put and don't clog the drain (this is especially useful if you don't have a garbage disposal). When I'm done with my prep, it's easy to dump the contents of the colander into the trash.

A gold mesh coffee filter works overtime

—TONYA RUBIANO, Westfield, New Jersey

My kitchen is very small, so I try to get the most out of every kitchen tool I have. I recently discovered that my reusable gold mesh coffee filter can do double duty as a strainer: After steaming clams, I wanted to reserve the broth but saw sand in the bottom of the pot. The coffee filter happened to be within reach, so I used it to strain the broth. Now I also use the filter for straining small quantities of sauce and gravy.

In-a-pinch colander

—R. B. HIMES, Vienna, Ohio

I once found myself in a friend's kitchen without a colander, so I made one on the spot. I rinsed an empty milk carton and opened the top. Then I took a sharp paring knife and cut a few vertical slits on all four sides. Using the tip of the knife, I made a bunch of small holes in the bottom. I ended up with a very serviceable drainer.

COOKBOOKS, MAGAZINES & RECIPE CARDS

Pyrex® pan is see-through protection for cookbooks

—G. JASKIEWICZ, Stoney Creek, Ontario, Canada

I have a thick muffin cookbook that refuses to stay open at the selected page. Searching for something to hold down the pages, I took out my large Pyrex baking dish. It's perfect, as it keeps the book open and protects the pages, yet I can easily read through it.

Protect your magazine while cooking

—AMY BARUCH, Boise, Idaho

When I'm baking from a *Fine Cooking* recipe, I don't want my magazine to get covered with flour and splashes of batter. So I open the issue to the page I need, fold the magazine, and insert it into a clear gallon-size zip-top bag. The magazine fits perfectly, and it stays nice and clean.

Trouser hangers hold food magazines

—DANN HOXSEY, Toronto, Ontario, Canada

I'm an avid *Fine Cooking* reader, and I cook from it quite often. But I sometimes find it difficult to hold the magazine open at the page I need while I'm juggling hot pans and kitchen appliances. Besides, it takes up precious counter space. So I use a trouser hanger to clip the magazine open, and then I hang it on a cabinet knob or utensil rack in the kitchen.

Skewer and clothespin hold recipe in view
—MARGIE KELLAND, St. John's, Newfoundland, Canada

When I'm following a recipe, I like to have the card or piece of paper in my line of sight yet out of the way of splatters and spills. I've found a way to do this using a skewer and a clothespin or plastic spring clip. I run the skewer through the spring of the clothespin and rest the skewer, with the clothespin in the center, on two adjacent upper cabinet handles. I then clip my recipe so that it's suspended at eye level.

JARS

A new use for old spice jars
—MARIA OLAGUERA, Overland Park, Kansas

I don't throw away old spice jars anymore. Instead, after washing and drying them thoroughly, I fill them with assorted dry ingredients for sprinkling. I have one with flour for dusting surfaces when I'm baking (the holes in the cover release just the right amount of flour) and another with confectioners' sugar for garnishing cakes. I also have one filled with cinnamon sugar for my morning coffee.

Shake up a vinaigrette in a sippy cup
—SHELDON PRESSMAN, via email

Now that our kids have outgrown spillproof sippy cups, I've discovered that they're perfect for making small batches of vinaigrette or other emulsions. Just dump in the ingredients, screw on the top, and shake.

Blend a slurry in a cocktail shaker
—JESSICA BUKER-VINCENT, Windham, Maine

When I need a quick thickener for sauce or gravy, I make a slurry by putting flour and water in a regular cocktail shaker and giving it a few good shakes. This produces a much smoother mixture than I've ever been able to make by stirring. And the shaker has a built-in strainer, which keeps any lingering lumps of starch from getting into the sauce.

ALL THE REST

Plastic ruler stands in for bench scraper
—ANGELA M. LYONS, Metuchen, New Jersey

▶ I don't have a bench scraper, but I've discovered that a plastic ruler is a perfectly good substitute when it's time to clean up doughy, floury countertops. The ruler scrapes up the flour and sticky bits of dough on the work surface, and it is easily wiped clean with soap and water.

Substitute bread peel
—DENISE RUNDE, Madison, Wisconsin

▶ The other day I had bread that needed to go in the oven, but I couldn't remember where I had stored my bread peel. I had a clipboard made of Masonite® hardboard handy and found that it filled in wonderfully. It takes a dusting of flour, and it easily slipped beneath the dough. Best of all, the clipboard is easy to clean.

At last, a tool for removing sticky fruit labels
—CHARLOTTE KORNHAUSER, Clark, New Jersey

▶ For years, I tried to find an easy way to remove those little produce stickers from tomatoes, stone fruit, apples, and pears without tearing the fruits' skin. When I recently bought a serrated peeler, I discovered that I could use it to lift the edge of the label away from the fruit and peel it off without taking a chunk of fruit with it.

Peelers aren't just for peeling
—JENNIFER ARMENTROUT, *Fine Cooking* contributor

▶ In the test kitchen, we don't just use peelers for trimming vegetables; we also shave and thinly slice foods like hard cheeses, summer squashes, small potatoes, and chocolate.

To make shaved fennel, trim and cut a fennel bulb into quarters. Remove most of the core, and then run your peeler down one of the cut sides. Keep shaving until you can no longer safely hold the piece of fennel.

For chocolate shavings, run the peeler over the edge of a block of chocolate.

For larger shavings and curls, warm the chocolate a bit, either by rubbing it with the palm of your hand or by microwaving it very briefly, about 5 seconds at a time. The warmer the chocolate, the larger the curls will be. To make it easier to grip and to keep your hand clean, you can hold the chocolate block with a paper towel.

A potato ricer juices pomegranates

—NIKKI GRAVELLE, Merville, British Columbia, Canada

When I had guests over for the holidays, we discovered an ingenious way to juice pomegranates: We used a potato ricer. The juice came right out, leaving the pith and seeds behind.

A potato masher breaks up ground meat easily

—REBECCA MORGAN, Pasadena, California

When browning ground meat or sausage out of its casings, I use a potato masher to break up the larger pieces as soon as they start to brown and firm up a little. It's much quicker than using a wooden spoon or spatula, and I get more even results.

Make anchovy paste in a garlic press

—LOUISE E. OATES, Salinas, California

I've discovered that anchovy paste is easy to make at home. I just put a few whole anchovies in my garlic press and out comes anchovy paste, which can be mixed with a little extra-virgin olive oil for a smooth consistency.

Makeshift muddler

—CAITLYN SASSAMAN, via email

My wooden honey swizzler turns out to be the perfect substitute for a muddler, and now it gets much more use as a muddler than as a swizzler.

Versatile chopsticks

—PHILIP MAY, Chicago, Illinois

I like to keep some chopsticks on hand in my kitchen because they're so useful. It's best to save the wooden chopsticks you get from Chinese take-out restaurants rather than using nice lacquered ones.

- Slide one or two under the lid of a pot when you want it partially covered.
- Slide a couple under a hot pot in place of a trivet to protect your table or countertop.
- Lay two chopsticks across the top of a pot of boiling pasta water while the pasta cooks. Set your serving bowl on top of the chopsticks for a few minutes to warm it.

Grapefruit knife carves bread easily

—TINA PETOK, Davidson, North Carolina

I used to have a hard time cutting neat lids out of loaves of bread to create bread bowls for soups and dips. Because a grapefruit knife is serrated on both sides, it quickly cuts through the top of a loaf and gives me a perfect lid every time.

Multiple uses for a fish poacher

—BARBARA MATHERS-NASH,
Needham, Massachusetts

➤ I use my fish poacher for cooking many foods other than fish. Because the pan is long and roomy, it's perfect for boiling lasagna noodles and corncobs and for steaming long vegetables such as asparagus.

- -

A cool way to use cast-iron pots in summer

—REBECCA PETERSON, Atlanta, Georgia

➤ I have a large collection of beautiful enameled cast-iron pots that I hate to put away in the summer, even though I rarely make soups or braises in hot weather. Now I've found another use for them. Cast iron retains cold as well as it does heat, so a chilled cast-iron pot turns out to be a great way to keep summer dishes cool. My homemade ice cream easily travels across town when stored and served from one of my smaller enameled cast-iron pans, and I've used the larger ones for salads and cold fruit soups. They also work well for backyard picnics. Just chill the pot in the fridge for several hours before filling.

- -

A hair dryer dries food quickly

—RICK MORRISON, Bloomfield Hills, Michigan

➤ I always keep a small travel hair dryer in a kitchen cabinet. I use it to dry a variety of foods, such as water-soaked potatoes for french fries before they go in the hot oil. It's quick and saves a lot of paper towels. Make sure to use it on the cool setting.

- -

Hot packs keep picnic items warm

—VALARIE PELISSERO, Portland, Oregon

➤ I went to a potluck last summer and needed to keep corn on the cob hot until dinnertime. I heated a hot pack in the microwave (make sure yours is the microwavable kind) and put it in the bottom of a small insulated cooler. Then I wrapped each cob of corn in aluminum foil, piled them on the hot pack, and set a platter on top. It was more than 2 hours before we ate, and the corn was still hot. This idea would also work with casserole dishes right from the oven. Wrapping the dish in foil offers an extra layer of insulation.

- -

Keep buns warm with heated rice

—BARBARA MILLINGTON,
Palatine Bridge, New York

➤ I have a neat trick for keeping fresh-from-the-oven muffins or rolls warm at the table for a long while. Put a couple of cups of uncooked rice in a fabric sack (you can use a clean cotton tube sock, a kitchen towel, or cheesecloth made into a little satchel, or sew a "beanbag" of rice together just for this purpose). Heat the satchel of rice in the microwave until it's warm to the touch, about 2 minutes. Then hide the satchel between two cloth napkins in a serving basket and put the rolls or muffins on top. The rice stays warm for about a half hour.

Medicine dropper for exact extract
—ROXANNE WINSTON, Eugene, Oregon

Pure vanilla extract has gotten quite pricey, and, unfortunately, when I pour it out of the bottle, I invariably lose several precious drops as they trickle down the side of the bottle. To prevent this, I bought a medicine dropper from the drugstore for less than a dollar. I use it to measure out my precious extract.

Toothpaste "squeezer" works for tomato paste
—SARAH SELIS, San Diego, California

When taking advantage of the convenience of tubed tomato paste (or anchovy paste), I use a toothpaste "squeezer." This makes the job of squeezing the tube easier, and it ensures that every last bit of paste is used. I prefer the kind that you slide along the tube rather than the kind that rolls up with the tube.

Use shower caps as plastic wrap
—D. HOLZINGER, Maple Grove, Minnesota

I always bring home one of those complimentary plastic shower caps when I stay in a hotel. They're perfect for covering bowls of food. They're easier than regular plastic wrap, and they're reusable.

A paper coffee filter serves as an herb sachet
—GARY KRAUSE, via email

When making stocks or soups, many recipes call for an herb sachet, traditionally made with cheesecloth. But I never seem to have cheesecloth around when I need it, so I use a paper coffee filter instead. I put the herbs and aromatics inside the coffee filter, tie the top with twine, and add it to the liquid at the required time.

Use a straw to fill kitchen sink soap dispenser
—ROSEMARY WEBER, Dunlap, Illinois

I love the soap dispenser that is a part of my new kitchen sink. However, adding liquid soap can be a challenge, as the soap bubbles up and makes a mess. Now I put a flexible plastic drinking straw into the opening and then add the liquid soap. The air escapes through the straw, so the soap doesn't bubble up. Just be sure to bend the straw first, or it will fall all the way into the dispenser.

Make an herb sachet ►

—KIMBERLY PORTER, via email

When I need to make a sachet to hold herbs for flavoring soups or broths but have no cheesecloth, I put my herbs in a large tea ball. The small chain attached to the tea ball allows me to lower the herbs into the simmering pot and to pull out the ball easily when I'm done cooking.

Use a cereal box liner bag as waxed paper . . . ►

—SO ARONSON, Montreal, Quebec, Canada

I always save the bags lining the inside of cereal boxes and use them instead of waxed paper. I cut along the side and bottom of the bag to straighten it out and use the sheet to wrap cheese or other leftover foods. In a pinch, it's a great substitute. Don't use them to line cake pans, though, as the plastic might melt.

. . . or when pounding meat ►

—BETH HAINES, Guelf, Ontario, Canada

I save the empty liner bags of cereal boxes and use them instead of plastic wrap when pounding meat. I cut off the bottom and along one side of the bag to obtain a flat, rectangular sheet and lay it on top of the meat. It saves plastic wrap and works just as well.

Reach in all nooks with a toothbrush ►

—LAURA B. FIFE, Bend, Oregon

I use a toothbrush to clean in small places where a sponge won't fit, like the wheels of a can opener or the base of a blender. A regular toothbrush works fine, but I like to use an electric toothbrush with a round tip. (I keep the tip in a kitchen drawer so I don't mistake it for my real toothbrush.)

Olive oil dispenser doubles as dish soap container ►

—NANCY GOLD, Lexington, Massachusetts

I fill a glass olive oil dispenser with blue or orange dishwashing liquid (yellow soap could be mistaken for olive oil). Because the dispenser's spout is designed to provide good control over the amount of liquid being poured, you never use more soap than you need to. Plus the glass dispenser looks much nicer than the soap's original plastic container.

A clear bowl lets you see the water when double-boiling ►

—TIZI YOUNG, San Francisco, California

When I set up a double boiler, I use a heatproof clear bowl (such as Pyrex) so that I can monitor the simmering through the glass and make sure there's always enough water in the pot.

PRODUCE

FRUIT

Keep cut-up apples from browning

**—GINGER FULTON BENNETT,
Santa Cruz, California**

➤ When I'm prepping a salad ahead of time that includes fresh apples, pears, or avocados, I toss the cut fruit with a little of the salad's dressing (which I also make ahead), using just enough to prevent the fruit from browning. It beats drizzling with lemon juice, which prevents browning but can lend a harsh flavor to the fruit. If the salad dressing is apt to stain the fruit, I use a little bit of nut oil with Champagne vinegar for the same result.

· NOT EVERY APPLE BELONGS IN A PIE ·

It's hard to think of another fruit that's available in more varieties than apples. With all those choices, picking one for a pie or other apple dessert can be tricky, because each variety behaves a little differently when cooked. To cut down on the guesswork, contributing editor Pam Anderson has classified some of the most common varieties into these three helpful categories. For pies, Pam recommends mainly using apples that hold their shape, along with a few apples that soften to tie everything together. If you're considering a variety that isn't listed, test its flavor and texture yourself by sautéing a few slices in butter.

Apples that hold their shape

Rome Softens but holds its shape nicely. Quite juicy, with a complex sweet-tart flavor.

Golden Delicious Holds its shape fairly well but gets a bit mushy. Very juicy but flavor lacks complexity.

Granny Smith Holds its shape fairly well. Flavor is not as appley as others but is fine when teamed with a softer, perfumey apple.

Braeburn Great texture—soft but still holds its shape. Flavor is on the sweet side.

Apples that soften

Empire Fairly juicy, tart, and perfumey.

Cortland Good complex flavor with well-rounded sweetness.

McIntosh Practically purées itself when cooked. Sweet with a pretty pink hue. Great in applesauce and preserves.

Macoun Not very juicy. Nice pink color and great flavor.

Apples to avoid in cooking

Red Delicious Flavorless when cooked. Save this one for the lunch box.

Fuji When cooked, flavor is flat and texture is like reconstituted dried apple.

—Fine Cooking Test Kitchen

AVOCADOS

Keep halved avocados green
—JANET C. DECARTERET, Bellevue, Washington

To keep cut avocados from turning brown when you want to store them, refrigerate them flesh side down in a bowl of water into which you have squeezed a little bit of lemon juice. The avocados will keep beautifully for a few days this way. The same method can also be used when preparing slices of avocado ahead of time for salads or garnishes.

Mash avocado in a quick and easy way
—ANTOINNE VON RIMES, Santa Barbara, California

For a quick and easy way to make a sublime guacamole, mash the avocado by putting the flesh through a potato ricer. The ricer gives the avocado a uniform consistency that is unequaled by any other mashing method. Be sure to mix in a few drops of lemon juice to prevent the avocado from browning.

Make guacamole with a whisk
—HELEN M. SCHWIND, Glastonbury, Connecticut

I love guacamole, and, after 30 years of experimenting with different tools and techniques, I've come to the conclusion that a wire whisk is a much better tool than a fork or a mortar and pestle, particularly when I am making a big batch. With a whisk, I can mash the avocado to a perfect consistency (leaving some small, toothsome chunks) and then stir in all the other ingredients.

BANANAS

Mash bananas in the peel
—EVA REED, Castine, Maine

When making banana bread or any other recipe calling for mashed bananas, I've found a way to save a bowl. I keep the fruit in the peel and smack the banana against the counter a couple of times. Then I roll it back and forth on a flat surface, pressing down until the skin splits. Finally, I open the peel where it split, and inside is a mashed banana ready to be mixed with the other ingredients.

Wash those berries ➤
—Fine Cooking Test Kitchen

Always wash fresh berries, even if you picked them yourself. Like any other produce, berries can pick up bacteria or other contaminants from water, soil, and handling; washing helps reduce these risks. Keep your berries cold and dry until shortly before you're ready to use them, and then wash them in a colander under a gentle spray of cool water. Shake lightly to remove excess water, and then spread the berries on paper towels to air dry until you need them.

Store summer fruits ➤
—CONNIE LOTHKAR, Olney, Maryland

I love cooking in the summertime when fresh berries and cherries are at their peak. To keep the fruit fresh between trips to the market, I put an ice pack in the bottom of a large stainless-steel bowl and set a colander of fruit on top; then I leave the setup on the counter. The air around the fruit stays cool and keeps the fruit fresh longer than when it is kept in the humid refrigerator. Of course, I check the ice pack often and replace it when necessary.

Seek out big blueberries ➤
—Fine Cooking Test Kitchen

When shopping for cultivated blueberries, look for the fattest berries you can find; they should be grayish purple and covered with a silvery bloom. Don't bother sniffing: Unlike many other fruits, ripe blueberries aren't very fragrant.

White is sweeter than red with cranberries ➤
—Fine Cooking Test Kitchen

Before using cranberries, pick them over for stems and shriveled berries. Any stray white cranberries are fine to leave in; they're sweeter than red ones.

Get perfect strawberry slices ➤
—KATHLEEN PROBST, Richville, Minnesota

When I need evenly sliced strawberries, especially for topping desserts, I use an egg slicer. First I stem the strawberries, and then I slice them just as I would a boiled egg. It's fast and easy, and the slices come out clean and flawless.

Baking with dried cranberries

—NICOLE REES, *Fine Cooking* contributor

➤ I generally prefer to buy dried fruit that hasn't been sweetened, but cranberries are the exception. For my baking, I want moist, plump, sweetened dried cranberries. Unsweetened ones are remarkably dry, astringent, sour, and even bitter. Fortunately, most producers lightly sweeten the berries during the drying process; it helps keep them tender and tasty but doesn't mask their tartness.

Hull strawberries with a grapefruit knife

—LORRAINE SHANK, Summit, New Jersey

➤ A serrated grapefruit knife makes an ideal tool for hulling strawberries quickly and easily.

CITRUS

Scrub before zesting

—LORI LONGBOTHAM, *Fine Cooking* contributor

➤ The first thing to do before zesting a lemon or other citrus fruit is to wash it thoroughly. Most of the insecticides and fungicides used on commercially grown citrus fruits are washed off in the packinghouse after harvesting, and the lemons are disinfected. To replace the natural wax that is removed during the washing process, the lemons are then coated with a small quantity of water-soluble food-grade wax for protection during shipping and to prevent shrinkage. The waxes are approved for use on foods and meet the requirements of the FDA. It's advisable, however, to wash citrus fruits thoroughly, even scrub them with soap and warm water, to remove the wax. If you want to avoid the pesticides completely, use organic fruits, but even those should be washed thoroughly before using, as they may also be coated with wax.

Flavor sugar with citrus zest

—KATE JOHNSTON, Sacramento, California

➤ Instead of garnishing desserts with confectioners' sugar, I sometimes like to use an orange-lemon sugar. I combine the zest of 2 oranges and 1 lemon with about 1 cup of granulated sugar in a food processor and process until it's fine but not powdery. The zest gives the sugar a wonderful fragrance and a bit of color, too. I love the sugar over lemon bars and other desserts, but it's also great for sweetening a cup of tea or sprinkling over buttered toast.

3 tools to remove the zest
—Fine Cooking Test Kitchen

Remember that the colored outer layer of peel is what you're after; avoid cutting into the bitter white pith directly underneath.

GRATER

Forget the box grater. A rasp-style grater like a Microplane® gives feathery, moist threads (and no pith) that are perfect for cakes, sauces, or any recipe that calls for grated zest.

PEELER

To infuse flavor into custards, syrups, or broths, use a vegetable peeler to cut wide sections of skin. Trim away the white pith by laying the strips flat and holding a sharp knife at a nearly flat angle. For very fine julienned zest, slice the pieces into thin strips.

ZESTER

A citrus zester has five small holes for peeling thin shreds of zest, which can be used much the same as grated zest. A channel knife has a single, larger hole, which produces thicker strips that are ideal for garnishes. Some tools include both of these cutting options in one.

· A BUYER'S GUIDE TO ORANGES ·

Here's a brief guide to the most common orange varieties—Valencia, navel, and blood oranges. With a few exceptions (see below), most subvarieties of these oranges aren't labeled at the market. That's because the differences have little to do with flavor and more to do with when the fruit matures during the year—only a grower would know one from the other.

Valencia Originally from Spain, Valencia oranges are thin-skinned and almost seedless. They're your best bet when you need lots of juice. But Valencia oranges are also a great choice for any recipe that calls for sweet oranges.

Navel Native to Brazil, navel oranges get their name from a second, smaller orange that develops at the base. (This undeveloped twin looks a little like a belly button.) Seedless, with thick skins, navels are the best eating oranges around. Though a little less juicy than Valencias, they're virtually interchangeable when it comes to cooking. At the store, most navels are labeled simply "navel," but you might see some called cara cara; these have dark pink flesh, an orange exterior, and a sweet, mildly acidic flavor.

Blood oranges Blood oranges have a much sweeter flavor and less acidity than navels or Valencias, with overtones of raspberries or strawberries. Their thin skins may be blushed with red, and the flesh is a distinctive blood red. If you want sweetness, blood oranges are the way to go, especially if paired with slightly bitter ingredients. At the market, you might find varieties like Moro or Tarocco. Moros have dark purple flesh and a deep reddish rind. Taroccos (sometimes called half-blood oranges because they aren't as red as the Moro) have a blushed rind.

—**JOANNE WEIR**, *Fine Cooking* contributor

3 tips for getting the most zest
—**LORI LONGBOTHAM**,
Fine Cooking contributor

➤ • Thick-skinned lemons, which tend to have pebbly-textured skin, are easiest to zest.
• Zest citrus fruit before you juice it.
• Save the flavor: You can freeze zest in a sealed container for up to 3 months.

Don't pack the zest
—**Fine Cooking Test Kitchen**

➤ When measuring zest, you should pack it just enough to get it into the measuring spoon. Don't pack it tightly unless the recipe says you should. Otherwise you may end up with a flavor that's more bitter than brilliant.

Recycled fruit bowls ▶
—KAREN ANN BLAND, Gove, Kansas

Halved and hollowed-out citrus fruit—like lemons, oranges, and grapefruit—make unusual and colorful individual bowls for serving ice cream, fruit salad, or even a gelatin dessert. To keep the bowls from wobbling, cut a thin slice from the bottom, taking care to leave the rind intact so there are no leaks.

How to squeeze a lemon ▶
—CYNTHIA A. JAWORSKI, Chicago, Illinois

Here's how to slice lemon wedges that won't squirt in your eye when you squeeze them: Cut a lemon wedge and make three or four small vertical slits across the wedge's edge. These cuts prevent the juice from squirting out forcefully. When you squeeze the lemon wedge, the juice will run out gently.

How to squeeze a lemon harder ▶
—DOTTIE UHRICH, Crofton, Maryland

I find that the metal squeeze-type lemon juicers extract the most juice, but sometimes the thickness of the fruit's skin can make it difficult to squeeze the handles. Slicing off a bit from each end of the lemon before cutting it in half to put in the juicer makes it easier to squeeze.

Getting the most lemon juice ▶
—LORI LONGBOTHAM,
Fine Cooking contributor

- The juiciest lemons tend to be those with thin skins. If the lemon skin is smooth rather than textured, that's a tip-off that the skin is thin. And small to medium-size lemons are generally thinner skinned than large ones.
- Juicers or reamers get the maximum juice from lemons.
- If you squeeze the fruit using only your hands, first roll the lemon on the counter and then microwave for 30 seconds. You'll get more juice.
- One lemon yields 3 to 4 tablespoons juice.
- Don't waste a drop: Extra juice freezes well for up to 3 months.

A rasp grater doubles as lemon juice strainer ▶
—KATIE DUMO, via email

When I need both the zest and the juice of a lemon, I use my rasp-style grater. First, I use it to grate the zest. Then I flip it over, remove any residual zest, and squeeze the lemon juice over it. This strains out seeds and any undesired pulp.

Use lemon juice to season a dish

—JENNIFER MCLAGAN,
Fine Cooking contributor

➤ Use lemon juice as you would a pinch of salt: It works wonders as a flavor enhancer. Don't be afraid to add a tablespoon or two of lemon juice to a stew or braise at the end of cooking to bring all the flavors together.

MELON

Choosing a ripe melon

—JENNIFER ARMENTROUT,
Fine Cooking contributor

➤ At first glance, those melons in a mound at the market all look the same. But we all know they don't taste the same. To find a ripe one:

Lift it. A melon should feel heavy for its size; compare a few.

Look at it. It's mainly what you *don't* see that counts: no blemishes, bruises, soft spots, wrinkles, or bumps.

Smell it. A fragrant aroma, especially near the stem end, is a good sign.

Thump it. Hold the melon to your ear and give it a few knocks. It should sound more cavernous and hollow than muffled.

Cutting watermelon mess-free

—FAYE P. WHITAKER, Verona, Wisconsin

➤ Cutting and seeding watermelon can make a drippy, sticky mess. So when I have one to slice, I do it on a cutting board placed in a rimmed baking sheet that's larger than the board. When I'm done, the sweet juices are contained in the baking sheet, ready to be used for a refreshing beverage or for making a sorbet. This method works well with all foods that release a lot of liquid when cut.

Pitting olives without an olive pitter

—JENNIFER ARMENTROUT,
Fine Cooking contributor

➤ I use my chef's knife or a small skillet or saucepan to pit olives. The action is the same for both tools: Apply pressure with the bottom of the pan or the side of the knife until the olive splits, exposing the pit enough so that it can be plucked away by hand. For soft black olives, I use the knife. For firm green olives, I use a skillet because more pressure is needed and the knife might slip. Plus, with a skillet, I can crack more than one olive at a time.

PASSIONFRUIT

What to know about passionfruit

—DABNEY GOUGH,
Fine Cooking contributor

➤ Passionfruit adds an exotic, tropical flavor to summery fruit salads, sorbets, and frozen blender drinks like daiquiris. Native to South America, these eggplant-colored orbs are like inside-out Fabergé eggs—their dull, leathery exterior belies the jewel-like seeds and heady, fragrant pulp contained within.

If it sloshes, it's ripe. Passionfruits get uglier as they ripen, so choose ones that have wrinkly or dimpled skin and feel heavy for their size. The best indicator of ripeness is the gentle sloshing sound they make when shaken. If you can find only underripe ones, let them sit out at room temperature for a few days to ripen.

Scoop and strain. When you're ready to use them, cut them in half with kitchen shears over a fine strainer set in a bowl to catch the juices. Then scoop out the seedy flesh and press it through the strainer. (The seeds are edible, but most recipes call for strained pulp.) A ripe passionfruit yields about 1 tablespoon pulp with seeds or 1½ teaspoons strained.

· A SIMPLE GUIDE TO HANDLING FRUITS & VEGETABLES SAFELY ·

For a long time, if we worried at all about getting sick from food, we focused on undercooked hamburger or tainted oysters. In light of outbreaks of illness from contaminated spinach and scallions, it's hard not to think about fresh produce, too. But there's no need to swear off it. You can reduce your risk by following a few guidelines.

Cross-contamination is to blame.

The pathogens that are often responsible for illness linked to fresh produce are the salmonella and E. coli O157:H7 bacteria, which are the same pathogens we associate with meat and poultry. Fruits and vegetables can become contaminated at many points in the food chain, from the open fields where they're grown through distribution and retail stores all the way through to preparation in your kitchen.

When the contamination occurs in the kitchen, it's usually due to contact with raw meat or poultry. To avoid this, designate separate cutting boards for raw meat and fresh vegetables, and wash hands and surfaces thoroughly after working with raw meat and before working with produce.

Identifying the sources of contamination that occur in the field has been very difficult, but irrigation water, improperly composted manure, and workers (from poor hygiene) are all considered possible origins.

Cooking will kill the bacteria.

You may not have the power to prevent contamination from occurring in the field, but in your kitchen, there's one certain way to ensure the safety of your fruits and vegetables, and that's simply to cook them. As long as the temperature hits 160°F, pathogens will be killed. But we don't always want to cook these foods, so here's what you need to know to minimize your risks.

Shop with safety in mind. When

you're choosing produce, you're probably thinking about quality not food safety. There's nothing wrong with that, but here are a few pointers that have produce safety in mind.

Shop in clean markets. Cleanliness is a good indication that the market takes its role in food safety seriously. The display cases should be cleaned regularly to prevent cross-contamination, and damaged fruits or vegetables (which may carry more pathogens) should be removed on a regular basis.

Refrigeration is key. If you're buying cut-up produce or packaged greens, be sure they've been kept cold, either in a refrigerated display case or surrounded by ice.

When a fruit or vegetable is cut, the cells are ruptured, releasing the moisture and nutrients bacteria thrive on. Keeping things cold holds the pathogens in check (and protects against spoilage). The packaging on cut produce should be cold to the touch. Don't buy it if it isn't. Be sure to store the food in the fridge once you get it home. The temperature inside your refrigerator should be 40°F.

Always bag your produce. Those rolls of plastic bags in the produce section aren't just for weighing vegetables; they're also important for sanitary reasons. Even if you're buying only one avocado, it's worth putting it in a bag. Grocery carts are rarely cleaned and conveyer belts at the checkout aren't cleaned often enough, so a bag provides another barrier to germs. Also, to avoid cross-contamination, keep your fruits and vegetables separate from raw meats, poultry, and seafood, both in your grocery cart and in the checkout bags.

How to wash depends on what you're washing. You might think

that simply rinsing produce with

water would wash off any potential pathogens, but it's not that easy. Washing can reduce contamination, but it can't completely eliminate it. One reason for this is that bacteria can be sticky. Rinsing them off isn't as easy as wiping dust off a table; it's more like removing grease or garden dirt from your hands. And like your hands, the surfaces of fruits and vegetables aren't perfectly smooth. Even fruits like apples and tomatoes aren't as smooth as they look. When you're the size of bacteria, the surface of an apple has lots of nooks and crannies to wedge into. And the craggier the surface, the more places there are to hide.

Scrub firm produce. For firm produce, such as apples, melons, and tomatoes, rub well while rinsing under water. For these foods, rinsing and rubbing is quite effective at removing tiny pathogens. Just use your hand or a vegetable brush under running water. (If you use a brush, be sure to replace or wash it regularly.) Don't worry so much about the length of time—5 seconds is about as effective as 20 seconds—but rather focus on rubbing the whole surface, which will take longer for a cantaloupe than for an apple.

Rinse more delicate produce. For produce with softer or complex texture, such as berries, broccoli, and spinach, a simple rinse is sometimes the only option. For this type of produce, rubbing

individual pieces is more difficult. It's tricky to quantify the effectiveness of washing techniques since there are many variables at play, but we do know that merely rinsing can help, even if only a little.

Cooking vegetables results in better than a 100,000-fold reduction in pathogens (if the bacteria are present). When you rinse, rub, and dry an apple, you might achieve a 1,000-fold reduction in bacteria. For soft fruits and vegetables that you can only rinse, you might get a 10-fold decrease. But that translates into a 90% reduction, so even though a simple rinse doesn't produce the kind of numbers that get microbiologists excited, it does still have an impact.

Peeling isn't an excuse to skip washing. Wash fruits and vegetables even if you're going to peel them. If there are bacteria on the rind, they're easily transferred to the inner surfaces during peeling or cutting. And once you've peeled or cut up a vegetable, it's virtually impossible to wash off any contamination. Cut surfaces provide more places for a microbe to hide, and they also tend to be difficult to rub.

Don't forget to dry. Drying fruits and vegetables with a paper towel or in a clean salad spinner provides another measure of safety. This is because bacteria become suspended in water droplets after washing, so by removing

the water, you're increasing the efficiency of the wash.

Rinse, don't soak, leafy greens. For leafy greens, rinsing is more effective than soaking. When cooks talk about the best way to store and wash fruits and vegetables, they're usually most concerned with flavor and aesthetic matters: preserving freshness or eliminating grit, for example. But as a food-safety expert, I'm also looking for the most effective way to remove or minimize numbers of bacteria. Usually, the same method can satisfy both cooks and food-safety folks. But when it comes to lettuce, spinach, or other leafy greens, we part ways. Cooks like to wash their greens by soaking them in a big bowl of water. This is a very good way to remove sand and grit, but it can actually increase the risk of moving contamination around—from one leaf to everything in the bowl. A much more effective way to remove pathogens is to discard the outer leaves, which is where most contamination would be, and wash each individual leaf under running water. So as a home cook, you have a choice. You can focus on grit removal and soak in a bowl of water. Or you can decide to make the very low risk of contamination even lower by rinsing under water.

—LINDA J. HARRIS, PH.D.,
Fine Cooking contributor

PEARS

Give pears the thumb test for ripeness
—Fine Cooking Test Kitchen

➤ The best way to judge ripeness in pears is to gently press the neck of the fruit near the stem with your thumb; if the flesh gives, the pear is ready to eat. Also use the sniff test. A ripe pear will often give off a delicious, sweet aroma. For cooking, pears should generally be "firm-ripe," or just at the beginning of the ripening window. In this case, look for ripe fruit that yields only slightly when pressed near the stem.

Use a melon baller to core
—RUTH LIVELY, *Fine Cooking* contributor

➤ A melon baller does a neat job of coring pears. Or use the smallest paring knife you have (I use a 2½-inch blade), cutting with only the tip of the blade.

· A COOK'S GUIDE TO PEARS ·

Anjou Juicy and very sweet, the Anjou becomes creamy when ripe. It appears in October and is available well into the early summer.

Bartlett A ripe Bartlett is bright yellow. A ripe red Bartlett is bright red. Aromatic and sweet, this pear is perfect eaten raw. It's the first pear to appear in late August.

Bosc It comes into season in September and can be available well into spring. Its dense, grainy flesh has an elegant, aromatic flavor that's perfect for cooking.

Comice This very sweet, very juicy pear is wonderful raw. Its season starts in early September and lasts into December.

Forelle The slightly crunchy texture of this pear, which appears in September, means it holds up well when cooked, but it's also delicious raw and in salads.

Seckel The smallest of pears, it has extremely sweet, very dense, crisp flesh, and it's lovely poached or roasted. Its season is September through December.

—Fine Cooking Test Kitchen

Tips for selecting a ripe pineapple

—Fine Cooking Test Kitchen

- Look for a fresh, dark green top and taut, shiny skin.
- Pick it up. It should feel heavy for its size and give a little when pressed, but there shouldn't be any large, very soft spots.
- It should have a light, sweet pineapple fragrance, especially at its base. A pineapple with a heavy, cloying fragrance may be overripe.
- Contrary to popular belief, a pineapple with greenish skin may actually be ripe; skin color varies with variety.
- You may also have heard that the ease with which a leaf can be pulled free is a sign of ripeness, but this isn't necessarily so.

Cut perfect pineapple rings

—JENNIFER ARMENTROUT,
Fine Cooking contributor

1 Cut off the top and bottom of the pineapple and stand it on a cut end. Slice off the skin, cutting deeply enough into the pineapple to remove the eyes, too. You'll lose some edible flesh this way, but it's the best way to get nice round rings.

2 Cut the pineapple into ¼-inch-thick slices, and then trim any pointy edges from each slice to round it off.

3 Remove the core from each slice with a small round cutter or a paring knife.

Use pineapple cores in marinades

—CHRIS RASCATI, via email

After I've cut all the juicy flesh from the core of a fresh pineapple, I chop up the tough core and use it, along with the juices that accumulated on the cutting board, to add flavor to marinades for chicken, pork, and beef.

VEGETABLES

(All vegetables are tossed with extra-virgin olive oil, kosher salt, and freshly ground black pepper, plus fresh lemon juice if you like, and roasted at 475°F.)

VEGETABLE	SERVINGS PER LB.	PREP	HOW TO ROAST
Asparagus (medium or large, not small)	3 to 4	Rinse, pat dry, and snap off tough bottom ends.	Roast for 5 minutes, flip, and roast until tender and a bit shriveled, 5 to 8 minutes.
Beets	4	Trim, peel, and cut into ¾- to 1-inch-thick wedges.	Roast for 15 minutes, flip, and roast until tender, 10 to 15 minutes.
Broccoli crowns	2 to 3	Trim and peel stem; slice into ¼-inch-thick disks. Where stem starts to branch out, split florets through stem so each piece is 1½ to 2 inches wide.	Roast until floret tops begin to brown, 8 to 10 minutes. Stir and continue to roast until tender, 3 to 6 minutes.
Brussels sprouts	3 to 4	Trim and halve lengthwise.	Arrange cut side down on baking sheet. Roast until tender and browned, about 15 minutes. No need to flip.
Butternut squash	4	Peel and cut into ¾- to 1-inch pieces.	Roast until browned on bottom, 15 minutes. Flip and roast until tender, 5 to 10 minutes.
Carrots	3 to 4	Peel. (If thick, cut in half crosswise to separate thick end from thin end; halve thick end lengthwise.) Cut crosswise into 1-inch lengths.	Roast until lightly browned on bottom, 12 to 15 minutes. Flip and roast until tender and slightly shriveled, 3 to 5 minutes.
Cauliflower	3 to 4	Trim and cut into 1- to 1½-inch florets.	Roast, stirring every 10 minutes, until tender and lightly browned, 20 to 25 minutes total.
Fennel	3 to 4	Quarter lengthwise. Trim base and core, leaving just enough of core intact to hold layers together. Cut into ¾- to 1-inch wedges.	Roast until pieces begin to brown on edges, 15 minutes. Flip and roast until tender and nicely browned, about 10 minutes.
Green beans	4	Trim stem ends.	Roast until tender, a bit shriveled, and slightly browned, about 15 minutes. No need to flip.
Mushrooms (cremini or small white)	3 to 4	Wipe clean and trim stem flush with cap.	Roast stem side down until brown on bottom, 20 to 25 minutes. Flip and roast until browned on top, 5 to 10 minutes.

continued

Parsnips	2 to 3	Peel, halve crosswise, halve or quarter thick end lengthwise, and then cut all crosswise into 2-inch lengths.	Roast until browned on bottom, about 10 minutes. Flip and roast until tender, about 5 minutes.
Potatoes	2 to 3	Peel or scrub well and dry. Cut into 1-inch pieces.	Roast until browned on bottom, 10 to 15 minutes. Flip and continue to roast until tender, about 5 minutes.
Rutabagas	3 to 4	Peel and cut into ½- to ¾-inch pieces.	Roast until browned on bottom, 13 to 15 minutes. Flip and roast until tender, 5 to 10 minutes.
Sweet potatoes	3 to 4	Peel and cut into 1-inch pieces.	Roast until lightly browned on bottom, 10 minutes. Flip and roast until tender, 5 to 10 minutes.
Turnips	3 to 4	Peel and cut into ¾- to 1-inch pieces.	Roast until browned on bottom, 10 to 15 minutes. Flip and roast until tender, about 5 minutes.

GAS GRILLER'S GUIDE TO VEGETABLES —Fine Cooking Test Kitchen

VEGETABLE	PREP	HOW TO GRILL*
Asparagus	Trim off tough ends. Brush liberally with olive oil and season with plenty of kosher salt.	Heat gas grill to high. Put spears on grate at an angle and grill, rolling over once, until lightly marked and slightly shriveled, 3 to 5 minutes total.
Bell peppers	Leave whole.	Heat gas grill to high. Put peppers on grate, cover, and cook until skins are blackened on all sides, turning with tongs as needed, 3 to 4 minutes per side, or 10 to 15 minutes total. Wrap peppers in foil or put in a paper bag to cool completely. When cool, peel off blackened skins and remove stems and seeds, reserving flesh and juices.
Corn	Shuck corn, removing all husk and silk. Lay each ear of corn on a 12-inch square of aluminum foil. Rub each ear with 1 tsp. butter and season all over with kosher salt and freshly ground black pepper. Tuck a sprig or two of fresh thyme or other herb next to corn and wrap corn tightly in foil.	Heat gas grill to high. Put foil-wrapped corn on grate, cover, and cook, turning every 5 to 6 minutes, for 15 to 20 minutes. Remove from grill and open foil loosely. Corn should be blackened in places. If it isn't, rewrap it and return it to grill for another 5 minutes. Let cool.

Eggplant	Use a vegetable peeler to peel lengthwise strips of skin from eggplant—it will look striped. Alternatively, use a fork to score skin deeply. (Cooked eggplant skin can be tough; smaller eggplant have thinner skins, so you can leave it all on, if you prefer.) Trim ends. Cut eggplant crosswise into rounds about ⅜-inch thick. Brush both sides of slices with plenty of olive oil and season well with kosher salt just before grilling.	Heat gas grill to high. Put eggplant slices on grate and cover grill. Grill, checking occasionally with tongs, until slices are well browned on both sides, 3 to 4 minutes per side. Move slices from heat and stack them to finish cooking (put them on an upper rack, set them over a turned-off burner, or wrap them in foil off the grill). Let sit for 15 to 20 minutes. (This last step lets residual heat steam flesh to guarantee that it's cooked throughout.)
Onions	Trim ends, peel, and cut into ½-inch-thick slices. Thread slices on thin metal skewers (poultry lacers work great) or soaked wooden skewers. Brush liberally with olive oil and season with kosher salt.	Heat gas grill to high. Put onion skewers on grates and cook until slices are well browned on both sides (they will have dark marks on them), about 15 minutes total. Turn one of grill burners down to low and move skewered slices to that area. Stack them loosely and leave there for 10 minutes to finish cooking through. Alternatively, remove them from grill and wrap in foil to finish softening.
Portabella mushrooms	Wipe off any dirt with a damp paper towel. Cut or snap off stem at base. With a spoon, scrape out dark gills on underside of cap and discard. Brush both sides of mushroom cap with plenty of olive oil and season with kosher salt just before grilling.	Heat gas grill to high. Put mushrooms stem side up on grate. Grill mushrooms as long as they need to get very well browned (a lot of liquid will pool up in cap), 5 to 8 minutes. When cap is brown, turn it over and press down to gently push out as much liquid as possible. Grill for another 4 or 5 minutes, until they're much thinner and drier.
Zucchini and summer squash	Trim off both ends. To make lengthwise slices, trim a little off two long sides of zucchini and cut remainder into length-wise strips, each about ¼ inch thick. To use zucchini and summer squash on platters or in salads, trim ends and cut slices on a sharp diagonal into ovals between ¼ and ⅜ inch thick. Brush both sides of strips or slices with plenty of olive oil and season with kosher salt just before grilling.	Heat gas grill to high. Put strips or slices on grill at a 45-degree angle to grates and grill, covered, until well browned and limp, 3 to 4 minutes per side. Check occasionally and move slices around gently with tongs as necessary so they brown evenly; don't undercook. When done, remove from grill and drape them over a cooling rack (to keep them from steaming as they cool).

Using charcoal instead? If you grill over charcoal, build a two-level fire (see p. 194) so that you have hot and medium-low areas. Grill your vegetables uncovered over the hot coals to sear both sides (cooking times will depend on the heat of your fire). Then move them to the cooler area and cover as directed to finish cooking.

4 tips for roasting vegetables

—JENNIFER ARMENTROUT,
Fine Cooking contributor

Roast in a very hot oven (475°F). The vegetables will cook quickly but still have a chance to brown nicely on the outside by the time they become tender inside.

Cut even pieces. It's very important that you cut the vegetables in pieces of about the same size. Unevenly sized pieces won't roast and brown in the same amount of time, and you'll end up with both over-roasted and under-roasted vegetables.

Line the pan. To prevent sticking, line the pan with a sheet of parchment; otherwise, when you have to pry stuck vegetables off the baking sheet, it's the tasty brown bottoms that are left on the pan.

Position vegetables near the pan's edges. If the vegetable pieces cover the pan sparsely, arrange them more toward the edges of the pan. Pieces near the edge brown better.

---

8 tips for grilling vegetables

—ELIZABETH KARMEL,
Fine Cooking contributor

- Always coat the vegetables with a thin layer of olive oil to help them cook evenly.
- Sprinkle with kosher salt or sea salt (and freshly ground pepper, if you like). The salt is essential: It helps draw out moisture and promote caramelization.
- When grilling vegetables, watch the heat. If the grill is too hot, the vegetables will burn on the outside and be undercooked inside.
- Arrange the vegetables across the cooking grate to keep them from falling into the fire.
- Turn the vegetables with tongs. Slide the tongs gently under the center of the food in the thickest part when turning. In general, turn the vegetables only once, halfway through the cooking time.
- Remove vegetables like zucchini and asparagus when they're crisp-tender; they'll continue to cook after they come off the grill. Bell peppers and eggplant, however, should be grilled until soft all the way through.
- Taste the grilled vegetables while they're still warm, and if they need more salt, add it before they cool.
- Toss grilled veggies with flavorful accents like fresh basil or thyme, olives, or sun-dried tomatoes.

To avoid cabbage odor, cook sprouts quickly

—KIMBERLY Y. MASIBAY,
Fine Cooking contributor

Brussels sprouts, as well as other potentially malodorous vegetables like kale and collard greens, are members of the cabbage family. These plants contain sulfur compounds called isothiocyanates in their cells. During cooking, these compounds break down, forming other compounds, some of them terribly stinky; hydrogen sulfide, for example, smells like rotten eggs. The longer these sulfur compounds cook, the more they break down and the stinkier they get, so to minimize offensive odors, you have to minimize cooking.

Try a quick-cooking method such as sautéing, steaming, stir-frying, or blanching, and cook just until the Brussels sprouts are crisp-tender—they'll taste great. But if you and your family love Brussels sprouts, no one's likely to object to their odor, so go ahead and roast them or make your favorite gratin recipe—just open a few windows to air out the kitchen. And, honestly, as long they're not cooked to mush, the sprouts really shouldn't smell too bad.

Cut an X for quicker cooking

—Fine Cooking Test Kitchen

To help Brussels sprouts cook evenly when boiling or braising them whole, cut a ¼-inch-deep X into the stem end to help the liquid penetrate.

Smaller is sweeter

—EVA KATZ,
Fine Cooking contributor

Brussels sprouts are grown on large stalks, and some markets carry them in this impressive form. If you encounter them, look for the stalk with the smallest sprouts, which will be sweeter.

Shredding cabbage

—Fine Cooking Test Kitchen

Whether you're preparing cabbage for a sauté, a salad, or a soup, more often than not you'll be shredding it. For large quantities, use a food processor fitted with a slicing blade, but for small amounts, it's quick to shred by hand. Quarter and core the head of cabbage. Thinly slice each quarter crosswise, keeping the fingertips of your guiding hand curled under so you don't cut them. If the quarter gets too awkward to hold, flip it onto another side and finish slicing.

CARROTS

Carrots and the seasons

—DAN BARBER,
Fine Cooking contributor

Carrots are available all the time at the grocery store, and they'll always look and taste the same. But when you grow them yourself or buy them from a farmer, you'll notice that their character changes with the seasons. The young carrots at the farmers' market in late spring and early summer have a delicate flavor and juiciness that are best appreciated fresh—shave them into a salad for an afternoon lunch and you needn't do much more. But in late fall, after the first soft frosts have spoken, their flavor becomes more complex and sweet, a result of the cold temperatures converting the roots' starches to sugars. To highlight this natural sweetness, roasting is the best option—apply just enough heat to caramelize the sugars.

Cut fine julienne strips with a zester

—MARYLIN VOGEL, Mississauga,
Ontario, Canada

I love the flavor and color of carrots in my tossed chef's salad, but I don't like the hard texture of chunks or slices. Instead, I grate my carrots with a channel zester for fine julienne strips.

A shortcut to julienned carrots

—DR. CHARLES A. GUTWENIGER,
Camas, Washington

I skip the initial step of finely slicing carrots to make julienne by using my vegetable peeler to create long ribbons; I press a little deeper into the carrot than usual to get thicker strips. I usually discard the first two to three slices and select large carrots with less taper for the task. To julienne, all I have to do is stack the thin, wide carrot ribbons and slice them into thin sticks. The julienne is a little thinner than typical, but it works great.

Finding the freshest carrots

—Fine Cooking Test Kitchen

Your best guarantee of freshness is to buy carrots in bunches, with their leafy green tops still attached. Even when they're very large, carrots with tops should still be tender, juicy, and full of good flavor. Look for firm roots and fresh, dark greens. Once you get them home, cut off the tops so they don't draw moisture from the roots. Instead of throwing away the tops, which are full of nutrition and flavor, try adding them to soups or chopping them and using in salads. When buying packaged carrots, look for plump, firm, fresh-looking roots with no sign of shaggy hair-like protrusions.

CAULIFLOWER

Keep cauliflower florets intact
—ALPHONDA S. THORN, New York, New York

➤ Whenever I try to separate a head of cauliflower into whole florets with a knife, I invariably slice through some of the florets. So after trimming the stem end as close to the base of the head as I can, I set aside my knife, get out my melon baller, and start scooping out the remaining stem. It takes just a few scoops to remove most of the flesh. Now the lovely florets are only loosely attached to one another, and it's very easy to separate them, whole and intact.

CELERY

Celery without strings
—CHRIS WHITE, Yardley, Pennsylvania

➤ I love the taste and crunch of raw celery in salads or with hummus, but I don't like those pesky strings that get caught between my teeth. So before slicing or dicing celery, I peel it with a vegetable peeler, just as I would a carrot.

Extend celery's shelf life
—LISA CIHLAR, Brodhead, Wisconsin

➤ I end up throwing a lot of celery away because it loses its texture and turns slimy too quickly in the refrigerator. I found out that if you wrap it tightly in aluminum foil, it will last at least three times longer, about a month.

Remove silk from corn cobs in no time

—MARGARET PRECKEL,
West Lafayette, Indiana

Fresh corn on the cob is delicious in summer, but the silk can be tedious to remove. I found that the last threads are quickly burned off by turning the cob over a gas flame for a few seconds. The kernels are scarcely heated, and the blackened silk can be brushed off easily.

Cutting corn off the cob

—MELISSA PELLEGRINO,
Fine Cooking contributor

So often when you're removing kernels from an ear of corn, they miss the cutting board completely and end up scattered all over the counter and floor. To keep those kernels in their place, insert the tip of the ear of corn into the center hole of a bundt pan. Cut the kernels away from the cob in long downward strokes, letting them fall into the pan.

Keep fresh kernels at the ready

—RUTH LIVELY,
Fine Cooking contributor

Here's a simple way to preserve the sweetness of fresh corn and to keep corn kernels on hand for tossing into salads, side dishes, sautés, and other weeknight dishes. Cut the kernels off the cobs and blanch them in boiling water for 1 to 2 minutes. Drain, let cool, and store in a covered container in the fridge for up to 5 days. Or freeze the kernels in a single layer on a baking sheet until hard, and then store in an airtight container in the freezer, where they'll keep for up to 3 months.

Keeping fresh corn fresh

—MARYELLEN DRISCOLL,
Fine Cooking contributor

When you're buying sweet corn, don't get hung up on varieties. Instead, keep in mind that timing is everything. Corn's sugars quickly turn into starch as the corn ages, so freshness should be your priority.

Buy local. To start, find a reliable source for locally grown produce, one that's closely linked to the fields where the vegetables are grown. Ideally, this means buying straight from the farm, either at a farmstand or a nearby farmers' market.

Don't husk the corn before buying it. The husks protect the ears of corn within, keeping them fresh and moist. Most people husk the corn to make sure it's worm-free and fully developed, but there are ways to find good ears without husking:

- Choose ears that are snugly wrapped in their husks, which should appear fresh, green, and moist. It's all right if the tassel seems a little dry at its end, but it should feel fresh around the tip of the ear.
- Run your fingers along the ear, feeling the formation of the kernels through the husk. They should feel plump and densely packed in even rows. You can feel if the kernels are immature.
- Look for wormholes. If you see one, move on to another ear. If you find a worm after husking the corn, it's not a big deal. Just cut it out.

Eat it or chill it. At home, use fresh corn as soon as possible. If you must store it, don't remove the husk, which protects the corn from moisture loss. Wrap the ears in damp paper towels, seal them in zip-top bags, and store in the fridge for no longer than 2 days.

Keeping corn on the cob warm
—NADIA COLLINS, via email

Whenever I cook corn on the cob for a dinner party, I take the corn out of the boiling water with tongs, put the cobs in a colander, and then set the colander over the cooking pot of water while I assemble the rest of the dinner. Even with the burner off, the steam from the boiled water keeps the corn moist and hot until it gets to the table.

Use Styrofoam to organize corn holders
—LISA SPRAGGINS, Dallas, Texas

I grew tired of searching for my corncob holders and getting pricked by their sharp ends, so I cut a piece of Styrofoam to fit in my utensil drawer and stuck the holders in the Styrofoam. Now they're easy to find.

Stick corn holders in a cork
—CINDY JOHNSTON, Lakewood, Washington

After pricking my fingers too many times searching for corncob holders in my drawer, I now store each pair in a wine cork. One goes on each end of the cork, and they're easy to spot in my drawer.

CUCUMBERS

An apple corer makes neat cucumber rings
—ELLEN GILMORE, Baton Rouge, Louisiana

An apple corer works great for removing cucumber seeds. I slice the cucumber in half widthwise and then push the corer down the center of each half. Then I can slice the cucumber into rings, which I sometimes serve with a halved cherry tomato in the middle for a simple appetizer.

EGGPLANT

Salt first for less oily eggplant ►
—Fine Cooking Test Kitchen

Eggplant soaks up oil like a sponge, but you can reduce its ability to absorb oil by salting the cut flesh and letting it sit for 30 minutes or more. Drain, pat dry, and proceed with cooking.

Easier eggplant ►
—MICHAEL WODJENSKI,
New Milford, Connecticut

When preparing eggplant—especially for grilling—I like to leave the skin on for flavor and because it helps keep the tender flesh from falling apart. But sometimes the skin can become a chewy mess. I compromise by scoring the entire eggplant from top to bottom with a dinner fork. The fork's closely spaced tines leave fine "stripes" on the eggplant's skin, not unlike the way cucumbers are often left with stripes of peel. When cooked, the skin is much more manageable.

GARLIC

Minced vs. pressed: can you taste a difference? ►
—Fine Cooking Test Kitchen

Garlic presses aren't for everyone. Some cooks find it simpler to mince garlic with a knife; others argue that pressed garlic has inferior flavor. We've long wondered whether minced and pressed garlic actually taste any different. So to find out, we held a blind taste test, serving two versions of a quick marinara, sautéed Swiss chard, and gremolata (a garnish of minced garlic, lemon zest, and parsley). For each dish, we made one batch with minced garlic and one with garlic crushed in a press. Almost everyone found that garlic crushed in a press gave dishes a more aggressive garlic flavor. Many tasters found the pungency offensive in the gremolata, which featured raw garlic, but acceptable in the marinara, which was cooked.

Get rid of the germ ►
—JENNIFER MCLAGAN
Fine Cooking contributor

The sprout in the center of each garlic clove is known as the germ. When the garlic is fresh, the germ is tiny and pale in color. As garlic ages, the germ grows and turns green, becoming bitter. So always remove the germ, especially in recipes that call for raw or quickly cooked garlic.

WHEN I COOK EGGPLANT, IT ALWAYS COMES OUT BITTER. HOW DO I AVOID THIS?

There's plenty of disagreement among cooks about whether or not to salt eggplant before cooking. Some claim salting is essential to remove bitter juices; others believe it improves texture. I find that a ripe, carefully selected eggplant is not bitter and has a delightful texture, even without salting.

In my experience, you can avoid the bitterness problem by buying eggplant when it's in season. The best ones arrive in the market around mid-summer. The earliest crops have fewer seeds and consequently better flavor and texture. Look for ones that are evenly firm and deep in color, with shiny, unwrinkled skin. When you press gently on the flesh, it should bounce back. If it leaves a dent, the eggplant is old. Try to shop at farmers' markets, where you have a better chance of getting recently harvested vegetables.

The biggest difficulty in storing eggplant is that it does best at about 50°F. Most refrigerators are set at 41°F or lower, which is too cold for this tropical vegetable. If you can, buy eggplant the day you plan to cook it. If this isn't possible, find a cool spot in the kitchen to store it.

—TASHA DE SERIO, *Fine Cooking* contributor

6 easy ways to peel garlic

—DABNEY GOUGH, *Fine Cooking* contributor

Don't be put off by the prospect of peeling garlic—here are some ways to get the job done quickly and effortlessly. Start by separating the cloves and pulling off any loose, dry, papery skins. Then try one of the following methods. Each will break and loosen the skins enough so that it peels off easily.

- Blanch the cloves in boiling water for about 15 seconds and then shock them in ice water.
- Put a few cloves in the center of a silicone potholder. Fold the potholder in half and, keeping it on the counter, roll the potholder with the palms of your hands.
- On a cutting board, position the broad side of a chef's knife on a clove of garlic. Carefully and gently smack the knife with the heel of your hand. You will hear a quiet "crack" when the skin breaks open.
- Put cloves in a bowl of very hot water and whisk briskly until the skins are loosened.
- If the recipe calls for chopped or sliced garlic, cut the cloves in half and peel the skins from each half.
- Put cloves in a small or medium-size lightweight mixing bowl and then invert another similar bowl over it. Firmly hold the two bowls together and shake vigorously for about 30 seconds.

Plus 1 more ➤

—KASPAR SHIU, Stow, Ohio

I love garlic. It's gotten to the point where I put it into just about every-thing I cook. To save time peeling it, I use the flat side of my meat mallet to crush multiple cloves with one strike. The skin comes off easily, and the cloves are lightly smashed to bring out their flavor.

A neat approach to roasted garlic ➤

—Fine Cooking Test Kitchen

There's more than one way to roast garlic. You can roast whole heads of garlic with their tops cut off so that you can just squeeze the cloves of roasted garlic right out of their skins. That approach is all right, but the garlic gets squished, your fingers get sticky, and annoying flakes of papery skin stick to your fingers. Here is a neater method.

1 Separate a head of garlic into individual cloves. Don't peel the cloves, but do rub off any flaky or papery skin. Use a paring knife to nip off the stem end of each clove. You want the peel to stay on, but it's fine if a little comes off.

2 Put the cloves in the center of a square of aluminum foil, drizzle with a little olive oil, and use your fingers to rub the oil evenly on the cloves. Add fresh herb sprigs for aroma, if you like.

3 Gather the foil into a beggar's pouch and set the pouch directly on the rack of a 350°F oven. Roast until the garlic becomes very soft and lightly browned, about 1 hour. You can roast two heads' worth of cloves in one pouch, but for more than that, make another pouch.

4 Open the pouch and let the cloves sit until they're cool enough to han-dle. Squeeze each clove gently at the untrimmed end and the roasted flesh should slide right out in one piece.

GREEN BEANS

Trim beans by the handful ➤

—MARIA REID, via email

Here's how to quickly trim green beans: Grab a handful, and, holding them loosely, tap the stem ends on the cutting board until all the stems line up. Then lay the beans on the board and slice off the stems in one cut. Repeat the process to remove the tips of the beans, if you like.

**Keep green beans ➤
vibrant with
quick cooking**

—KIMBERLY Y. MASIBAY,
Fine Cooking contributor

Green beans get their color from the pigment chlorophyll. But chlorophyll, unfortunately, loses its luster in the presence of acids, and when a green bean cooks, its cells break down, allowing natural acids to escape and react with the bean's chlorophyll. To curtail color loss, simply limit the cooking time—toss the beans in a hot sauté pan or wok for a few minutes and serve them crisp-tender, or, if you prefer your beans cooked through, steam or boil for up to 5 minutes and promptly drain them. And be sure you don't dull the beans' brilliance by dressing them too early with an acidic sauce—wait until right before serving.

GREENS

**The secret to ➤
tender kale**

—BILL TELEPAN,
Fine Cooking contributor

Stuff washed kale in a heavy-duty zip-top bag and freeze it for a few hours or up to a month. Cook it straight out of the freezer. Freezing breaks down its fibers in a way that no amount of cooking can.

Stem-free spinach ➤

—Fine Cooking Test Kitchen

Remove stems from spinach by folding the leaf lengthwise and pulling down as you would a zipper.

HERBS

Buy fresh herbs for less ➤

—ANDREA REUTZEL, Chute, Texas

I get tired of the high prices and low quality of fresh herbs in the grocery store. So when I find myself out of a particular fresh herb, I head to the nursery. I've found that I get a lot more out of one plant for the same price or less. Plus, the potted herbs are truly fresh, and they last longer than cut herbs.

**Getting the most from ➤
fresh herbs**

—JENNIFER ARMENTROUT,
Fine Cooking contributor

STORAGE

Treat fresh herbs like a bouquet of flowers: stems down in a few inches of water. Keep the bouquet loosely tented with a plastic produce bag and store in the refrigerator. This treatment keeps herbs hydrated but not too wet. Many herbs, like parsley, mint, and cilantro, may last for up to 2 weeks this way. The exception is cut basil, which is happiest around 55°F, colder than room temperature but warmer than the fridge. Test-kitchen experience has taught me that if basil is purchased already refrigerated, it should stay that way. If cut fresh or bought unrefrigerated, keep the basil at room temperature unless it's very hot out. Regardless, cut basil rarely keeps longer than a week.

CLEANING

When ready to use the herbs, hold them by their stems and vigorously swish them around in a bowl of cool water until they seem free of dirt. Shake the herbs over the sink and then spin dry or blot dry with paper towels. (Curly parsley can be squeezed partially dry before blotting with paper towels.) The drier the herbs, the better they'll withstand chopping.

- -

Coarsely vs. finely ➤ chopped herbs

—JENNIFER ARMENTROUT,
Fine Cooking contributor

Coarsely chopped herbs are good for garnishing and mixing into salsas and cold salads. The leaves are chopped just enough to break them into smaller pieces and release their flavor but are left large enough that some pieces have intact edges, so they're identifiable by sight rather than being anonymous chopped green bits.

Finely chopped herbs are usually best for mixing into dishes in which the flavor of the herb is more important than its appearance. Though by no means a firm rule, fresh herbs are generally added near the end of cooking, giving them enough time to infuse a dish without overcooking and muddying their flavor nuances.

Here are some tips for chopping herbs:

- Choose your sharpest knife. This is crucial. A dull knife mashes and bruises; a sharp knife cuts cleanly.
- Use a rocking-chopping motion by adding wrist action as you chop, rocking the knife back and forth in a slight slicing motion. This motion cuts the herbs more cleanly, so the flavor stays in the herbs rather than leaking out onto the board (which happens with a dull knife and a straight up-and-down chopping motion).
- Chop herbs just before using for the freshest flavor—if possible, that is. Sometimes you have to work ahead, and in these cases, chopped herbs (covered and stored in the fridge) will stay reasonably fresh tasting for several hours. Just try to avoid chopping them any sooner than necessary.

Freeze an herbal bounty into cubes

—RENEE SHEPHERD,
Fine Cooking contributor

Freezing works best with delicate herbs that don't taste very good when dried, such as basil, dill, chives, chervil, and parsley. Just chop the herbs, portion them generously into ice cube trays, and add a little chicken broth. The frozen herb cubes are a great way to add a flavor lift to vegetable sautés, rice pilafs, noodles, or soups. I do this with mint, too, but I use water instead of chicken broth so that I can add the mint to iced tea and other cold drinks. Resinous herbs such as rosemary, thyme, sage, and oregano keep better dried because they contain more essential oils. Just hang the leftover herbs by their stems in a cool, dark place.

Freeze herbs whole

—MARY ROWSELL, Russell, Ontario, Canada

I freeze extra herbs from my garden by putting them on baking sheets in the freezer. Once they're frozen, I transfer them to a plastic bag. They retain most of their vibrant flavor, and hardier herbs like rosemary and thyme can practically be interchanged for fresh. Leafy herbs like basil and parsley suffer in the looks department, though, turning dark and mushy, so they're best used only for cooking.

Slicing and mincing basil

—JESSICA BARD, *Fine Cooking* contributor

FINE SHREDS

Stack leaves on top of one another and roll into a tight tube. (For smaller leaves, bunch as tightly together as possible before cutting.) Cut the rolled leaves using a single swift, smooth stroke for each slice. The width is up to you. This is known as a chiffonade.

MINCED

Turn the chiffonade slices (keeping them together with a gentle pinch) and make a few perpendicular cuts as wide or as narrow as you like. Don't go back over basil as you might when finely chopping parsley.

TREAT BASIL WITH CARE

This sun-loving herb is vigorous in the garden, but once cut, it's fragile and susceptible to bruising, so careful handling and storing are a must. In my early restaurant days, on herb duty, the chef made me sharpen my knife every few minutes when cutting herbs to avoid bruising the tender leaves. Perhaps that was overkill, but I did learn to make friends with basil. I've heard of many ways of cutting basil to keep the edges from blackening, from slicing the leaves vertically to drawing the knife toward you as you cut. A sharp knife really does make all the difference: The less you mash, the less you'll damage the leaf. If it's appropriate for your recipe and you have the time, gently tearing the leaves instead of cutting them is a nice alternative and seems to reduce blackening.

Slice basil with kitchen shears

—CAROL A. VOLLMER, Durham, North Carolina

For the thinnest chiffonade of basil, I roll up a stack of leaves and use a sharp pair of kitchen shears instead of a knife.

Freeze pesto in plastic egg cartons

—SHEILA DAVIS, Ottawa, Ontario, Canada

A clear plastic egg carton is just the thing for storing leftover pesto. I clean the carton, portion the pesto into each egg cup, snap the top shut, and stash it in the freezer. It's really easy to pop the frozen pesto out of the cups when I want to stir some into pasta sauce.

Keep your chives from wandering

—RUTH LIVELY, *Fine Cooking* contributor

I often use scissors to snip chives. To prevent the snippets from scattering, I cut them into a small, deep dish. If you chop chives on a cutting board, use a very sharp, thin-bladed knife so you don't bruise the tender leaves.

Don't throw out cilantro stems

—JENNIFER ARMENTROUT, *Fine Cooking* contributor

When preparing cilantro for chopping, you don't necessarily have to remove all of the stems. Cilantro stems are quite flavorful, so if they're thin and tender-crisp (bite one to check), just chop them up along with the leaves.

Freeze lemongrass to have on hand

—LINDA RITTELMANN, Baltimore, Maryland

Many recipes that call for lemongrass require only part of a large stalk. Instead of wasting the pricey herb, I found a way to extend its life. I buy 3 or 4 stalks at a time, cut away the woody exterior, and grind the stalks in a food processor. I store this ground lemongrass in zip-top bags in the freezer and have found that it keeps for a long time. I can take out just a tablespoon or so to use for that night's recipe.

· SUBSTITUTING FRESH FOR DRIED HERBS ·

The general rule when substituting fresh herbs for dried in a recipe is to use twice as much. The essential oils in fresh herbs are less concentrated than they are in dried form, and as a result the flavors are less potent. A more specific answer depends on the type of herb you're using and how pronounced you want its flavor to be in the finished dish.

When cooking with milder, tender herbs such as basil, parsley, and dill, you can even use up to three times as much fresh as dried, and sprinkle more onto each serving for garnish. More assertive, hardy herbs such as sage, oregano, and rosemary can quickly overwhelm the balance of flavors in a dish. Start judiciously, holding back up to 1½ times as much fresh as dried. Then, taste and add a pinch more at a time until you reach the amount that suits your taste.

Most recipes calling for dried herbs instruct you to add them early in the cooking process. This isn't always the best approach when using fresh herbs in their place. To preserve the vibrant flavor of tender herbs, add them during the final stages of cooking. With delicate herbs like cilantro and chives, it's better yet to add them off the heat. When using hardy, strong-scented fresh herbs, add them during the early stages of cooking to temper them and build a background of herbal flavor.

—LYNNE SAMPSON, *Fine Cooking* contributor

Substitute lime zest ➤ for lime leaf
—SU-MEI YU, *Fine Cooking* contributor

Kaffir lime leaf is the secret ingredient that brings a Thai curry together. The leaves come from the makrut lime tree and are sold at Asian markets. Expect to see less and less of the term *kaffir*, because it's derogatory in Arabic and in some southern African languages. More and more recipes now refer to the ingredient as *mah krud* (its Thai name) or wild lime leaf. When I can't find fresh leaves, I don't bother with dried or frozen versions, because they lack the fresh version's essence. Instead, substitute grated lime zest, which will add a citrusy dimension, although not the perfume for which this Thai ingredient is renowned.

Quick-pick parsley ➤
—DABNEY GOUGH,
Fine Cooking contributor

There's a certain Zen-like state that can be reached while performing menial tasks like washing dishes or picking parsley leaves off their stems. But for a recipe that calls for a lot of parsley, the meditative state can sometimes turn maddening. In these cases, try a technique used in restaurant kitchens: Rather than picking the leaves individually, "shave" them right off the bunch. Hold a rinsed bunch of parsley with the leaves facing away from you. Graze a chef's knife along the length of the bunch, starting near the base of the leaves and keeping the blade almost parallel to the main stems. As long as you have a sharp blade, the leaves (and some of the more tender stems) will come right off.

**Strip those stems ▶
when using thyme**

—LYNNE SAMPSON,
Fine Cooking contributor

When using fresh thyme leaves, don't pick but rather strip the thyme leaves from their woody stems. Hold the sprig in one hand and use the fingers of the other hand to slide down the stem, stripping off the tiny thyme leaves. It doesn't matter whether you strip from base to tip or tip to base; either will work. Some of the thyme's tender, green stems will break off along with the leaves; simply chop these up with the leaves, and they won't even be noticed. It's not always necessary to stem thyme leaves. When making stews, braises, soups, or other long-cooking dishes, you can just throw in whole thyme sprigs. The leaves will fall off during cooking, and you can extract the woody stem before serving.

MUSHROOMS

**Store mushrooms ▶
in a paper bag**

—RUTH FAIRALL, Eldorado, Texas

Mushrooms get slimy if you leave them in a plastic produce container or bag for more than a day or two. So when I bring mushrooms home from the market, the first thing I do is remove them from the plastic container. I line the bottom of a paper bag with a folded paper towel, arrange a single layer of mushrooms on the towel, and cover them with another folded paper towel, continuing until the bag is almost full. Before stashing the bag in the refrigerator, I fold down the top and secure it with a binder clip. Stored this way, really fresh mushrooms last for up to 2 weeks.

**When to wash ▶
mushrooms**

—ALLISON EHRI KREITLER,
Fine Cooking contributor

Mushrooms grow in compost and other not-so-tasty things like rotting logs and leaves. When they come to market, they often still have bits of this stuff clinging to them, so they seem to demand some cleaning. But mushrooms absorb water, and waterlogged mushrooms resist browning in the sauté pan. And we like our mushrooms well browned. Because of these opposing facts, there are different schools of thought on how to clean them. One approach is to brush them off with a dry or damp towel or a soft brush.

This method works well if the mushrooms aren't very dirty, but if they are, I prefer to wash them, albeit gently. I rinse them briefly, one at a time, under running water, then transfer them to a dry towel and give them a little pat to blot away surface moisture. This method removes the grime without completely soaking them. Mushrooms tend to exude lots of moisture when they're heated, particularly if they've been rinsed. This is why we like to sauté them, in plenty of oil or butter, over medium-high to high heat—the high temperature helps the moisture evaporate quickly so that the mushrooms can then brown well.

Remove bitter portabella gills
—JENNIFER ARMENTROUT,
***Fine Cooking* contributor**

Whether you plan to grill a portabella or cook it any other way, there's an important but often overlooked prep step you should take: Remove the gills on the underside of the cap. They have a bitter taste, and they exude an unattractive black liquid when they're cooked. To get rid of them, just scrape them off with a table knife or the side of a spoon.

Clean mushroom caps with a melon baller
—CHERYL L. BEAUCHAMP, Scotia, New York

When I'm stuffing mushrooms, I use a melon baller to dig out the stem and gills, creating perfectly round, unbroken caps for stuffing. I use a smaller melon scoop for button and cremini mushrooms and a larger scoop for portabella and other large-stemmed mushrooms.

French press keeps mushrooms submerged
—JUDY GORDON, Bend, Oregon

I use my French press coffeemaker to submerge dried mushrooms in hot water to rehydrate them. The top of the press will keep them under the water until you're ready to use them. And the fine mesh acts as a strainer for the flavorful liquid, keeping grit behind.

Rehydrate dried mushrooms with wine
—JOHN DELZANI, Rocky River, Ohio

Instead of using hot water to rehydrate dried mushrooms, I use warmed wine, either white or red. The wine adds richness and depth to a number of dishes, many of which might already include wine. This method is also great for rehydrating dried cherries and cranberries.

Dried mushrooms for seasoned flour

—BRUCE WOOD, Ottawa, Ontario, Canada

▶ If I have leftover dried mushrooms, I grind them to a fine powder in a coffee grinder. I then mix the powder with flour and other seasonings, such as smoked paprika, ground fennel seeds, or chopped fresh herbs, and dredge meats or fish in this seasoned flour before pan-searing or braising. It adds great flavor.

LEEKS & ONIONS

Getting leeks grit-free

—RUTH LIVELY, *Fine Cooking* contributor

▶ Since leeks are grown with soil piled all around them, there is plenty of opportunity for dirt and grit to settle between their onion-like layers. The easiest way to clean a leek is to trim the root end and the dark green tops and cut it in half lengthwise (or, if you want to retain the appearance of whole leeks in your dish, just cut about two-thirds of the way through the stalk). Hold the leek root end up under cold running water and riffle the layers as if they were a deck of cards. Do this on both sides a couple of times until all the dirt has been washed out.

Slicing onions: direction makes a difference

—ALISON EHRI KREITLER, *Fine Cooking* contributor

▶ **LENGTHWISE**

When you slice lengthwise, you're cutting with the grain of the onion. These slices hold up better during cooking, so they're a good choice for dishes like pot roast or French onion soup, in which you want to see pretty strips of onion after a long cooking time.

CROSSWISE

When you cut the onion crosswise (across the grain), you get slices that cook down and lose their shape quickly. This cut is ideal if you want melt-in-your-mouth onions for a marmalade or for topping a steak sandwich.

What's in a color?
—ANNIE WAYTE,
Fine Cooking contributor

➤ Many people don't realize that most bell peppers start out green and ripen to become red, orange, and yellow peppers. The longer the pepper ripens on the plant, the more the flavor mellows and the more sugar the vegetable develops, which explains why green bell peppers have a sharp and sometimes bitter flavor. The color the pepper turns when fully ripe depends on the variety.

How to roast a red pepper
—JENNIFER ARMENTROUT,
Fine Cooking contributor

➤ 1 Coat each pepper with a little oil. If you have gas burners, you can roast a pepper directly on the grate over high heat, turning the pepper occasionally until it's charred all over. To char a batch of peppers, a hot charcoal or gas grill is best, but the broiler works too. Put the oiled peppers on a foil-lined baking sheet and broil as close to the element as possible, turning them so they char evenly.

2 Put the charred peppers in a bowl while they're still hot and cover with plastic wrap. Let them rest until they're cool enough to handle. Pull on the stem. The seed core will pop out. Cut the pepper open, flick off any seeds, and turn skin side up.

3 Use a paring knife to scrape away the charred skin. Don't rinse the peppers with water or you'll dilute their flavor.

Roasted peppers with less mess
—DARLENE WONG, Toronto, Ontario, Canada

➤ I used to steam roasted red bell peppers in a paper bag, but it tended to create a soggy mess. Now I place the charred peppers in a steamer insert set inside a pot and cover with a lid. As the peppers steam and their skins loosen, the juices conveniently accumulate in the bottom of the pot.

A simpler way to steam off skins
—CATHY CARTER, Ann Arbor, Michigan

➤ When roasting chiles in the oven, I line the pan with foil, set the chiles on top, and char them under the broiler. Then, instead of transferring them to a covered bowl, as is often recommended to steam off the skins, I simply use the foil to wrap and steam the chiles after roasting. If you are lucky, this results in two fewer items to wash (the roasting pan and the bowl).

Even with a sharp knife, slick pepper skins can be difficult to slice through. Make it easier on yourself by arranging the pepper segments skin side down on the cutting board. This positions the soft, easier-to-cut flesh on top, with the tougher skin against the board, so it takes less effort to slice through the skin.

· A COOK'S GUIDE TO CHILES ·

Anaheim These are one of the only chiles most New Mexicans and West Texans use, so they just call it a "green chile" (until it ripens and becomes a "red chile"). In the rest of the country, most of us call it an Anaheim. This light green chile has a pleasant vegetal flavor and ranges from slightly warm to medium hot. Anaheims are usually roasted and peeled before they're used.

Heat: Mild to medium.

Good in: Roasted and cut into strips called rajas, Anaheims can be used as a condiment on tacos and fajitas, and they make a great garnish. Use them diced or puréed for green chile sauce.

Also called: Long green, Hatch, New Mexico, Chimayo.

In dried form: Called red chile or chile Colorado.

Jalapeño The classic Tex-Mex hot chile and one of the world's best known. Originally grown in Mexico, it's named for Jalapa, a town in the state of Veracruz. The fresh jalapeño has a strong, vegetal flavor to go with the heat. Although many Americans prefer to cook with fresh jalapeños, the jalapeño is most widely consumed in the United States in its pickled form. Red jalapeños are common in the fall.

Heat: Hot.

Good in: Salsas, stir-fries, soups, vegetable stews; Chinese, Vietnamese, Thai, and Indo-Pakistani cuisine; Mexican and Tex-Mex cooking.

In smoke-dried form: Called a chipotle.

Poblano Fat, wide, and dark green, the poblano is rich in flavor. Poblanos are one of the most commonly used chiles in central Mexican cooking, both fresh and dried. Named after the Mexican city of Puebla, where they probably originated, poblanos are generally roasted and peeled before use, though they can also be sautéed.

Heat: Medium.

Good in: Chile relleno dishes, quesadillas, any melted cheese dish. Like Anaheims, poblanos are good roasted, cut into strips, and used as a flavoring for tacos, fajitas, or quesadillas.

Also called: Ancho or pasilla.

In dried form: Called an ancho.

Serrano Similar to the jalapeño, the serrano is hotter and usually smaller. Often serranos have a fuller, more herbaceous flavor than jalapeños.

Heat: Hot.

Good in: Salsas and any place you'd use a jalapeño.

In dried form: Called a chile seco.

—**ROBB WALSH,** *Fine Cooking* contributor

❓ WHY CAN ONE CHILE BE HOT AND ANOTHER NOT?

Chiles can be unpredictable. Sometimes a chile you expect to be hot, like a jalapeño, will have next to no heat. And sometimes a chile that's supposed to be mild, like an Anaheim, will make your mouth tingle noticeably. There are a couple of explanations for this variation.

Growing conditions Warmth and water play a large part. "The main reason for heat difference in the same variety of chile is stress on the plant—specifically, hot temperatures and lack of water. Chiles grown in drier, hotter weather will produce more capsaicin," says Denise Coon of the Chile Pepper Institute at New Mexico State University.

Seed source Horticulturists provide chile growers with seeds that have been certified to be a particular variety and that usually produce chiles of a predictable heat level. But when you buy your chiles at the store, there's no way to know the seed source. And growers sometimes report wide variations in heat levels even from two chiles grown on the same plant. In the end, the only way to tell the exact heat of a chile is by tasting it.

—ROBB WALSH, *Fine Cooking* contributor

A great way to clean hands after handling chiles
—SARAH KINGSTON, Provo, Utah

► I've found an easy way to clean my hands thoroughly after chopping hot peppers: I rub a small amount of vegetable or olive oil on my fingers for a minute and then wash them with a little dish soap. The oil removes the capsaicin, which is what irritates the skin and can so easily be transferred to your eyes or mouth.

POTATOES

What's in a name? New potato or not?
—EVA KATZ, *Fine Cooking* contributor

► Red potatoes, especially small ones, are often labeled in the supermarket as "new potatoes," but chances are they aren't new potatoes at all. Technically, a new potato is harvested from the potato vines while the leaves are still green. At this stage, the immature potatoes are thin skinned and haven't developed their full complement of starch. So regardless of their variety, new potatoes are low in starch and high in moisture, even if they're actually a high-starch variety. Since mature red potatoes and new potatoes are both low in starch, they can be used interchangeably, and subsequently the term *new potato* is used quite loosely.

Storing potatoes properly

—MOLLY STEVENS,
Fine Cooking contributor

- Refrigerating potatoes turns their starches to sugars. Instead, store them in a cool, dark, well-ventilated place—in a paper bag in a low cupboard, for instance.
- Don't wash potatoes before storing. Dampness can cause decay.
- Remove any rotten spots, as they'll cause the other potatoes to spoil.
- Avoid storing potatoes near onions, which will cause both to spoil sooner.

- -

Trim potatoes gone green

—ROY FINAMORE,
Fine Cooking contributor

Potatoes with green skins have a high level of solanine, which is toxic in large amounts. You can eat potatoes that have some patches of green, though, as long as you peel them completely, being sure to remove at least ⅛ inch of the outer layer of flesh. It's not enough to remove just the green patch, and most peelers don't remove enough of the outer layer to get rid of the solanine. Sprouts also contain high levels of solanine.

If your potato has one or two sprouts, cut them out and peel the potatoes well. If many of the eyes have sprouted, chances are the potato has started to decay and just won't make good eating. When you're deciding whether it's worth your time to rescue a green or sprouted potato, keep in mind that many of the nutrients in potatoes are in and near the skin.

- -

A better way to peel a potato

—WILLIE ZEE, Lincolnwood, Illinois

Sometimes peeling potatoes drives me nuts: The peeled part gets really slippery. To make the job easier, I peel one end of the potato and sink a fork firmly into that area. Then I hold the fork in one hand while I run the peeler down the length of the potato, quickly removing long strips of peel. It's so much easier than fumbling with a slippery potato.

- -

The 3 secrets of fluffy mashed potatoes

—KIMBERLY Y. MASIBAY,
Fine Cooking contributor

- **The right taters** High-starch varieties, such as russet and Idaho, give the fluffiest results because of the way their starch behaves during cooking. The microscopic starch granules in these potatoes' cells separate and swell as they sponge up moisture that's naturally present in the potato; as a result, the cooked potatoes' texture seems dry and fluffy. The starches in medium- or low-starch varieties such as Yukon Gold and red potatoes, on the other hand, tend to stick together, giving them a denser, moister texture that becomes creamy (or even sticky) when mashed.

- **The right technique** Dry out the potatoes, and add the fat before the liquid. Waterlogged potatoes will give you a gummy mash, so if you cook the potatoes by peeling and boiling them, then you should return the potatoes to the pan after you've drained them and mash them over low heat, letting the potatoes dry out for a few minutes. Or use a cooking method that prevents the potatoes from sopping up too much water in the first place: steaming, for example, or boiling the potatoes whole in their skins. Then, after you've mashed them, stir in the butter—the fat will coat the starches and help prevent them from absorbing too much additional moisture when you add the milk, cream, or other liquid.

- **The right tool** Use a ricer, a potato masher, or a food mill, because any tool that you need to plug in (such as a food processor or electric mixer) is likely to overwork the potatoes, causing the starch granules to burst, release their sticky contents, and turn your mashed potatoes into a gluey mess.

? WHY ARE RUSSET POTATOES DRY AND FLUFFY? WHAT DISHES ARE THEY BEST FOR?

Not only do russet potatoes have more starch than other varieties, but they also have more of a particular type of starch known as amylose. These starch granules are relatively large, and when they're heated they absorb water from surrounding cells, which makes the potato dry. The amylose starch also swells up and separates, and this makes the potato seem light and fluffy. The result is a potato that's perfect for baking.

When to choose russets

Russets' high-starch, low-moisture content makes them great in many dishes. They make first-rate mashed potatoes—soft and light and able to absorb an impressive amount of liquid or other enrichments. When sliced thinly, layered in a baking dish, and covered with milk and cream, russets bake up into a tender, toothsome gratin. The potatoes absorb flavor along with the liquid, so you can infuse the cream with aromatics (like bay leaf and garlic). And finally, russets make the best french fries. Again, it's their low moisture content. As the potato fries, what little moisture it contains gets pushed out, leaving the fry crispy outside and dry inside.

When not to choose russets

Russets fall apart easily when boiled and can become waterlogged, so avoid using them for simple boiled potatoes or for potato salads. Also, they'll absorb too much dressing if used in a salad. And though russets make delicious smooth soups, it's not a good idea to use them in any soup where you want the potatoes to stay in small, intact chunks.

—**MOLLY STEVENS,** *Fine Cooking* contributor

Keep potatoes from discoloring

—CHERIE TWOHY, via email

As I'm slicing potatoes for a gratin, I keep the slices in a bowl with enough of the liquid I plan to use in the recipe to cover. The potatoes don't turn brown, and the liquid, such as milk, cream, or broth, gets enriched with the potato starch, which only helps to thicken the sauce when the gratin bakes.

Boil potatoes in a pasta pot

—COLLEEN LANIGAN-AMBROSE, Seal Beach, California

I boil potatoes in a pasta pot with a colander insert because it's much easier to drain the cooked potatoes by lifting out the colander than it is to lug a pot of boiling water to a colander in the sink.

---

3 tips for boiled potatoes

—ROY FINAMORE, *Fine Cooking* contributor

- Start the potatoes in cold water; it gives them the chance to cook more evenly.
- Drain cooked potatoes in their skins on a rack rather than in a colander, where they continue to steam and get overcooked as they cool; in addition, those on the bottom often get crushed.
- Use a fork or a skewer to test boiling potatoes for doneness; a knife will just cut into them, making them seem more tender than they are. Also, the smaller the hole you make in the potato, the less the chance it will get waterlogged.

Creative potato ricer

—JENNIFER CHARLTON, Fountain Valley, California

I adore potatoes, especially when mashed or in gnocchi. But due to limited kitchen space, I don't have room for a potato ricer. Instead, I press cooked potatoes through a small-holed colander with a rubber spatula with very satisfactory results.

Use a double boiler to warm mashed potatoes

—JENNIFER ARMENTROUT, *Fine Cooking* contributor

You can't hold mashed potatoes directly over a burner because they'll dry and scorch. The secret to keeping them hot is to put them in a covered double boiler or to put them in a metal bowl covered with a lid or foil, set over a pan of barely simmering water. This way, the mash stays soft and moist. Check the water occasionally to be sure it's not either boiling or fully evaporated.

Warm potatoes in a slow cooker

—RACHEL W. N. BROWN, Mt. Sidney, Virginia

► When mashed potatoes are on the menu, I like to make them first and put them in my slow cooker. I put the cooker on the sideboard, set it on low, and finish preparing the meal. When I'm ready to serve, I spoon just enough potatoes into a serving bowl for one pass around the table. Seconds and thirds remain in the slow cooker, steaming hot and at the ready.

Quicker mashed potatoes

—BOB ZAUKE, Normal, Illinois

► When making mashed potatoes, I boil whole potatoes with their skins on to save myself the peeling time. When they're tender, I drain them, cut them in half, and place them in a potato ricer. The flesh goes through the ricer while the skins remain inside, where I can easily remove them.

Boil potatoes and steam vegetables together

—VEE ROBILLARD, via email

► When I boil potatoes, I steam fresh vegetables in a steamer insert placed over the pot. I save energy and free up a burner on my cooktop at the same time.

SALAD GREENS

5 tips for perfectly dressed salad

—ANNIE WAYTE, *Fine Cooking* contributor

► • Thoroughly dry the leaves before adding the dressing. Droplets of water will dilute your dressing and prevent it from clinging to the leaves.

• Dress your salad just before you serve it. Tossing the greens with the dressing any earlier will cause them to become limp and soggy.

• Use just enough dressing to lightly coat the greens. Pick up and taste a leaf as a test. If it needs a little more moisture, add a few additional drops of dressing. But keep checking the leaves to make sure they don't become too wet.

• Toss with your hands rather than utensils. It's easier on the leaves. You can also get a feel for whether the leaves have enough dressing.

• Scatter a few toppings on the salad for excitement. Just be sure to use a light hand. Chopped or whole fresh herbs such as basil, mint, parsley, chives, cilantro, chervil, tarragon, dill, and celery leaves contribute a bright, aromatic note. Thinly sliced raw vegetables like fennel, zucchini, radishes, and mushrooms add flavor and texture. Toasted whole sunflower, poppy, or sesame seeds are good for crunch. And toasted and chopped nuts add both crunch and richness.

Spin cycle

—ROBERT GALFORD,
Concord, Massachusetts

The key to a great salad is to dry washed salad greens completely before tossing them with vinaigrette. But my salad spinner rarely does the job to my satisfaction. Now I add a paper towel to the basket of the spinner along with the greens. The towel efficiently absorbs the excess moisture, and it's easy to spin until dry.

Reuse grape bags for washed greens

—JUDY WONG, Oakland, California

I buy grapes at the supermarket in perforated zip-top bags, which I've found to be perfect for storing washed greens. Because the bags allow air to circulate, the greens hold up in the refrigerator without moisture condensing in the bag.

Rip, don't cut, greens

—*Fine Cooking* contributor

When you're ready to assemble your salad, gently rip washed and dried greens by hand into manageable pieces, discarding any thick ribs. Using your hands prevents the leaves from bruising and keeps them fresh and beautiful.

Quick, make-ahead salad

—JULIE TURNER,
East Kingston, New Hampshire

I line a large bowl with paper towels and prepare several days' worth of salad on top of the towel layer (excluding wet ingredients like tomatoes, which I add at the last minute). I cover the salad with another layer of paper towels and cover the bowl with plastic wrap, and I have the week's fresh salad waiting for me.

Evenly season vinaigrette

—MARIA HELM SINSKEY,
Fine Cooking contributor

Dissolve a measured amount of salt in the vinegar before whisking in the oil. (When salt is suspended in oil, it won't dissolve unless it works its way into a pocket of vinegar.) Because acid, whether from fruit or vinegar, accentuates salt, do the final seasoning toward the end of tossing your salad.

Stack your salad

—Fine Cooking Test Kitchen

To shape salad greens into tall stacks, lightly dress the greens and pack them loosely in a clean plastic container; pints work well. Invert the container onto a salad plate, lift it away, and voilà—a statuesque salad.

How to handle a big winter squash

—IVY MANNING, *Fine Cooking* contributor

► **1** Prick the squash several times with a fork and microwave for 3 minutes; it will soften slightly, making it easier to cut open. Or bake the whole squash directly on the rack in a 350°F oven until slightly softened and the skin begins to change color, about 10 minutes.

2 Set the squash on a towel on a cutting board to prevent it from slipping, and push the tip of a sharp chef's knife into the squash near the stem. Carefully push the knife through the squash to the cutting board to cut off the stem.

3 Then cut lengthwise through half of the squash, starting with the tip of your knife in the center of the squash. If the knife sticks, don't try to pull it out; this is dangerous, since it may come out suddenly. Instead, tap the handle with a rubber mallet or meat tenderizer until the knife cuts through the squash.

4 Rotate the squash and cut through the other side the same way.

5 Push the halves apart with your hands. With a soupspoon, scrape the seeds and stringy bits away from the flesh and discard.

Ice cream scoop works for squash

—BRIAN WIGLEY, via email

► Squash is so plentiful in the fall that I cook with it a lot. I prefer to roast butternut and acorn squash, because roasting intensifies their natural flavor. I've found that an ice cream scoop is excellent at removing the squash from the shell after baking.

TOMATOES

Chop canned tomatoes with a spatula

—CAT FRESHWATER, Rockaway Beach, Oregon

► Instead of using kitchen shears to cut tomatoes, I like to use a sturdy, straight-ended stainless-steel spatula. Using careful, steady movements, I plunge the spatula through the tomatoes until they're chopped. The spatula cuts all the way to the bottom of the can without having to remove each layer of tomatoes as they are chopped. It works well every time.

Don't refrigerate a cut tomato

—DENNIS KIHLSTADIUS,
Fine Cooking contributor

Keeping a tomato out of the refrigerator is crucial to preserving its flavor. Once a tomato falls below 50°F, its flavor enzymes are destroyed. This also causes the texture of the tomato to break down and become mealy. After slicing a tomato, if you don't plan to use all of it at once, cover the cut side only (not the entire tomato) with plastic wrap. Then set the tomato, cut side down, on a flat plate. Storing it this way on the countertop, not in the refrigerator, should allow you to safely keep the tomato for at least another 24 hours. It's most important to cut the tomato with a clean knife, not one that was used to slice meat for your sandwich or to spread mayonnaise. This prevents cross-contamination of other organisms to the tomato.

Squeeze seeds out of a tomato

—PENNY COHEN, Rancho Mirage, California

When a recipe calls for seeding a tomato, I simply cut off ½ inch from the bottom and squeeze the tomato to release the seeds and pulp. It's much faster than halving each tomato and scooping out the seeds.

· CHOOSE TOMATOES BY FRAGRANCE AND COLOR ·

When choosing tomatoes, don't hesitate to smell them; if there's no tomato fragrance, there will be little tomato flavor. Color, on the other hand, is also a good indicator of flavor.

With heirloom tomatoes, color is the key.

With heirlooms, the color is an indicator of flavor, be it sweet or tart. Here's a guide to taste and texture, by color:

Red or pink varieties offer a balance of acid and sweetness that tastes closest to what is thought of as the classic tomato flavor. Brandywine is the heirloom you'll see most often because it's the hardiest and travels best. Roma-shaped varieties such as Opalka are meaty, with low seed counts, making them good for sauces or pastes.

Yellow or orange varieties such as Lemon Boy are the lowest in acid of the heirloom tomatoes, with a mild, sweet flavor. The Garden Peach has an unusual fuzzy skin and a sweet, fruity flavor.

Purple or black heirlooms usually appear more deep maroon or brown, like Cherokee Purple and Carbon. Most have a smoky-sweet flavor and are more acidic than the yellow or green varieties.

White varieties like White Beauty tend to have a yellow tinge and a slightly lower acid content than red heirlooms. Their much higher sugar content makes them the sweetest of the heirlooms.

Green varieties such as Green Zebra are lower in acid than red ones, with a flavor both sweet and tart.

Cherry tomato heirlooms, such as Sugary, Fond Mini, Red Currant, and Mirabel, are very sweet and juicy. They add nice textural variety when used whole in salads or other dishes alongside sliced larger heirlooms. —ERIC RUPERT, *Fine Cooking* contributor

Substituting canned tomatoes for fresh

Fine Cooking Test Kitchen

➤ If a recipe calls for fresh tomatoes, you can substitute your canned big buy. Here's how:

- One 28-ounce can of tomatoes equals 10 to 12 whole tomatoes, peeled (or about 2 pounds).
- One 14.5-ounce can of tomatoes equals 5 to 6 whole tomatoes, peeled (or about 1 pound).

Use sun-dried tomato oil in marinades

—STEPHANIE SHERMAN, Watertown, Massachusetts

➤ When I have leftover oil from oil-packed sun-dried tomatoes, I use it to make a marinade for fresh vegetables before grilling them. The oil gives the vegetables a pleasant sun-dried-tomato flavor.

TURNIPS & RUTABAGAS

Turnips vs. rutabagas

—JENNIFER ARMENTROUT, *Fine Cooking* contributor

➤ Because they're sometimes marketed as yellow turnips or wax turnips, rutabagas are frequently confused with turnips. Both of these root vegetables are members of the brassica family, which includes cabbages, but the rutabaga is probably a hybrid of a cabbage and a turnip. Turnips are usually white fleshed with white or white and purple skin. Rutabagas usually have yellow flesh and a purple-tinged yellow skin, and they're bigger than turnips. (There are also yellow-fleshed turnips and white-fleshed rutabagas, but you won't generally find them in supermarkets.) Both vegetables have a slightly sweet but snappy flavor reminiscent of cabbage. Rutabagas are sweeter than turnips.

When purchasing either, choose those that are firm and feel heavy for their size. Turnips tend to get woody as they grow, so look for ones that are less than 4 inches in diameter. If the greens are still attached, remove them before storing the roots in a plastic bag in the refrigerator for up to 2 weeks. Store the turnip greens separately if you plan to eat them.

- Before peeling a turnip or rutabaga, trim off the top and bottom; this gives you a flat surface on which to stand the vegetable and will eliminate wobbling.
- Turnip skin is usually tender enough to pare with a vegetable peeler.
- Rutabagas are often sold coated in food-grade wax and usually require paring with a knife.

MEAT, FISH & POULTRY

MEAT

Understanding beef labels

—Fine Cooking Test Kitchen

As the demand for safer, sustainably raised beef grows, we're seeing more language relating to farming and production methods—or how the animal was raised—on beef packages. That's the good news. The bad news is that some of these terms have loose standards and are not verified by anyone other than the producer. (If the beef in your market doesn't carry any of these terms, tell the meat manager you'd like to see more options.)

Grass-fed All cattle eat a natural diet of grass at the beginning of their lives. The question is whether the animal was switched to grain to fatten up before slaughter or whether it continued to eat grass and hay throughout its life. From a health standpoint, exclusively grass-fed beef has more nutrients and less saturated fat, lower rates of the dangerous E. coli O157:H7 bacteria, and no risk of mad cow disease.

The United States Department of Agriculture (USDA) grass-fed standards (look for the "process verified" USDA shield on beef packages) specify a grass-only diet as well as continuous access to pasture during the growing season. However, there is no restriction on the use of antibiotics, hormones, or pesticides, which means a producer can state "grass-fed" on its labels without verification. Look for terms like 100% grass-fed or grass-finished or look for the sign of for another third-party verifier, such as the American Grassfed Association (whose standards are stricter than those of the USDA).

Free-range or free-roaming Neither of these terms have any legal definition when applied to beef (though they do for poultry). While they suggest, at minimum, that the animal had access to the outdoors, there are no standards that producers need to follow.

Organic Beef that carries the USDA organic logo has met the department's standards, which prohibit the use of growth hormones, antibiotics, genetically modified feed, and animal byproducts, among other things. The standards do not require a grass-only diet; the animal may be fed organic grain.

Raised without antibiotics This implies just what it says: that antibiotics were not given to the cows. The producer must submit documentation supporting the claim, but unless otherwise noted, it isn't independently verified.

No hormones administered This suggests that the animal received no growth-stimulating hormones. The producer must submit documentation supporting the claim, but unless otherwise noted, it isn't independently verified.

Natural As defined by the USDA, "natural" or "all-natural" beef has been minimally processed and contains no preservatives or artificial ingredients. Since virtually all fresh beef conforms to these standards, the term has no real significance.

Naturally raised The USDA is working on a new standard for naturally raised beef that would prohibit the use of hormones, antibiotics, and animal byproducts but might not address other production concerns, such as animal welfare, diet, or access to pasture. Once the final standard is released, you may start to see this term accompanied by the USDA "process verified" shield. However, the program will be voluntary, so producers may use the term even without verification.

Dry-aging beef pays off with big flavor
—JENNIFER ARMENTROUT,
***Fine Cooking* contributor**

If you've tasted dry-aged beef, then you know that it has a remarkable depth of flavor. Unfortunately for those of us who don't have a high-end butcher nearby, dry-aged beef can be hard to come by. But the good news is that, if you have a refrigerator, you can dry-age beef at home.

WHY DRY-AGED BEEF TASTES BETTER

All fresh beef is aged for at least few days and up to several weeks to allow enzymes naturally present in the meat to break down the muscle tissue, resulting in improved texture and flavor. These days, most beef is aged in plastic shrink-wrap—a process known as wet-aging. Dry-aged beef, on the other hand, is exposed to air so that dehydration can further concentrate the meat's flavor. It's a more expensive process than wet-aging, however, because the meat loses weight from dehydration, and it also must be trimmed of its completely dried exterior.

HOW TO DRY-AGE BEEF AT HOME

1 Buy a prime or choice boneless beef rib or loin roast from the best meat source in your area.

2 Unwrap the beef, rinse it well, and pat it dry with paper towels. Do not trim. Wrap the roast loosely in a triple layer of cheesecloth and set it on a rack over a rimmed baking sheet or other tray.

3 Refrigerate for 3 to 7 days. The longer the beef ages, the tastier it gets. After the first day, carefully unwrap and then rewrap with the same cheesecloth to keep the cloth fibers from sticking to the meat.

4 When ready to roast, unwrap the meat and, with a sharp knife, shave off the hard, dried outer layer of the meat and dried areas of fat, leaving the good fat. Roast whole or cut into steaks.

A FOOD SAFETY NOTE

Home refrigerators aren't as consistent or as cold as commercial meat lockers. Before aging meat at home, get a refrigerator thermometer and be sure your fridge is set below 40°F. Cook or freeze the meat within 7 days of beginning the dry-aging process.

Treat grass-fed beef right for best results

—SHANNON HAYES,
Fine Cooking **contributor**

Grass-fed beef and other types of meat come from animals that feed on pasture, which is their natural diet, rather than being fattened with grain. As a result, grass-fed meat (also called pasture-raised meat) has great flavor but less fat and therefore less buffer against drying out during cooking.

Whether you're cooking grass-fed beef, lamb, or pork, there are some easy tricks to overcome meat's tendency to toughen and dry out.

- Don't cook the meat beyond medium. Aiming for medium or medium-rare doneness means the meat will be juicier and more tender. The exception to this rule is ground meat, which for safety reasons should be cooked so the center is no redder than light pink.

- Use an instant-read thermometer to check the internal temperature. There's less room for error with grass-fed meat than there is with fattier grain-fed meats.

- Cook grass-fed meat at a lower temperature than usual. Because it's leaner, grass-fed meat cooks faster. For quick-cooking thin cuts, such as steaks or chops, sear the meat on medium-high heat briefly to brown it, and then turn the heat to medium-low. This minimizes the loss of fat and juices as the meat reaches the desired internal temperature. (When grilling, sear briefly, and then move the meat to a side of the grill that isn't lit.) With roasts, try using a technique that I call super-slow roasting, in which you cook the meat at 170°F for several hours. This low heat keeps the juices inside the meat and reduces the likelihood that it will be overdone.

KNOW YOUR STEAKS —SARAH JAY, *Fine Cooking* contributor

CUT, ALTERNATIVE NAMES	DESCRIPTION	COOKING TIPS
FROM THE SHORT LOIN		
TENDERLOIN STEAK filet steak, filet mignon, tournedos, filet de boeuf	These very tender special-occasion steaks are cut from the long, narrow tenderloin muscle. When cut from the smaller end, they're usually 1 to 2 inches thick and 1½ to 2 inches in diameter and called filet mignon. Tournedos are cut from the wider end and are thinner and larger. Figure 1 steak per person.	Good match for rubs, sauces, or flavored butters.
T-bone	A carnivore's delight, this steak consists of two muscles separated by a T-shaped bone. Cut from the front end of the short loin, the larger muscle is the juicy, flavorful top loin, and the smaller muscle is part of the tenderloin. Look for ample marbling. Steaks will weigh 1½ to 2 lb. and serve 3 or 4.	Excellent with rubs, sauces, or flavored butters.
Porterhouse	Essentially the same as a T-bone except that it has a larger tenderloin muscle and a smaller top loin muscle than the T-bone (it's cut from the rear of the short loin, where the tenderloin is bigger). Ample marbling. Magnificent when cut to a luxuriously thick 2 inches, which can weigh 2 lb. and serve 3 or 4.	The tenderloin muscle cooks quickly, so keep it over lower heat. To carve, cut the two muscles off the bone, slice, and then reassemble so everyone can sample from both sides.
TOP LOIN STEAK *Boneless:* strip steak, Kansas City steak, New York strip steak, boneless club, and more • *Bone-in:* New York strip loin, shell steak, strip steak, club steak, club sirloin steak, Delmonico steak	Think of these popular steaks as a T-bone or porterhouse with the tenderloin section removed, leaving you with the very tender and juicy top loin muscle. May be boneless or bone-in. Look for ample marbling. Ideal thickness is 1½ inches, giving you a ¾- to 1-lb. steak serving 2 or 3.	Firm enough to take a marinade but also great with sauces or flavored butters.
FROM THE FLANK AND PLATE		
FLANK STEAK London broil, jiffy steak, flank steak filet	From the underbelly of the steer, flank is a lean cut with a visible longitudinal grain that absorbs marinades well. It's known for its beefy flavor and firm texture. Oblong in shape, with a thinner, tapered end. One steak weighs 1 to 2 lb., serving 3 or 4.	Superb with marinades. Slice thinly on the bias (and across the grain) to increase tenderness. Keep thinner end over less-intense heat and flip occasionally for even cooking.

HANGER STEAK hanging tenderloin, flap meat, butcher's steak, butcher's tenderloin	This cut "hangs" from the last rib just below the tenderloin. It's not often found in supermarkets (there's only one per steer, and butchers like to keep it for themselves), but this flavorful, tender, and juicy cut is worth seeking out. A 1½- to 2-lb. hanger steak will feed 3 or 4.	Good for marinating. Ask for the central nerve to be removed, which results in two smaller steaks, or grill whole and cut around nerve during carving. Grill briefly over high heat and avoid cooking beyond medium rare. Slice across the grain.
SKIRT STEAK Philadelphia steak, fajitas meat	From the plate, this steak is the long, thin diaphragm muscle. It has a fairly coarse grain, which runs crosswise rather than lengthwise (as with flank steak). Though it's sometimes confused with flank, it's fattier, more tender, and offers even more beefy flavor. A 1½- to 2-lb. skirt steak will feed 3 or 4.	Ideal for marinades. Grill quickly over high heat, just a few minutes per side. Keep to medium rare to avoid drying out. Carve lengthwise across the grain.

FROM THE RIB

RIB-EYE AND RIB STEAK *Boneless:* Spencer steak, Delmonico steak, beauty steak, entrecote, market steak • *Bone-in:* rib steak	Ask for cuts from the small end of the rib (closer to the short loin), where the tender eye muscle is larger, rather than from the large end (near the chuck), where there are tougher shoulder muscles. Should have ample marbling. Exceptionally tender and juicy. Ideal thickness is at least 1½ inches, serving 2 or 3. Boneless, figure 6 oz. per person; bone-in, figure 8 oz. per person.	Excellent when paired with a dry rub, marinade, or sauce.

FROM THE SIRLOIN (HIP)

TOP SIRLOIN sirloin butt steak, London broil, top sirloin butt, center cut	The sirloin consists of several muscles, and steaks cut from this area vary in tenderness and marbling. Top sirloin is the most desirable (those labeled simply as "sirloin" are tougher). Look for steaks at least 1½ inches thick, weighing 1½ to 2 lb., to serve 2 or 3.	Marinades and rubs can help counter the steak's leanness. To carve, slice thinly or portion into smaller individual steaks.
TRI-TIP STEAK culotte, triangle steak, triangle tip, Newport steak, sirloin bottom butt	Cut from the triangle-shaped tri-tip muscle in the slightly tougher bottom sirloin area, these small, lean steaks are prized for their great beefy flavor. Tri-tips can come in packages of 2 or 3 and are typically 1 to 1¼ inches thick. Figure 1 steak per person.	Excellent with spice rubs and marinades; slice thinly across the grain.

FROM THE CHUCK (SHOULDER)

CHUCK-EYE STEAK boneless chuck filet steak, boneless steak, bottom chuck, center-cut chuck steak	This boneless steak, found under the steer's backbone closest to the rib section, has good beefy flavor and is relatively tender, though it may also have a fair amount of fat and gristle. Steaks can weigh from 1¼ to 2½ lb. and serve 2 to 4.	Good choice for marinades; slice very thinly.
TOP BLADE STEAK flat iron steak, lifter steak, book steak, top chuck steak, butler steak, chicken steak	A flavorful steak from the chuck, this cut is quite tender yet moderately priced, making it an excellent value. Figure one 1¼- to 1½-inch-thick steak per person.	Recommended for marinades; remove line of gristle running down middle either before or after cooking; slice very thinly.

GRILL YOUR STEAK THE WAY YOU LIKE IT —SARAH JAY, *Fine Cooking* contributor

THICKNESS OF STEAK	TOTAL GRILLING TIME, HIGH HEAT	TOTAL GRILLING TIME, MEDIUM-HIGH HEAT
½ inch	3 to 4 minutes for medium rare; 4 to 5 minutes for medium	4 to 5 minutes for medium rare; 5 to 6 minutes for medium
1 inch	6 to 7 minutes for medium rare; 7 to 8 minutes for medium	8 to 9 minutes for medium rare; 9 to 10 minutes for medium
1½ inches	10 to 12 minutes for medium rare; 12 to 14 minutes for medium	11 to 13 minutes for medium rare; 13 to 15 minutes for medium
2 inches	N/A (steak will burn before it's cooked through)	18 to 22 minutes for medium rare; 22 to 24 minutes for medium

7 tips for perfect medium-rare steak

—SARAH JAY, *Fine Cooking* contributor

- Before you grill, remove the chill. Take the steaks out of the fridge about 30 minutes before cooking so that they'll cook evenly and quickly.

- Go ahead and touch. With practice, you can gauge doneness by pressing on the meat. Rare feels quite soft, medium rare is slightly resilient, and medium has a bit more spring. If it's firm, you've overshot into medium-well or well-done territory.

- If you're not sure, take a peek. Although cutting into the steak allows some juices to escape, it isn't the worst offense. Use the tip of a paring knife and cut near the center of the steak for a view of what's happening inside.

- Pull the steak off just before it reaches your target doneness. Meat continues to cook a little after it's off the grill, so be sure to allow for this "carryover cooking" when you're checking doneness.

- For thicker cuts, use a digital instant-read thermometer. Steaks should be at least 1½ inches thick to get an accurate reading. For rare, remove the steak at 120° to 125°F; for medium rare, aim for 125° to 130°F; and for medium, 130° to 135°F.

- Let it rest before you carve. When you cook meat, the juices converge in the center. A 5- to 10-minute rest on a cutting board allows that moisture to redistribute, and your steak will be juicier for it.

- Slice against the grain. When slicing steak—especially the leaner cuts from the tougher parts of the steer—always cut across the grain for the most tender result. This means cutting perpendicular to the long parallel muscle fibers in the steak, so that the fibers in each cut piece are shorter and easier to chew.

CHOOSE THE RIGHT MEAT

When it comes to hamburgers, ground round or chuck is the only way to go, and if you've ever heard the saying "Fat is where the flavor is," then you understand why. Ground round is a good choice for pan-seared burgers because it has enough fat (10% to 15%) to keep the meat moist but not so much that the burger ends up swimming in melted fat in the pan. For grilled burgers, ground chuck is our favorite. At 15% to 20% fat, it's able to withstand the intense heat of the grill and still make for a mouthwateringly juicy burger. Excess fat simply drains through the grill grate.

COOK EXTRA FLAVORINGS FIRST

Smooth out the flavor of garlic, onions, and chiles by gently cooking and then cooling them slightly before mixing them into the beef. You can toast any spices you want to use at the same time: Cook the aromatics over medium-low heat in a tablespoon or two of oil until they soften, and then add spices and cook briefly until they become fragrant. Add salt and pepper directly to the meat (even if you're not using any other flavors).

USE A LIGHT HAND

The worst thing you can do to a burger is mash and compact it into shape. Too much pressure makes a dense, heavy burger. Instead, wet your hands to keep the meat from sticking to them, and then gently pat the meat into patties. Make a deep impression in the center of each patty; this helps the burger cook evenly and keeps it from plumping into a flying saucer shape as it cooks.

COOK IT SAFELY

It's an unfortunate part of modern life that we have to be cautious with ground meat, but the grinding process increases the chance of bacterial contamination. If you want to be on the safe side, cook burgers to a minimum of 160°F. That's medium well, but if you've used the right meat (see above), your burger will still be juicy and delicious.

EASY DOES IT FOR A JUICY BURGER

When you cook burgers, flip them only once and never press down on the meat with your spatula. You want to keep the flavorful juices inside the burgers, not spilled out onto the grill or in your skillet.

IS MY BURGER READY? —Fine Cooking Test Kitchen

Here are some ballpark guidelines for grilling burgers over a medium-hot fire. The times given are for a 6-ounce patty that's 1 inch thick.

DESIRED DONENESS	COOK TIME, SIDE 1	COOK TIME, SIDE 2	DONENESS FEEL
Rare	4 minutes	3 minutes	Center very soft; inside red.
Medium rare	5 minutes	4 minutes	Center slightly springy; juices not yet flowing from interior.
Medium	5 minutes	5 minutes	Center very springy; juices flowing from interior; inside moist.
Medium well	7 minutes	5 minutes	Center firm; inside texture dry, slightly crumbly.
Well done	7 minutes	7 minutes	Center hard; inside texture crumbly.

Choose chuck for the best beef stew

—MOLLY STEVENS,
Fine Cooking contributor

One of the best cuts for making beef stew is chuck. Chuck comes from the well-exercised shoulder and upper foreleg of the steer, so it has lots of tough connective tissue and sinew. Slow, moist, gentle cooking (stewing or braising) transforms that toughness into delectable fork-tenderness and rich flavor.

Chuck is a big part of the steer—it accounts for more than 25% of the animal—and it consists of several different muscles, each with its own characteristics affecting texture and cooking times. At the market, you'll have a choice of cuts from the chuck, and some are better for stews than others. To avoid confusion, head to the store with the cheat sheet below. Cuts labeled with any of these terms will give you a stew with more uniform texture and great flavor.

- Top blade
- Blade
- Flat iron
- Shoulder
- 7-bone roast (named after the number-7-shaped blade bone)
- Chuck short ribs (purchase extra since they're fattier and need heavy trimming)

Bone-in ham delivers more flavor

—BRUCE AIDELLS,
Fine Cooking contributor

I find that any meat cooked on the bone has better flavor, and in the case of ham, it also has better texture. When producers remove the bone from a ham, they then have to reshape the meat (in a machine called a vacuum tumbler) so that it won't fall apart when sliced. This can give boneless ham a bit of a spongy texture. And there's one more reason I like bone-in hams: The leftover bone is great for flavoring soups, beans, and other dishes. If you can find only boneless ham, try to pick one that has the natural shape of the leg, which indicates that it was minimally tumbled.

Spiral-cut hams are partially boned hams that have been sliced before packaging. I don't recommend them because they tend to dry out when baked, and they often come already coated with a commercial-tasting glaze.

How to straighten your bacon

—ALLISON EHRI KREITLER,
Fine Cooking contributor

I love really crunchy bacon, so sometimes I weight it down as it cooks to keep the edges from curling up and staying soft. This little trick works especially well for bacon that will be crumbled. It means there's another pot to wash, but to me, that's a fair price to pay for bacon that is perfectly flat and crisp all over.

Here's how to do it: Place your bacon in a large sauté pan, being careful not to crowd the pan. Place a pot that's slightly narrower than the bottom of the sauté pan on top of the bacon to weight it down and keep it flat. Cook the weighted bacon over medium heat so the fat renders slowly and completely. After the bacon is browned on one side, 2 to 3 minutes, carefully lift the pot (it'll drip), flip the bacon, and replace the pot. Cook the bacon on the other side until it's completely browned and crisp, 2 to 3 more minutes.

Freeze unused bacon

—ANNETTE PEDROZA, via email

When a recipe calls for a slice or two of bacon and I have no immediate use for the rest of the package, I roll each slice of bacon into a spiral and place the rolls on a baking sheet in the freezer. Once they're frozen enough not to stick to one another (2 to 3 hours), I put them in a zip-top bag for future use. The spiral shape makes them compact and easy to grab.

FISH

&

SHELLFISH

Clues for fresh fish ➤
—JAY WEINSTEIN, *Fine Cooking* contributor

- When buying fish fillets, examine the flesh, which should be moist and glistening and without any large gaps. Dry-looking flesh is a sign of age.
- Fresh fish should not smell strong or fishy but should have a mild, fresh scent suggestive of the sea.
- When buying skin-on fillets, look for intact skin and make sure the scales were properly removed. Most fish skin is edible and delicious, especially when cooked until crisp.

Gel ice keeps fish fresh ➤
—DIANE MCCANN, Flower Mound, Texas

Instead of keeping fish and shellfish on watery, messy ice in the refrigerator, I use packets of gel ice (the kind used to ship perishable goods). I always keep a couple in the freezer. When I buy fish that I need to store in the refrigerator, I place an ice packet on a glass or ceramic dish, cover it with plastic wrap, lay the fish on top, and store it, covered, in the fridge. Once I've cooked the fish, I give the ice packet a thorough rinse and put it back in the freezer for later use.

Nonstick fish ➤
—Fine Cooking Test Kitchen

Fish loves to stick to the sauté pan. Using a nonstick pan helps, but sometimes it will even stick to that. Here are a few tips to prevent sticking.

Start with perfectly dry fish. Pat it with paper towels before it goes in the pan.

Make sure the fat is hot. Test it by dribbling a drop of water or two in the pan. It should sizzle.

Shake the pan when adding the fish. While putting the fish in the pan, shake the pan back and forth so that the fish moves over the pan's surface for the first 5 to 10 seconds of cooking.

Turn the fish only once. This won't necessarily keep it from sticking, but it lessens the chance of the fish falling apart if it does stick. Begin with the best-looking side facing down in the pan. If the fillets have their skin, start with that side down. If they're skinless, cook the bone side first; the skinned side may have some harmless but unsightly discoloration.

How to store fish ▶

—DABNEY GOUGH, *Fine Cooking* contributor

The first step in making a great fish dish is to buy great fish (no surprise there). So you go to the market, bring home your "catch," and then what? Keeping your fish in prime condition is all about good storage.

- Put your fish away before anything else. The less time it spends out of refrigeration, the better. Make your visit to the fish counter your last stop when shopping, and ask them to pack the fish on ice if you won't be going home immediately.

- Rinse fish in cold running water to help reduce surface bacteria. Pat dry with a paper towel.

- Wrap fish in waxed paper, and then put it in a tightly covered container. This helps the fish maintain just enough moisture and keeps any liquid runoff from contaminating other food.

- Use within a day or two. Always do the sniff test—if it smells off or overly fishy, change your menu plans. When it comes to fish, follow the adage "When in doubt, throw it out."

----

4 tips for great grilled fish ▶

—MARIA HELM SINISKEY, *Fine Cooking* contributor

Grilled fish steaks are a wonderful choice for entertaining because you can grill them to your guests' individual preferences. Follow the tips below, and the steaks will look great, too.

- Begin with a clean, well-oiled grill, and let it heat up. A major culprit behind sticking fish is the debris left on the grates. Clean and oil the grill for best results. Hot grates keep fish from sticking by causing the proteins in the fish to contract and release, so be sure your grates are thoroughly heated before you start to grill.

- Don't move the steaks for the first few minutes of cooking. You need to give the side that's facing down time to cook (and contract) before turning the fish.

- Use tongs and a spatula to move fish steaks. Tongs work really well for turning sturdy fish steaks, but sometimes a little unseen debris on the grill rack will cause the fish to stick. If this happens, slide a thin spatula underneath the stubborn spot to release it.

- Cut into the fish to check for doneness. With experience, you'll know by feel when fish steaks are done to your liking. Until then, cut into the side of the fish with a paring knife to see what's going on inside. (Poke it with your finger, too, so that you learn what different degrees of doneness feel like.)

Picking and prepping hard-shell clams and mussels

—Fine Cooking Test Kitchen

➤ **Spot the good ones.** At the fish counter, use your eyes and your nose to guide you. Fresh hard-shell clams and mussels should look tightly closed or just slightly gaping open. If they're yawning wide, they're dead or close to it. Once you have them in hand, take a sniff. They should smell like the sea. If they're really fishy smelling, don't use them.

Keep them fresh. Shellfish will suffocate in plastic, so take them out of the bag as soon as you get home, put them in a bowl, cover with a wet towel, and refrigerate. It's best to cook them as soon as possible, but if they were fresh to begin with, they should keep stored this way for up to 2 days.

Clean them up. Just before cooking, look for any that have opened and tap them on the counter. If they don't close, discard them. Check closed mussels by pressing on the two shells in opposing directions. Dead ones will fall apart. Once you've weeded out the bad ones, scrub the remaining mollusks under cold running water with a stiff brush to get rid of any grit. If the mussels have "beards," or black hairy fibers sticking out of their shells, pinch them and yank them off.

LOBSTER

Lobster 101
—JENNIFER ARMENTROUT,
Fine Cooking **contributor**

➤ • Compare lobsters of similar size. If one is heavier than another, it's meatier.

• Pick a frisky lobster. When held by its body, it should flap its tail and wave its claws around. Avoid lethargic lobsters, as well as those with short antennae or with algae growing on them, which are signs of long storage.

• Cook the lobster the same day you buy it. Keep the lobster in its bag in the refrigerator until you cook it.

• Don't blindly put your hand in the lobster bag. Lobsters have spiny surfaces that can puncture your skin and cause infections. Instead, gently dump the lobster out of the bag.

• Don't remove the claw bands until the lobster is cooked. Those claws are sharp, and they'll cut if you get pinched.

Killing a lobster
—MELISSA PELLEGRINO AND JENNIFER ARMENTROUT, *Fine Cooking* **contributors**

➤ No matter how you plan to cook your lobster, you should kill it first. While it's tempting to skip the execution part and just boil the live lobster—it'll die as it cooks, after all—that's a slow and cruel death. Here's the most humane way to quickly dispatch a lobster before cooking.

1 Chill the lobster in the freezer for 20 minutes—this numbs it and slows down its movements, making it safer to work with.

2 Set the lobster on its back on a cutting board. Position the tip of a chef's knife in the middle of the lobster just below the claws, with the cutting edge facing the lobster's head.

3 In one swift motion, forcefully insert the point of the knife into the lobster and then chop down through the head, splitting it in half—this kills the lobster quickly. It isn't necessary to cut completely through the shell on the top of the head, and, in fact, if you don't, the cooked lobster will look more appealing.

Roll out the lobster
—CHRISTINE ADAMS, Charlottesville, Virginia

➤ When I splurge on lobster, I don't want to waste a single delicious morsel. To get the meat out of those long skinny legs, I remove the leg and run a rolling pin over it, from the "foot" up. The meat pops right out.

Shrimp at the ready ➤
—Fine Cooking Test Kitchen

Shrimp is one of our absolute favorite go-to ingredients for making a fast meal. Keep a bag of unpeeled shrimp in the freezer and you're always ready to make a stir-fry, a shrimp curry, or shrimp with pasta.

THAWING

Thawing shrimp in the fridge overnight definitely works, but when we need to quickly defrost a pound or two, here's how we do it: Take the shrimp out of the freezer, open the package, and put them in a large bowl of cold water placed in the sink. Let a trickle of cold water run into the bowl while the excess spills over the sides and into the drain. The shrimp should be ready to shell, devein, and cook in about 15 minutes.

FROZEN SHRIMP ARE ACTUALLY FRESHER

Because there's a lot of variation in quality, it helps to know what to look for when shopping for shrimp.

BEST BET, ICE BLOCKS

The best shrimp are flash frozen in blocks of water, like giant ice cubes, within hours of pulling in the net. This is the best way to preserve the flavor and texture of the shrimp—it seals the shrimp and prevents it from getting freezer burn. If you can buy a block of shrimp from your fishmonger (usually 4- or 5-pound blocks), that's the best way.

NEXT BEST, IQF BAGS

Your next-best bet is to buy frozen unpeeled shrimp in a bag and thaw it yourself. Your supermarket or fishmonger will have bags of frozen shrimp. If you don't see them, ask. Most likely, this shrimp has been individually quick frozen (IQF) and is just as fresh as the ice-block shrimp, just not as protected from freezer burn. So check for excessive ice crystals.

LAST CHOICE, FISH COUNTER

Unless you live where shrimp is caught locally, the shrimp that's displayed at the fish counter won't be fresh; it will have been previously frozen and conveniently thawed for you—but the problem is that you don't know how it was thawed or how long ago it was thawed. If this appears to be your only option, take the time to ask: The store may have some of the very same shrimp in the back that is still frozen. Ask for that instead.

WHEN SHOPPING, LOOK FOR SHRIMP THAT ARE BIG

Larger shrimp are generally better because they offer more of a buffer against overcooking. Bigger shrimp are more expensive, but they're also easier to peel and clean. Look for 21 to 25 count, which refers to the number of shrimp per pound, rather than size designations like "jumbo" or "large," which are not standardized.

LOOK FOR SHRIMP NOT TREATED WITH STP

Many shrimp these days are soaked in a salt-water solution called STP (sodium tripolyphosphate), which helps shrimp maintain moisture during processing and cooking. This may not sound like such a bad thing, but this solution can give shrimp a saltier flavor and a bit of a spongy texture. To avoid shrimp that contain STP, check the ingredient list on bags of frozen shrimp. If you're buying from a fish counter, ask if it's been treated. If you can find only STP-treated shrimp, be sure to reduce the salt in the recipe.

LOOK FOR WILD SHRIMP

We think wild shrimp tend to have a sweeter, more pronounced flavor and a firmer texture than the farmed variety. If you're lucky enough to find some wild-caught shrimp (frozen shrimp will be labeled wild or farmed), grab them, as only about 20% of shrimp sold in the United States are wild caught.

SHELLFISH ON THE GRILL —ELIZABETH KARMEL, *Fine Cooking* contributor

When you're shopping for shellfish, freshness is key. Always buy shellfish on the day you plan to use it and refrigerate it as soon as you can. Not only will fresher shellfish taste better, but it will also cook faster.

Here's what to look for when buying shellfish, how to store it properly, and how long to grill it.

SHELLFISH	WHAT TO BUY	HOW TO STORE	GRILLING TIME (OVER MEDIUM-HIGH HEAT)
Shrimp	• Unless you live close to where they are fished, the freshest shrimp are frozen. That's because they're usually flash frozen within hours of being caught. Most nonfrozen shrimp sold in stores have been previously frozen and are less fresh. • Choose IQF (individually quick frozen) shrimp in the shell. • Look for jumbo 16- to 20-count shrimp, which means there are 16 to 20 shrimp in a pound (in general, the lower the number of shrimp per pound, the larger the shrimp).	Keep shrimp frozen until ready to use; thaw under cold running water. Store thawed shrimp in the refrigerator in a loosely closed plastic bag on a bed of ice in a large bowl or dish with sides. Refresh ice as it melts, and use within a day.	2 to 3 minutes per side
Lobster	• Purchase whole live lobsters and kill them just before grilling (for directions, see p. 102). • One 1½- to 2-lb. lobster per person is usually enough. But if buying "chicken" lobsters, which weigh less than 1 lb., count on two lobsters per person.	Store live lobsters in the refrigerator in a damp paper bag on wet newspapers or paper towels in a large pan or platter with sides. Use within a day.	*Small* (about 1½ lb.), 8 to 10 minutes *Large* (about 2 lb.), 12 to 14 minutes
Lobster tail	• An IQF (individually quick frozen) lobster tail is a good alternative to a whole lobster. Not only is it easier to handle, but it's also less expensive.	Keep frozen until ready to use. Thaw under cold running water just before cooking.	8 minutes
Mussels, clams, and oysters	• When buying mussels, clams, and oysters, make sure their shells are closed or that they close immediately when given a gentle tap. That's an indication they're still alive. • Discard any whose shells open prior to cooking. • Buy more than the quantity required, since you'll likely have to discard a few that don't open during cooking.	Store in the refrigerator on a bed of ice in a large bowl or dish with sides. Refresh ice as it melts, and use within a day.	*Mussels*, 3 to 7 minutes *Clams*, 6 to 10 minutes *Oysters*, 4 to 6 minutes

Deveining shrimp in the shell

—JENNIFER ARMENTROUT,
Fine Cooking contributor

For dishes in which you plan to serve shrimp still in their shells, try this method for deveining them before cooking. Bend the shrimp so that the shell sections nearest the tail separate, exposing the flesh. Insert a toothpick or wooden skewer into the shrimp, digging in deeply enough to get under the vein. Lever the skewer to begin pulling the vein from the shrimp. If you're lucky, you'll get it on the first or second try. Once it pulls out completely, pinch off the end to separate it from the tail. If the vein breaks at the first tail section, try the next one. Sometimes you can pull out just enough to grasp and finish the job with your fingertips before the vein breaks.

Peel shrimp in a jiffy

—DOUG PRYOR, Key West, Florida

We eat a lot of shrimp here in Key West, and the best tool I've found for peeling them is a zip letter opener (the small hand-held plastic kind that are often given away as promotional items). It quickly splits open the shell and separates the flesh for easy deveining.

Boil shrimp in the shell for full flavor

—Fine Cooking Test Kitchen

Boiling shrimp yourself instead of buying it precooked is quick and easy and guarantees freshness. For best flavor, start with shell-on shrimp. (The shells help keep the shrimp moist.) To cook 1 pound of shrimp, bring a medium-size saucepan of salted water to a rolling boil. Drop the shrimp into the water and cook until they turn pink and opaque, 1 to 2 minutes. Drain in a colander and rinse with cold water until the shrimp are cool. Peel and devein, if needed.

Keep shrimp cocktail chilled

—JUDY TINKHAM, via email

I often serve shrimp cocktail at parties. To ensure that the shrimp stay chilled, I fill my serving bowl halfway with water a couple of hours ahead and put it in the freezer. When ready to serve, I arrange the shrimp over the ice. (Be sure to use a freezer-proof serving bowl; glass and ceramic may crack.)

POULTRY

If you want the best-tasting, most humanely raised chicken with no unnatural additives, look for one or more of these labels on the wrapping.

Best bet

USDA organic certified The official organic seal means the chicken was raised under a specific set of humane guidelines, including requirements for shelter and an organic diet without antibiotics or synthetic pesticides.

Next best

No antibiotics used These chickens are not necessarily organic, but they have been raised without antibiotics of any kind.

Certified humane chickens with the Humane Farm Animal Care seal meet requirements for humane treatment, which include access to clean water, no antibiotics, and no cages.

Pastured poultry or "grass-ranged" poultry This term is most often used to label chickens that have been raised on small farms in uncrowded conditions and been allowed to feed on grass in addition to grain.

Keep an eye out for

Air chilled Most chickens are chilled in water, but a new process called air chilling prevents them from absorbing excess water, which can mean a tastier, crispier bird. There are brands that are both air chilled and certified organic.

Kosher Kosher chickens are slaughtered according to Jewish dietary laws. The process includes brining the chicken in a salt solution, which not only removes any remaining blood and bacteria but enhances flavor as well. There are brands that are both kosher and organic.

Don't be fooled by

100% natural This means nothing. Many of these birds are injected with saline solution to add weight. They may also contain "natural" additives, such as carrageenan, broth, tenderizers, or marinades.

Hormone-free All chickens are hormone-free because the use of hormones in poultry is prohibited by law.

Cage-free The birds may still be tightly packed into sheds without room to move, access to the outdoors, or clean surroundings.

Free-range This popular label does not mean much other than that the birds are "allowed" to wander outside the barn for a few short weeks of their lives.

—SUSIE MIDDLETON, *Fine Cooking* contributor

Thin chicken cutlets without a mallet

—SARAH GREENE HOPKINS,
North Yarmouth, Maine

Instead of flattening chicken breasts with a mallet, I freeze the breasts just long enough to get them firm but not rock hard. Then I halve them through the middle to get two thin cutlets. As I heat the pan and prepare other ingredients, the breasts have time to thaw and are ready for cooking.

Put a lid on it ➤

—FRANK FAILLACE, Reston, Virginia

Supermarkets often sell delicate greens in large disposable plastic containers, and I have found a use for the container lids, which otherwise would end up in the trash. Instead of pounding boneless chicken breasts between waxed paper or parchment, which shreds, I use a plastic lid. It's large enough to fully cover one or two large pieces of meat, and it doesn't break or shred when I pound on it. After use, it can be washed and used again, or simply thrown away or recycled.

Use a wire twist tie ➤
to truss chicken legs

—MARY ANN PALCHIKOFF, Fairbanks, Alaska

I often find myself without butcher's twine when I need to truss chicken or turkey legs before roasting. As an alternative, I use those large paper-covered wire twist ties used to wrap lettuce and other produce in grocery stores. I save these twist ties, rinse them to remove any dirt, and stash them in a drawer, ready to use. I throw them away after I've roasted the chicken or turkey.

· HOW TO POUND A PAILLARD ·

Paillard (pronounced pie-yard) is the French term for a boneless chicken breast or other cut of meat that's been pounded into a broad, thin sheet about ¼ inch thick. Start by removing the tenderloin if it's still attached. (That's the little strip of meat often dangling from the back of each chicken breast.)

If you have a small chicken breast, set it skinned side down—the more pliable cut side of the breast is more pounder friendly—on a large sheet of plastic wrap and cover it with a second sheet of plastic wrap. Using a pounder, lightly pound the chicken breast to the desired uniform thickness.

For a larger chicken breast, cut it in half horizontally, put the halves between the two sheets of plastic wrap, and pound as described above. When they're cut in half this way, though, you'll find the chicken breasts need very little, if any, pounding.

My favorite pounder is a disk-style one with a handle in the middle. For quick weeknight cooking, however, I've found that my fist works pretty well, too. And although their pounding surfaces aren't flat, a can or rolling pin can also be used to even out a cutlet. Whatever you use, make sure that it's relatively lightweight with a smooth surface. Unlike tough red meat, which can stand sharp, heavy blows, chicken breasts are delicate and need only gentle coaxing to thin out.

—PAM ANDERSON, *Fine Cooking* contributor

Use spaghetti instead of toothpicks

—MATT PINNOW, Atlanta, Georgia

▶ I like to make stuffed chicken breasts and have found that a short piece of uncooked dried spaghetti easily punctures the meat and substitutes nicely for a toothpick to secure the flaps of meat. When the dish is finished, the spaghetti is cooked, and you don't need to worry about removing it (or forgetting to take out the toothpick).

Hands-free spice-rubbed chicken

—JOHN DAVIS, Spring, Texas

▶ My family loves spice-rubbed chicken on the grill, but it's time-consuming and messy to rub each piece of chicken with the spice mix. Instead, I put all the chicken pieces in a 13 by 9-inch Pyrex baking dish or plastic storage container, add the spice mix, attach the pan's lid, and shake vigorously for about 10 seconds. Each piece of chicken is evenly coated, and the force of the shaking ensures that the spices adhere well. Even better, I take the pan directly out to the grill, eliminating another dirty dish.

Season chicken safely

—SARAH JAMESON, San Antonio, Texas

▶ Before working with raw chicken, I scoop kosher salt from my pinch bowl (a small ramekin) into a smaller bowl and add freshly ground pepper to the bowl as well. That way, my seasonings are in place, and I don't have to worry about cross-contaminating my bowl of salt or getting chicken goo on my pepper mill.

· A GUIDE TO MOIST MEAT & CRISP SKIN ·

Salt the chicken ahead. Salting seasons the bird, of course, but if you can do it a day, or even a few hours, ahead, you'll get more flavorful meat and crisper skin. You can also flavor the salt with herbs and zest.

Use a rack. A V-shaped roasting rack cradles the chicken and allows its juices to drip away, leaving even the bottom skin crisp.

Start breast side up and flip halfway through. Starting with the breast up ensures brown, crispy skin. Turning the bird over keeps the breast moist while the slower-cooking legs finish roasting.

Coax browning along with a sprinkling of sugar. To encourage browning, sprinkle the chicken all over with a little sugar before putting it in the oven.

Add water during roasting to keep the pan drippings from burning.

If the pan dries out and the drippings start to burn before the chicken is done, add a little water to the pan.

—Fine Cooking Test Kitchen

No-mess butter pats ▸

—K.L. WYRILL, San Diego, California

Rubbing butter under the skin of a chicken or turkey used to leave me with slick, greasy hands, and I'd get butter everywhere. A better way is to work with frozen butter: I slice the butter with an egg slicer to get even pieces, and then I separate the slices and put them in a plastic bag in the freezer. The frozen pats slip easily under the poultry skin.

A better way to stuff (and unstuff) a bird ▸

—KIM MARCHUK,
Vancouver, British Columbia, Canada

Before I stuff chicken or turkey, I line the empty cavity with a layer of rinsed cheesecloth—and then I add the stuffing. This makes removing the cooked stuffing much easier. Instead of digging around with a spoon, I simply grab the edges of the cheesecloth and pull out all the stuffing at once.

2 ways to reduce oven spatter ▸

—PAM ANDERSON, *Fine Cooking* contributor

When roasting a chicken, melting chicken fat hitting the hot roasting pan can cause messy spattering. Here are two options for reducing it.

Add water. Roast the chicken on a rack set over a thin layer of water in the roasting pan. The water will prevent the dripping fat from spattering. With this method, however, you lose those rich, dark pan drippings that are the foundation for a flavorful sauce or gravy.

Flatten it. Butterfly the chicken by cutting out its back, and then flatten it and place it in the roasting pan. Because the chicken is roasting flat and low to the pan, the drippings won't have as far to fall, thereby reducing (though not eliminating) the amount of spattering fat.

ROASTING TIMES & TEMPERATURES FOR CHICKEN —Fine Cooking Test Kitchen

TYPE OF CHICKEN	OVEN TEMPERATURE & ESTIMATED TIME	INTERNAL TEMPERATURE
Whole chicken (about 3½ lb.)	400°F for about 1 hour	170°F in thickest part of thigh
Butterflied chicken (about 3½ lb.)	475°F for about 40 minutes or 425°F for about 50 minutes	170°F in thickest part of thigh
Bone-in chicken parts	425°F for 50 to 60 minutes	Well browned and 165°F for white meat, 170°F for dark
Cornish hens (about 1½ lb. each)	425°F for 40 to 45 minutes unstuffed, 45 to 50 minutes stuffed	170°F in thickest part of thigh (center of stuffing should be 165°F)

Whether you buy a rotisserie chicken or have leftovers from your own roast chicken, it's good to know how much chicken meat you now have to make a second meal from. Amounts at right are based on a 4-lb. chicken.

LEFTOVER AMOUNT	YIELD (SLICED OR DICED)
1 whole chicken	5 cups
½ chicken	2½ cups
1 breast	1 cup
1 leg (thigh and drumstick)	1 cup

Browning a ▶ brined turkey

—KIMBERLY Y. MASIBAY, *Fine Cooking* contributor

When you soak a turkey in a brine, the meat's tightly wound protein strands loosen and form a spongy matrix that sops up the liquid, and the meat becomes packed with extra moisture, which helps the white meat stay juicy until the dark meat is fully cooked. All that extra juiciness, though, can potentially interfere with the molecular reactions that turn turkey skin brown and tasty. Brining leaves extra moisture on the surface of the turkey, preventing the skin from getting hot enough for browning reactions (which require hot, dry conditions) to occur.

But brining and browning aren't mutually exclusive. Simply pat the turkey's skin dry before it goes into the oven, preferably a very hot oven—the hotter the oven, the more quickly the skin will dry out completely and the browning can begin. Once you've got the browning underway, you can lower the oven temperature for the remaining cooking time.

Reheating turkey ▶

—LYNN PALERMO, Simcoe, Ontario, Canada

I often find myself cooking for 30 or more people around the holidays. To make things easier, I like to roast the turkey for at least a few hours ahead, if not the day before. To keep the sliced turkey moist while it's reheating, I layer it in a shallow pan and lay a clean, damp dishtowel over the slices. Then I pour warm chicken broth over the towel just until it's soaked through. I seal the pan tightly with foil and reheat the turkey in a 300°F oven until hot. The turkey stays juicy, and I have less to do on the day of the gathering. This technique also works well for reheating stuffing.

8 secrets for a moist and juicy roast turkey

—Fine Cooking Test Kitchen

A perfectly roasted turkey is the holy grail of every cook on Thanksgiving. Here are our tips to help you achieve this goal.

Choose a fresh turkey instead of a frozen one. Ice crystals that form during freezing damage a turkey's muscle cells. When the bird thaws and roasts, fluids leak more readily from the damaged cells, drying out the meat.

Roast two small turkeys rather than one large one. Smaller turkeys roast more evenly than large ones, so for feeding a crowd, two small turkeys are a better option. They'll cook quicker, too.

Brine the turkey. A turkey soaked in a salt-water solution absorbs both the salt and the water, so it's moister to begin with as well as seasoned on the inside. You can flavor a brine as well. (For more information, see Brining, p. 206.)

Rub soft butter under the skin. As it melts, it bastes the turkey and adds buttery flavor. For even more flavor, you can add herbs and spices to the butter.

Truss loosely or not at all. Legs tied up tightly against the sides of the turkey take longer to roast, putting the breast meat in jeopardy of overcooking while the legs take their time.

Roast the turkey upside down at first. Placing the turkey breast side down on a V-rack for the first hour or so of roasting essentially allows it to baste itself. Any marks left by the rack will disappear once you flip the turkey over and finish roasting it.

Don't overcook it. Use an instant-read or probe-style thermometer to monitor the temperature in the thickest part of the thigh (be careful not to hit the bone). You're aiming for 170°F.

Let the turkey rest before carving. The intense heat of the oven forces the juices into the center of the bird, so after roasting, let the turkey rest for roughly 20 minutes (enough time to make the gravy). The juices will redistribute, and you'll get moister slices.

Keep carved turkey slices moist

—IRENE MORETTI, Ridgeville, Ontario, Canada

Just before I carve my Thanksgiving turkey, I carefully remove the skin from the breast, trying to keep it in one piece. When I finish carving and slicing the breast meat, I cover it with the piece of roasted skin. This helps the meat stay warm and moist. I remove the skin just before serving.

DAIRY
&
EGGS

Where to store butter in the fridge
—Fine Cooking Test Kitchen

▶ To keep butter as fresh as possible, store it tightly wrapped away from light on a back shelf in your refrigerator (not in the butter compartment on the fridge door; the temperature fluctuates too much there). You can freeze butter, too. It may seem watery when it thaws, but if you're using it for baking, you'll find little difference in the final baked product.

Planing butter
—KATE THOMAS, Lynnfield, Massachusetts

▶ When preparing breakfast for my family, I often forget to take the butter out of the refrigerator to soften. In a pinch, I use a cheese plane to skim thin slices off the stick of butter. They melt instantly when applied to hot toast, bagels, or English muffins.

Soften butter in minutes
—CATHERINE EMERY, via email

▶ I often forget to bring butter to room temperature ahead of time when a recipe calls for softened butter. To do it quickly, I fill a water glass with very hot tap water and let it sit for a few seconds to warm the glass. I empty the water and turn the glass upside down over the amount of butter I need. The butter softens in less than a minute without melting (as it would if I had put it in the microwave it for a few seconds).

Use paper muffin cups for melting butter
—CHRISTINA WILLIAMS, South Norwalk, Connecticut

▶ When I need to melt a small amount of butter for a recipe, rather than dirty a bowl, I use a paper muffin cup and put it in the microwave for a few seconds. This only works for a few tablespoons of butter, which won't spill out of the cup once melted, and you need to take care not to slosh the hot liquid when removing it from the microwave. But anything that saves me washing another bowl is great.

Slice butter with a pastry cutter
—DELORES JESPERSEN, Grand Marais, Minnesota

▶ You can use a sharp-bladed pastry cutter to slice a cold stick of butter into perfect little pats.

Mix flavored butter in a plastic bag

—EILEEN GODFREY, Simi Valley, California

When making flavored (or compound) butter, instead of mixing the softened butter with the other ingredients in a bowl, I put all the ingredients in a zip-top bag, seal it tightly, and knead until well mixed. Then I lay the bag on a work surface and gently push the butter toward the bottom with a dough scraper or the back of a knife. I snip off a corner of the bag and pipe the butter onto a piece of parchment to form a log, which I wrap and store in the fridge. I find this method neater and easier, and there's no bowl to wash.

BUTTERMILK

Make faux buttermilk

—Fine Cooking Test Kitchen

An easy way to make a quick buttermilk substitute is to add 1 tablespoon white vinegar or lemon juice to 1 cup whole milk and let it stand for 10 minutes. This "sour milk" can pinch-hit for buttermilk in most baked goods. (Don't try using truly soured milk, which is milk that has spoiled and has an unpleasant flavor.) It will provide the acid for leavening and tenderizing, though the final flavor won't be as tangy or as pleasing as it would be with regular buttermilk.

Yogurt substitutes for buttermilk

—CATHERINE SUBICK, Philadelphia, Pennsylvania

I love the taste of buttermilk in baked goods, but somehow I never seem to have it on hand. However, I always have yogurt in the fridge, and I find it makes a good substitute when combined with milk. If the recipe calls for 1 cup of buttermilk, I use ½ cup milk combined with ½ cup yogurt. (Because buttermilk is low fat or nonfat, the yogurt and milk should be low fat or nonfat as well.)

Saving leftover buttermilk

—SHIRLEY POLK, Oliver, British Columbia, Canada

I can't always use an entire carton of buttermilk before it goes bad, so I portion it into zip-top plastic bags, which I then flatten, stack, and freeze for up to 2 months. When I need to use it, I immerse a bag in warm water or defrost it on the counter. The thawed buttermilk won't be as creamy as it once was, so it's not ideal for sauces, but it works fine in baked goods like scones or cakes.

Buttermilk has staying power ➤

—Fine Cooking Test Kitchen

Because of its acidity, which inhibits bacterial growth, buttermilk has good staying power. A fresh carton will keep for 3 to 4 weeks. You'll know it has gone bad if the texture is grainy and it smells off. Always shake the carton before using because the milk solids tend to settle. If you have extra buttermilk but don't plan on using it up in that time, you can freeze it for up to 6 months. Keep in mind that it will separate when it's thawed, and even after mixing it, the texture won't be the same.

CREAM

Keep it cold ➤

—JENNIFER MCLAGAN,
Fine Cooking contributor

When whipping cream, be sure it's well chilled. Cold cream whips up more easily into soft peaks.

No-mess whipped cream ➤

—NANCY ADAMS, Hancock, New Hampshire

When whipping heavy cream with my hand mixer, some of the cream always splatters onto the counter (and me). The solution? I set the bowl in my sink and whip away. A rubber mat underneath protects the sink, and any splatters hit the sink walls and are easily rinsed away. Best of all, my clothes and countertops stay clean. This is also great for beating in dry ingredients like flour when making cakes or cookies.

Bring whipped cream back from the brink ➤

—JENNIFER ARMENTROUT,
Fine Cooking contributor

There you are, whipping cream to go along with your dessert masterpiece, knowing that you're probably getting close to perfect peaks when—whoops!—all of a sudden you push it too far and the cream goes from fluffy to grainy in a split second. Do you start all over again? No, you don't.

Instead, you add a few tablespoons of fresh cream to the overwhipped cream and start whipping again. As long as the overwhipped cream hasn't begun to form clumps of butterfat (which means it's more than just a little overwhipped and is actually on its way to becoming butter), the fresh cream should quickly smooth out the graininess. But this time, stop whipping before you overdo it again. For extra insurance, you can whip the fresh cream in by hand with a whisk.

CHEESE

Humidity is key ➤

—LAURA WERLIN, *Fine Cooking* contributor

Keep cheese in a refrigerator drawer, where the humidity and temperature are higher than in other areas.

Let soft cheeses breathe ➤

—LAURA WERLIN, *Fine Cooking* contributor

Store soft and creamy cheese unwrapped in a plastic container, and poke a few small holes in the lid to keep the cheese from suffocating.

Tailor storage method to the cheese ➤

—TIM BUCCIARELLI, *Fine Cooking* contributor

Wrap your cheese based on its moisture content and age.

Younger, softer cheeses, such as Brie, Taleggio, or chèvre, are more active and need a wrapping that lets them breathe. Waxed paper or parchment works well—their loose folds and crimps allow air to get in yet still offer protection from the drying environment of the refrigerator.

Semifirm to firm cheeses, such as Morbier, Cheddar, or Gruyère, need to breathe less than young cheeses, while they need to be protected more from drying out. Keep these medium-aged cheeses in waxed paper or parchment with a loose overwrap of plastic.

Hard cheeses, such as Parmigiano-Reggiano or extra-aged Gouda, are the most susceptible to drying, and I've found that tightly wrapping in foil works best for them.

Avoid plastic wrap. In general, I avoid wrapping cheeses directly in plastic because I find that it often gives cheese a bitter flavor and unpleasant texture. If you do use plastic, I suggest changing the wrapping often and cutting off a thin layer of the cheese that was in contact with the plastic.

Crumble goat cheese without sticking ➤

—BARBARA MINISH, Ottawa, Ontario, Canada

To crumble goat cheese without it sticking to my fingers, I cut off the amount I need for a recipe and put it in the freezer for 20 to 30 minutes (I set a timer so I don't forget about it). When I take it out, it crumbles like feta.

Best cheese flavor ➤

—LAURA WERLIN, *Fine Cooking* contributor

Take your cheese out of the refrigerator at least 1 hour before serving to get the best flavor..

- -

Weighing grated cheese ➤

—JAN MATHIEU, Luck, Wisconsin

When a recipe calls for grated cheese by weight, I weigh the block of cheese before I start grating and weigh it again, at intervals, as I grate. If the cheese weighs 8 ounces to start with and I need 2 ounces of grated cheese for a recipe, I grate until the block of cheese weighs 6 ounces. It's much easier than grating cheese onto a scale.

- -

Freeze semifirm cheese before grating ➤

—VI ECKARDT, Sarasota, Florida

Grating semifirm cheeses, such as Gruyère, Fontina, or Cheddar, can be messy, especially if they're at room temperature. So I put the cheese in the freezer for 10 to 15 minutes to make it firmer and easier to grate.

- -

No-stick grating ➤

—MARY JANE KALOUSTIAN, Northville, Michigan

Before you shred cheese with a hand-held grater, spray the grater with cooking spray or rub it with a little oil. This will prevent the cheese from sticking and slowing down the job.

- -

Easy Parmigiano matchsticks ➤

—SUSIE MIDDLETON, *Fine Cooking* contributor

Most people are familiar with the technique of using a vegetable peeler to make shards of Parmigiano-Reggiano to top a dish. But if you use a julienne peeler, you get cool little matchsticks of cheese, which make a nice garnish.

- -

Easy onion soup cleanup ➤

—JUDY MCBRIDE, Harlingen, Texas

I love making French onion soup, but I always dread the heavy-duty cleaning job required to remove the crusted cheese from my soup crocks. I've started lightly greasing the inside of the crocks with olive oil before adding the soup, and now cleanup is a breeze. No scrubbing required.

· THE RULES OF MELTING CHEESE ·

RULE NO. 1: Use the cheese the recipe calls for, if you can. It's tempting to substitute a little bit of this for a little bit of that when you're cooking. With cheese, that's not always a good idea. There are well over a thousand distinguishable cheeses, and it's no exaggeration to say that they are made by a thousand different methods. This embarrassment of variables guarantees that no two cheeses will have exactly the same properties—they'll differ in appearance, flavor, and texture, as well as in their melting behavior. Over time, various cultures have created dishes that show off the unique qualities of their local cheeses. You're better off sticking to the tried and true—you'll never be able to make a saucy Swiss fondue from a stringy Italian mozzarella. But what if you don't have the exact cheese specified in a recipe, or what if you just want to throw together a cheese toast, a vegetable gratin, or a quesadilla? Follow the second rule.

RULE NO. 2: Choose a cheese that's known to melt the way you want it to. The problem is, when you're shopping for cheese, you can't necessarily predict its melting behavior by scrutinizing its appearance or the nutrition information label. Cheeses melt in lots of ways, and you can't depend on seemingly similar cheeses to melt identically. One semisoft cheese might behave quite differently from another for reasons that are as complex as the cheeses themselves. But there's no need to plow through dozens of scientific research papers on the properties of melted cheese. All you really need to know is that cheeses fall into three broad melting categories: stretchy and stringy, smooth and flowing, and nonmelting.

RULE NO. 3: Be gentle with the heat. Choosing the right cheese is important, but that's not the only secret to success. You must also treat the cheese kindly during cooking. Even if you're using the perfect cheese for a dish, too high a temperature or too much heating time can make its proteins tighten up, squeezing out both water and fat. Result: rubbery globs of protein awash in a pool of grease. When this happens to pizza (and it often does because pizza is baked in such a hot oven), it's not the worst thing in the world,

but when it happens to a cheese fondue, you've got a flop on your hands. And, unfortunately, these changes aren't reversible. But there are a few steps you can take to keep your cheese from meeting this sad fate.

Shred it. By shredding cheese, you increase the surface area that's in contact with the heat source, which reduces the amount of time the cheese will take to melt.

Give it a head start. Bringing cheese to room temperature before you hit it with heat also lessens the amount of time the cheese will need to be exposed to heat before it melts.

Use low heat. Although not all recipes call for it, cheese prefers low heat. At higher temperatures, the proteins in the cheese are more likely to seize up and squeeze out fat and moisture. So if you need to finish off a cheese topping under the broiler, keep a watchful eye on it and take care to expose it to the heat only long enough for the cheese to melt.

— ROBERT L. WOLKE,
Fine Cooking contributor

The melting characteristics of cheese When you want to get creative, choose a cheese that has the melting characteristics you want, and you won't go far wrong. The names of the cheeses in this table are generic, because cheeses go by many names and may have many variations.

STRETCHY & STRINGY MELTERS	SMOOTH & FLOWING MELTERS	NONMELTERS
These are the cheeses we love on pizza, in panini, and stuffed into croquettes. They stay pretty much where we put them, without running all over the place, and they can form long strings when pulled.	This category claims the largest number of cheeses. Some are viscous when melted, while others have little body. These cheeses are great for making toasted sandwiches; topping soups or vegetable tarts; stuffing into vegetables; adding richness to baked pasta dishes; and folding into biscuit, scone, and bread dough. They also blend smoothly into other dishes, such as polenta, mashed potatoes, risotto, and soufflés.	Some of these cheeses can be grilled, fried, or baked; though they may soften when heated, they won't lose their shape and flow. There are a few possible reasons that some cheeses don't melt: The cheese might be extremely high in salt, or it might be low or high in acid, or it may contain high levels of whey proteins (during the cheesemaking process, whey is removed from most cheese).
Mozzarella (aged and fresh) Fresh Cheddar cheese curds Provolone Queso Oaxaca Scamorza String cheese	Asiago Blue cheeses (*they melt around the mold*) Cheddar Emmentaler Fontina Gouda Gruyère Havarti Monterey Jack Muenster Soft-ripened cheeses like Brie and Camembert (*the rind will not melt*) Parmigiano-Reggiano*	Cottage cheese Feta Fresh goat cheese Fresh Mexican cheeses such as queso blanco, queso fresco, ranchero, cotija Haloumi Paneer Ricotta Parmigiano-Reggiano*

SOURCES: *Dr. Carol Chen and Dr. Dean Sommer of the Wisconsin Center for Dairy Research*

* *Very hard, aged cheeses like Parmigiano don't fit cleanly into these categories. If you finely grate them and add them to a sauce or a dish with moisture, they will melt smoothly, but due to their own lack of moisture, they won't melt very well alone.*

EGGS

Spot the freshest eggs ▶
—Fine Cooking Test Kitchen

You might be surprised to learn that some egg cartons tell you exactly what day the eggs were packed—a piece of information that's a lot more specific than a sell-by or use-by date. About one-third of the eggs in the United States are packed under the USDA's voluntary grading service. If the eggs in your market were graded by a USDA inspector, the carton will display a USDA grade shield, and a three-digit code that reveals the packing date will be stamped somewhere on the carton, usually on the short side near the expiration date. The code is actually an ordinal calendar date, meaning it represents a day of the year, not a day of a month. So, a carton marked "001" means it was packed on January 1; "365" means it was packed on December 31.

To find the freshest eggs in your store, look for the packing date that has the highest number (with the exception of the transition from December to January). Don't confuse the packing date with the packing plant number, which is always preceded by the letter "P." If the carton doesn't have a USDA shield, then it was packed under local regulations, which vary from state to state, and it may or may not carry a packing date.

Keep eggs in the carton ▶
to preserve freshness
—MARIE SIMMONS, *Fine Cooking* contributor

The refrigerator door, where many egg storage trays are located, is subject to constant temperature fluctuation as the door opens and closes, so it's not a good place to keep eggs. To keep eggs fresh, store them in their carton on a shelf in the coldest part of the refrigerator. The carton protects the eggshells from cracking, prevents the loss of moisture (which thins egg whites and accelerates staleness), and prevents the absorption of refrigerator odors.

How to break an egg ▶
—Fine Cooking Test Kitchen

Whenever you need to crack open an egg, rap it on a flat surface, like a counter, rather than on the rim of your bowl. Breaking eggs on a bowl rim causes more shell shatter and sometimes drives tiny shell shards—the kind that can be infuriatingly hard to fish out—into the egg white. If you crack your eggs on the counter (or on the inside wall of your bowl), shell fragments should appear in your bowl far less often.

Separating eggs smartly

—Fine Cooking Test Kitchen

► If you need to separate lots of eggs, separate each egg individually over a small bowl. This way, you'll be sure that each white is clean before adding it to the others in your beating bowl, and there's no chance that the last egg you separate will break its yolk and contaminate a bowl full of whites.

Be careful subbing different size eggs

—Fine Cooking Test Kitchen

► Eggs are classified by weight by the dozen. Because of this, there will be slight variations in the weights of eggs in every carton. A dozen extra-large eggs weigh 27 oz. (about 2¼ oz. each on average), a dozen large eggs weigh 24 oz. (about 2 oz. each), and a dozen medium eggs weigh 21 oz. (about 1¾ oz. each).

IF YOUR RECIPE CALLS FOR 4 OR MORE EGGS . . .

In nonbaking recipes, if you're substituting only 1, 2, or 3 extra-large or medium eggs for large eggs, simply make a one-to-one direct substitution. Beyond that, use these equivalents:

- In place of 4 large eggs, use 4 extra large or 5 medium.
- In place of 5 large eggs, use 4 extra large or 6 medium.
- In place of 6 large eggs, use 5 extra large or 7 medium.
- 1 extra-large egg = 4 Tbs. (2⅔ Tbs. white and 1⅓ Tbs. yolk)
- 1 large egg = 3¼ Tbs. (2¼ Tbs. white and 1 rounded Tbs. yolk)
- 1 medium egg = 3 Tbs. (2 Tbs. white and 1 Tbs. yolk)

Separate eggs cold

—JENNIFER MCLAGAN,
***Fine Cooking* contributor**

► It's easiest to separate eggs when they're cold because the yolks are firmer.

Eggshell grabber

—CHARMAINE SWENSON, Milaca, Minnesota

► The edge of a serrated grapefruit spoon easily grabs elusive bits of eggshell.

Freeze egg whites in ice cube trays

—HELEN PLODERER-KING,
Châteauneuf-du-Pape, France

► When a recipe calls for egg yolks, I freeze the remaining egg whites in an ice cube tray, taking care to put one egg white in each ice cube section. This way I know that when I need, say, three egg whites, all I have to do is push out three cubes. I let them come to room temperature and use them according to the recipe.

KEEP IT CLEAN

Whipped egg whites can billow up to eight times their original volume, but a single drop of yolk or a little grease lingering in a mixing bowl can reduce the egg whites' foaming power by two-thirds. That's because the fat bonds with the egg proteins before they can bond with one another and form those mesh-like protein sheets necessary for trapping bubbles.

GIVE EGG WHITES A LITTLE WARM-UP

Egg whites whip to their greatest volume at about 70°F. When whites are warm, they don't cling together as much, making it easier to incorporate air.

OLDER IS BETTER

When it comes to choosing eggs for whipping, opinions differ. As eggs age, the whites become thinner and whip easily to great volume. Fresher eggs are more viscous, so they take longer to beat, but some cooks think that the resulting foam is more stable. For making clouds of meringue in particular, we opt for older whites and extra volume and add a little cream of tartar to stabilize the foam.

USE 'EM OR LOSE 'EM

Have you ever beaten whites to perfect medium-stiff peaks, turned away for a few moments to measure the other ingredients, and returned to find your foam looking dry, clumpy, and overbeaten? That's because egg white foam exposed to air quickly begins to coagulate and lose its elasticity. So if you're beating egg whites to soft peaks without sugar for a cake or soufflé, be sure to have all the remaining ingredients ready to go, and add them as soon as the whites are beaten.

Reviving overbeaten ➤
egg whites

—ALICE MEDRICH,
Fine Cooking contributor

Sometimes it only becomes apparent that you've overbeaten your egg whites (they clump instead of blend) after you have begun to fold them into your batter. Happily, there is a fix. First, use a clean spatula to scoop about a quarter of the whites into the batter. If the whites clump badly as you fold, beat a fresh egg white into the remaining whites for a few seconds to remoisten them—they won't be perfect, but they should soften up. You can now fold the revived whites into your batter.

Poach leftover egg yolks

—JEANNE SCHIMMEL, via email

I recently prepared a recipe that called for egg whites, and I had several intact egg yolks left over. Instead of putting them in the fridge and forgetting about them, I poached them in simmering water just as I would whole eggs, until they were firmly cooked, and then I crumbled them into a potato salad.

Easy cleaning for poached egg pans

—MARLA POLLARD,
Stratford, Prince Edward Island, Canada

I make poached eggs almost every morning for breakfast and used to find the pot very difficult to clean afterward, because the egg whites would stick to the pan. Thinking back to biochemistry class, I remembered that bleach breaks down proteins, like those found in egg whites. Problem solved: Now I soak the poaching pot in a solution of 1 part bleach to 10 parts water while I eat my breakfast. The cooked-on egg whites wipe off easily.

Keep scrambled eggs from sticking to the pan

—Fine Cooking Test Kitchen

To keep scrambled eggs from sticking, don't pour raw eggs into a cold pan. This allows the eggs to get into any nicks or imperfections in the pan's surface, and the eggs will literally cook into the pan. Heating the empty pan first will expand the metal and effectively seal those imperfections, so your eggs will cook on the surface, not below it. Of course, you don't want the pan too hot, or you'll end up with fried eggs, so heat the pan and the butter gently.

Cookie cutters keep eggs from cracking

—DOROTHY HALBERG,
Battle Ground, Washington

To keep eggs from cracking when boiling them, I put each one in a small metal cookie cutter in the saucepan. The cutters keep the eggs from banging into one another, and I never get cracked eggs.

Slice eggs with a pastry cutter

—SHARON CURTIS, via email

I use a pastry cutter to slice hard-boiled eggs for egg salads. I get nice, even slices with only one hand motion for each egg.

Boiling an egg may not be rocket science, but timing is important. Here are some guidelines.

START EGGS IN COLD WATER

Put the eggs in a saucepan and add enough cold water to cover them by about 1 inch. Set the pan over medium-high heat, and as soon as the water reaches a brisk simmer, start timing according to the guidelines below.

SIMMER, DON'T BOIL, EGGS

As the eggs cook, adjust the heat as needed to maintain a brisk simmer. (Though we talk about hard-boiled eggs—and we're using that term here—the fact is that cooking eggs in boiling water cracks the shell and makes the eggs tough and rubbery. A simmer works much better.)

GIVE EGGS A COOL DOWN

When the eggs are cooked, carefully pour out most of the hot water, leaving the eggs in the pan. Set the pan in the sink under cool running water for a few minutes, until the eggs are barely warm.

OLDER IS BETTER WHEN IT COMES TO PEELING EGGS

If the shells are stubborn, try peeling them under running water. The fresher the egg, the more attached the shell, so for boiling, older eggs are preferable.

SOFT BOILED: 2 MINUTES

The white is solid, but the yolk is still runny. Serve in an egg cup for breakfast. Use the side of a small spoon to crack and remove the pointed end of the egg, making a hole in the shell large enough to fit the spoon. Or use egg scissors, if you have them.

MEDIUM BOILED: 4½ MINUTES

The yolk is solid but still dark orange-yellow, moist, and dense in the middle. Beautiful and delicious quartered on a salad.

HARD BOILED: 8 MINUTES

The yolk is completely solid, light yellow, and crumbly, with no sign of a green or gray ring around the yolk. Perfect for egg salad or deviled eggs.

THE BOIL-AND-WALK-AWAY METHOD

For another way to hard-boil eggs, begin as directed at left with the eggs in cold water, but once the water reaches a brisk simmer, turn off the heat and let the eggs sit uncovered in the hot water for at least 10 minutes and up to 30 minutes—the water cools gradually, preventing the eggs from overcooking. This is a great method when you're multitasking and can't pay careful attention to the eggs.

It's not always overcooking that causes a ring

—ELISA MALOBERTI,
Fine Cooking contributor

The gray-green discoloration you sometimes see on the surface of a hard-cooked yolk is caused by a reaction between the sulfur and the iron in the egg, but it affects neither the egg's flavor nor its nutritional content. This chemical reaction is usually brought on by overcooking, but it can also be caused by water that's high in iron (hard water, for example). If your problem is hard water, try cooking your eggs in bottled water. But if it's not the water, then the solution is to avoid overcooking the eggs.

DRY GOODS

How to store chocolate ►
—Fine Cooking Test Kitchen

Chocolate will keep for a year at room temperature, if kept below 70°F. Wrap it in a few layers of plastic to keep it as airtight as possible and put it in a dark cupboard, away from strong-smelling foods. (Chocolate, like butter, will absorb strong aromas.) You can store chocolate in the refrigerator or freezer if the cupboard gets too warm, but a moist environment isn't the best place. If you do chill your chocolate, bring it to room temperature while still wrapped to prevent condensation from forming, as any water on the chocolate can interfere with its ability to melt smoothly.

Chopping chocolate ►
—Fine Cooking Test Kitchen

Instead of chips, try chopping pieces of chocolate from a solid block— the chocolate will most likely be better quality, and the pieces add great texture. If you plan to melt chocolate, you'll have less chance of scorching it if you first chop it as evenly as possible.

- When chopping chocolate, tiny shards get everywhere. For easy cleanup, line a rimmed baking sheet with parchment and put your cutting board on top of that. Use the paper to gather the shards.
- To chop a thick slab of chocolate, set the blade of your biggest knife on a corner of the slab and bear down with both hands to break off a small bit; repeat. As that corner becomes a flat edge, turn the slab and begin cutting at another corner.
- For chopping large amounts of chocolate, a food processor can work. Break thin bars into pieces and pulse with the steel blade until chopped. For block chocolate, cut the block into chunks that will fit in the feed tube and use the coarse grating disk (heavy block chocolate might damage the machine if you use the steel blade).

Easy bittersweet chocolate shards ►
—ALICE MEDRICH,
Fine Cooking contributor

Here is a simple technique for making bittersweet chocolate shards.

1 Tear off two 16-inch-long sheets of waxed paper. Scrape melted chocolate onto one sheet and spread with an offset metal spatula in a thin, even layer to within about 1/3 inch from each edge. Cover the chocolate with the second sheet of waxed paper.

2 Starting at one short edge, roll the paper and chocolate into a narrow tube about 1 inch in diameter. Refrigerate the tube seam side down on a baking sheet for at least 2 hours.

3 Remove the tube from the fridge and quickly unroll it while the chocolate is still cold and brittle to crack it into long curved shards. Peel back the top sheet of waxed paper.

4 Immediately slide a metal spatula under the chocolate to release it from the waxed paper, and then slide the shards onto a rimmed baking sheet. Refrigerate until ready to use. Warm fingers will melt the shards, so handle them with a spatula or tongs.

How to melt chocolate ➤

—Fine Cooking Test Kitchen

Chop first. Chopping chocolate helps it melt more quickly and evenly. Because white and milk chocolates are delicate and scorch easily, it's best to chop them finely to melt them with minimal heat. Dark chocolate is more forgiving, so chop it into coarse, almond-size pieces. It will take a little longer to melt than if it were finely chopped, but it means less knife work up front and less frequent stirring.

Skip the double boiler, use a skillet instead. Most directions for melting chocolate suggest using a double boiler (in lieu of melting it in a pan directly on the heat, which could easily scorch the chocolate). But chocolate expert Alice Medrich has refined an even safer method. Instead of suspending the bowl of chopped chocolate over a pot of water, she puts the bowl right into a wide skillet of very hot but not simmering water. Here's why: In a double-boiler setup, you can't see what's going on with the water; it can easily start boiling without your knowing it since the water is completely hidden by the bowl of chocolate. Steam is hotter than boiling water, and it can scorch the chocolate. But with Alice's skillet method, you can see what the water is doing and control the temperature as needed.

Stir the chocolate. Occasionally stir the chocolate as well as any other ingredients you're directed to melt along with it, like butter, until melted and smooth. Remove the bowl from the pan, wipe the bottom of the bowl dry, and let the melted chocolate cool slightly (unless otherwise directed) before using it.

A microwave works well, too. Though you might find it fussier than using a water bath, the microwave is also a good tool for melting chocolate. Heat the chocolate on 50% (medium) power for 1 minute and then stir. Continue heating in 15-second bursts, stirring between each round, until the chocolate melts.

Watch out for water. If you're melting chocolate on its own, just a few drops of water can make the chocolate seize into an unworkable mass. Be sure that all the tools that come in contact with the chocolate are bone-dry before you start, and don't cover melting chocolate (condensation from the lid might drip into the chocolate).

Why chocolate seizes (and what to do about it)

—Fine Cooking Test Kitchen

Chocolate can seize while you're melting it if a small amount of moisture gets into it. There's no question whether your chocolate has seized because it will transform from a smooth state to a grainy, matte, clumpy mess.

Why it happens. Chocolate is composed of fine, dry particles (cocoa and sugar) in rich fat (cocoa butter). If a few drops of water (or even a bit of steam) get stirred into melted chocolate, the dry cocoa and sugar particles will clump together and form a dull, dry, grainy mess.

How to fix it. You can usually fix seized chocolate by whisking in more water, which will provide enough liquid to wet all the seized particles and smooth the chocolate (but this may change the proportions of your recipe).

How to prevent it. To prevent seized chocolate, you need to melt the chocolate with a sufficient amount of liquid from the recipe. The magic amount necessary is 1 tablespoon of water (or a water-type liquid) for every 2 ounces of chocolate, meaning your liquid must be at least 25% the weight of your chocolate (water's weight and volume are the same, so this is easy to calculate; for example, 1 tablespoon is ½ fluid ounce and also ½ ounce by weight).

The liquid can be pure water or milk, or you can use cream and butter, but you'll need to calculate the amount of water they contribute (cream is 60% water, and butter is only 20% water). Specialty chocolates with high percentages of cocoa may need a bit more liquid.

If your recipe doesn't call for adding any liquid to the melted chocolate, just be careful not to let water or steam get in the bowl, and be sure to use dry utensils.

Using high-percentage chocolates
—Fine Cooking Test Kitchen

Many high-quality bittersweet or semisweet chocolates contain significantly higher than average amounts of chocolate liquor, some as high as 80% or more. Despite the fact that these chocolates can be of excellent quality, using them in recipes not significantly designed for them can give you disappointing results: Cakes can turn out dry or overbaked, and ganaches can curdle.

Fine Cooking contributor and chocolate guru Alice Medrich has developed a way to convert recipes to work better with high-percentage chocolates: For chocolates labeled 66% or higher, use 25% to 35% less chocolate than called for in the recipe and add up to 1½ teaspoons more granulated sugar for each ounce of chocolate originally called for. For example, if a brownie recipe calls for 8 ounces of chopped semisweet chocolate and 1 cup sugar, you would use only about 6 ounces of high-percentage chopped chocolate and 1 cup plus 4 tablespoons of sugar.

Don't use chips
—Fine Cooking Test Kitchen

Chocolate chips contain significantly less cocoa butter than the same type of bar chocolate, so it's best not to substitute chips when semisweet or bittersweet chocolate is called for.

Treat white chocolate with care
—Fine Cooking Test Kitchen

White chocolate contains high percentages of both cocoa butter and milk solids, so it's the most temperature sensitive of the chocolates. Be careful when you melt it—it burns easily, so use very low heat. In addition, the milk solids can coagulate with too much heat, leaving tiny lumps in the chocolate, so be sure to use a water bath or very low power on the microwave.

Working with cocoa ➤
—Fine Cooking Test Kitchen

Substituting cocoa for chocolate. Cocoa can often be substituted for baking chocolate. Use 3 tablespoons cocoa and 1 tablespoon butter for each ounce of unsweetened baking chocolate.

Measure cocoa like flour. Spoon the unsifted cocoa into a measuring cup and level it off without compacting it. Sift it after measuring to remove any lumps. If the recipe calls for measuring sifted cocoa, sift the cocoa over the measuring cup and then level it off without compacting it.

Getting the lumps out. When dissolving cocoa in liquid, stir just enough of the liquid into the cocoa to make a stiff paste. Stir and mash the paste until it's smooth, and then stir in the rest of the liquid gradually. If you'll be adding sugar to the cocoa, do it before adding the liquid.

Dust cocoa powder ➤
—SHANNON SEEBACH, Las Vegas, Nevada

When I want to sprinkle a dessert with cocoa powder (or confectioners' sugar), I put the cocoa in a tea ball and dust it just as I would with a sieve. It gives me more control, especially when sprinkling over small items.

· COCOA: NATURAL VS. DUTCH-PROCESSED ·

Cocoa powder comes in two styles: natural (usually simply labeled "unsweetened cocoa powder") and Dutch-processed (or alkalized), which has been treated with alkali to neutralize its natural acidity. Both taste bitter out of the box, but natural has a fruitier, more acidic flavor, while Dutch-processed cocoa is mellower, with an almost nutty flavor.

In recipes without a chemical leavening agent such as baking soda, taste alone can be your guide, but for most baking recipes, it's best to use the style called for, as Dutch-processed and natural cocoas react differently to baking soda and baking powder. (Baking soda, which is alkaline, is generally paired with natural cocoa to neutralize its acidity; baking powder is paired with Dutch-processed cocoa because both ingredients are essentially neutral already.)

GELATIN

Cooking with gelatin ➤

—Fine Cooking Test Kitchen

Gelatin, a stabilizer derived from animal collagen, isn't an everyday ingredient, but learning to work with it can give you spectacular-looking desserts.

- Soften gelatin for success. Before adding gelatin to a recipe, it must be softened and then melted. For powdered gelatin, the softening process is also known as "blooming."
- Sprinkle or "rain" the powdered gelatin evenly over its softening liquid to keep lumps from forming.
- Set the gelatin aside for a few minutes until it swells or "blooms" as it absorbs the liquid.
- For every 2 teaspoons powdered gelatin, use about ¼ cup liquid for blooming. One ¼-ounce packet of Knox® brand powdered gelatin contains about 2¼ teaspoons.
- Always add softened gelatin to warm or hot mixtures; adding the gelatin to a cold mixture will make it firm up immediately, creating an unpleasant stringy or lumpy texture.

? I'M A VEGETARIAN. WHAT SORT OF GELATINS CAN I USE?

Of the vegetarian alternatives available, the one I like best is agar-agar, which is derived from red sea algae. Flavorless and colorless, agar-agar comes in powder, flake, or stick form and can be found at health-food stores or Asian markets. The most widely available and consistent brand I've found is Eden Foods®.

Agar-agar and gelatin behave differently in a couple of ways. Agar-agar, which usually sets up stiffer than gelatin, will set up and remain solid at room temperature. Gelatin, on the other hand, needs refrigeration to set up and will eventually melt at room temperature.

The two are similar in that you have to melt agar-agar in a hot liquid (above 140°F) as you do with gelatin. And agar-agar's gelling properties, like gelatin's, are sensitive to acids (vinegar and citrus), so depending on the concentration of acids you may need more dried agar-agar.

—ERIC TUCKER, *Fine Cooking* contributor

- Although powdered gelatin is the form most widely used by home cooks, sheet gelatin is preferred by some pros. The sheets are standardized regardless of thickness or dimension, so 2 sheets equal 1 teaspoon Knox brand powder (other powder brands may differ in their gelling power). Soften sheet gelatin by soaking it in cold water for about 10 minutes. Squeeze it to drain excess liquid before you melt it into the liquid ingredients in the recipe.

Not all fruits react well with gelatin
—KIMBERLY Y. MASIBAY,
Fine Cooking contributor

▶ Figs, guavas, kiwis, mangos, melons, papayas, pineapples, and fresh ginger contain enzymes that prevent gelatin from setting, no matter how long you let it chill. These enzymes have the unique ability to break down protein, and gelatin is, in fact, protein. It's all right to use cooked or canned versions of these fruits, though, because the heat of cooking and the canning process deactivates the enzymes. As a garnish, fresh fruits would be fine.

LEAVENERS

Make your own baking powder
—BRIAN GEIGER,
Fine Cooking contributor

▶ There are two reasons you might want to make your own baking powder:
- You get to choose the ingredients that go into it (and can avoid acids that contain aluminum, which may result in a metallic taste).
- It will be really fresh (if the purchased kind is kept on the shelf too long, moisture from the air can cause the acid to mix with the baking soda, thereby neutralizing both).

It's simple to do. Mix 2 parts cream of tartar with 1 part baking soda and 1 part cornstarch. Store in a cool, dry place for up to several months. How long it lasts depends on how airtight it's stored, how often you open it, and the humidity.

To test the freshness of your baking powder, either homemade or purchased, add 1 teaspoon to 1 cup of hot water. The mixture should bubble. If it doesn't, toss it.

Know your yeast

—PETER REINHART,
Fine Cooking contributor

Some bakers disagree about this, but nearly all breads and pastries will perform equally well with any of the available yeast products (fresh, active dry, quick rise, or instant).

Active dry yeast, developed about 150 years ago, is sold in sealed, foil-lined packets. In the packaging process, about 25% of the yeast cells die off, releasing a small amount of glutathione, which causes relaxation of gluten (this makes it a good yeast for pizza dough, but it's not ideal for all dough products).

Instant yeast, also called quick rise or rapid rise, came along about 30 years ago and has become more popular as its availability has increased. Because none of the yeast cells die during packaging, it requires 25% less instant yeast than active dry yeast to leaven a loaf. The biggest advantage of instant yeast is that it dissolves directly in dough without having to be hydrated in warm water the way active dry yeast often does.

Fresh yeast, also called compressed or cake yeast, is sold refrigerated in foil-wrapped blocks and cubes. It's a moist product and has a limited shelf life of about 3 weeks, even if refrigerated. It is also harder to find for home baking. Professional bakers have traditionally liked this type of yeast because it's what they learned to bake with, but many of them are now switching to instant yeast because of its extended shelf life and ease of use.

Substituting instant for regular active dry yeast

—PETER REINHART,
Fine Cooking contributor

Here's an easy rule: Instant yeast is 25% more concentrated than active dry. That is, if a recipe calls for 1 teaspoon of instant yeast, use 1¼ teaspoons active dry.

Conversely, if a recipe calls for 1 teaspoon active dry yeast, you'll need only about ¾ teaspoon instant. Instant yeast becomes "rapid rising" only if you use the extra 25% you'd use for active dry yeast. The shorter rising time, however, may have an impact on the flavor of baked goods, especially when you're working in big batches, because a faster rise (or fermentation) reduces the flavor-development period and increases the possibility of over-fermentation.

Toasting ahead ▶

—KAREN TANNENBAUM, Rhinebeck, New York

To save time and get ready for my holiday baking, I like to toast large batches of nuts and store them in the freezer. They keep for up to 3 months, and all I have to do is measure out the amount I need and let the nuts come to room temperature before adding them to my recipe.

· THERE'S MORE THAN ONE WAY TO SKIN A HAZELNUT ·

The skin of a hazelnut is bitter, and that's why recipes call for skinning the nuts. Here are two ways to skin them yourself. (For both methods: Let the nuts cool completely before using or before storing in a sealed container in the freezer for up to 3 months.)

The toasting method Spread the nuts in a single layer on a baking sheet and toast in a 375°F oven until the skins are mostly split and the nuts are light golden brown (the skins will look darker) and fragrant, about 10 minutes. Don't over-toast or the nuts will become bitter. Wrap the hot nuts in a clean dishtowel and let them sit for 5 to 10 minutes. Then vigorously rub the nuts against themselves in the towel to remove most of the skins. Try to get at least half of the skins off. This may take a lot of rubbing, so be persistent.

Pros: The nuts get toasted and skinned all in one step; uses the oven (which might be heating anyway for whatever you'll be making with the nuts) rather than dirtying a saucepan.

Cons: Almost impossible to get the nuts completely skinned; stains a dishtowel (so don't use one you really care about).

The blanching method For every ½ cup of hazelnuts, bring 1½ cups water to a boil. Add 2 tablespoons baking soda and the nuts; boil for 3 minutes —expect the water to turn black and watch out for boilovers. Run a nut under cold water and see if the skin slips off easily. If not, boil the nuts a little longer, until the skins slip off. Cool the nuts under cold running water, slip off the skins, blot dry, and then toast in a 375°F oven. (This method is adapted from *Fine Cooking* contributor Rose Levy Beranbaum.)

Pro: Completely skins the nuts.

Cons: Each nut must be skinned individually (which is easy but time-consuming if you're skinning a lot of nuts); nuts must be toasted in a separate step; nuts won't be as crisp as with the toasting method.

—JENNIFER ARMENTROUT, *Fine Cooking* contributor

Containing nuts ▶
while chopping

—CHARLES MCENIRY, Stoughton, Wisconsin

When chopping hard ingredients like roasted nuts, I put a cutting board inside my 13- by 11-inch baking pan and then use my chef's knife to chop away. Pieces may bounce and roll off the board, but they land within the confines of the pan instead of on the counter or the floor. This method works even better if your pan has tall sides—mine is 3 inches high.

OIL & VINEGAR

Taste nut oils ▶
before using

—JENNIFER ARMENTROUT,
Fine Cooking contributor

While all oils have a limited shelf life, nut and seed oils, like hazelnut, almond, sesame, and walnut, are more likely than others to turn rancid. The main reason is that they've sat for too long on the shelf, either at home or in the market. I've purchased nut oils that had gone bad before they were opened. The lesson: Be sure to taste your oil before every use. An oil can be rancid without smelling bad, so don't just take a whiff—try it. If its flavor is the slightest bit unpleasant, discard it.

HOW TO PROTECT THOSE PRICEY OILS

Rancid oil is inevitable, but you can do a couple of things to delay it. Air, light, and temperature are the enemies, so . . .

1 Purchase from a store that has high turnover; chances are the oil will be fresher when you buy it.

2 Transfer the oil to a metal or dark glass container if it didn't come in one, in order to block light.

3 Tightly close the container to keep air out.

4 Store the oil in the refrigerator to keep it cool.

Having olive oil on hand ▶

—SUSAN EVANS,
Martha's Vineyard, Massachusetts

I tend to buy olive oil for cooking in large containers, but they are too heavy and unwieldy to pour from every day. I used to decant the oil into a smaller glass bottle, but recently I discovered that pouring the oil into a small plastic squeeze bottle works best of all. It's light and easy to handle and is great for filling a measuring spoon with oil without spills, coating a piece of parchment, or drizzling oil over food before or after cooking. When I'm not using the squeeze bottle, I store it in a cool, dark place to prolong the shelf life of the oil.

Make your own seasoned rice vinegar

—DABNEY GOUGH,
Fine Cooking contributor

➤ If you already have some plain rice vinegar in the pantry and would rather not buy a separate bottle of seasoned vinegar, just combine ¼ cup of the plain rice vinegar with 4 teaspoons sugar and ½ teaspoon kosher salt.

Two-in-one pasta tip

—LILLIAN JULOW, Gainesville, Florida

➤ When draining cooked pasta, I place the serving bowl under the colander in the sink. That way the hot water spills into the dish, warming it up. If the sauce needs loosening, I can then scoop out some of the hot, starchy cooking water that's left in the bowl.

· HOW TO ACHIEVE PERFECTLY COOKED PASTA ·

Cooking pasta isn't difficult, but if you know a little about the science behind the cooking, you can help your pasta dishes really shine.

When you drop pasta into a pot of boiling water, starch granules on the surface of the pasta instantly swell up and then pop. The starch rushes out, and suddenly the pasta's surface is sticky with this exuded starch. Eventually, most of this starch dissolves in the water. Here are a few tips that will help you manage these surface starches for perfectly cooked pasta.

Use plenty of water. This helps prevent pasta from sticking together by quickly washing away the exuded starch. A big pot of water will also return to a boil faster after you've added the pasta.

Stir at the start. The first minute or two is the crucial period when the pasta surface is coated with sticky, glue-like starch. If you don't stir then, the pasta can fuse together as it cooks.

Add salt, but not oil. A generous amount of salt in the water seasons the pasta internally as it absorbs liquid and swells. Pasta that's cooked in oily water won't stick together, but it will become slippery and, as a result, the sauce will slide off the pasta rather than get absorbed.

Don't rinse. In addition to cooling the pasta too much, rinsing can wash off any remaining surface starch, which at this point you don't want to do. Any surface starch that remains on the pasta is now beneficial: it can help to thicken your sauce slightly.

Toss hot pasta with hot sauce. As pasta cools, the swollen starches crystallize and become insoluble, which means the pasta can't absorb very well. So to help the pasta really soak up your flavorful sauce, be sure the sauce is warm when the pasta is done.

—**Fine Cooking Test Kitchen**

2 tips for whole-wheat pasta

—LAURA GIANNATEMPO,
Fine Cooking contributor

▶ **Beyond al dente.** The texture of whole-wheat pasta is chewier and tougher than that of regular pasta, but we found that if you cook it a little beyond al dente, it gets better. We recommend setting the timer for the longest cooking time on the package instructions (if there's a range) and tasting the pasta when the timer goes off. If it still has an unpleasantly dry, gritty core, let it cook for another minute or two and taste again. Just don't let it overcook because, as with regular pasta, it will become gummy.

Pair it with the right type of sauce. Whole-wheat pasta can overwhelm subtle cream- or herb-based sauces, but it partners well with robust red or meat sauces and even bold Asian flavors like peanut sauce, soy sauce, and toasted sesame oil. Or try it as a substitute for hard-to-find soba noodles (Japanese buckwheat noodles).

Use a wire rack to drain lasagna noodles

—STEVEN FIELDS, San Francisco, California

▶ When you drain cooked lasagna noodles in a colander, they can tangle or break easily. To avoid this, I carefully pull out individual noodles as soon as they become al dente and drain them on a wire rack set over a rimmed baking sheet to collect any excess water. With this method, I have found that noodles cool quickly and are easier to work with.

Scissors cut lasagna noodles

—Fine Cooking Test Kitchen

▶ Use scissors to cut lasagna noodles to size—right in the pan. If one noodle doesn't cover the dish, cut a second noodle to fit, overlapping it slightly with the previous noodle.

Don't lose a single grain ➤

—IRENE MORETTI, Ridgeville, Ontario

When rinsing basmati or Thai jasmine rice before cooking, it's easy to lose grains down the drain. To avoid this, I measure the amount of rice I need into a fine-mesh strainer, which I set in a large bowl. I put the bowl in the sink and run cold water over the rice while stirring it gently. When the bowl fills with water, I lift out the strainer and pour out the starchy water. I continue rinsing until the water in the bowl runs clear.

· COOKING RICE: TAILOR THE METHOD TO THE RICE ·

Medium-grain rice, the absorption method

When cooked using the absorption method, medium-grain rice yields a tender, starchy, slightly creamy kernel that's ideal for saucy rice dishes. This method also ensures that the valuable fortified nutrients remain in the pot with the rice.

Absorption method basics: The rice cooks in a measured amount of water in a tightly covered pot so that by the time the rice is tender, all the water has been absorbed. As the water level drops, trapped steam finishes the cooking. Instead of a pot, you can use a rice cooker; just follow the manufacturer's directions.

Brown rice, the pasta method

Cooking brown rice by the pasta method is quick and results in tender, separate grains with a nice chewy bite instead of mushy, split-open kernels that often result when this variety is cooked in a covered pot. Unlike white rice, brown rice kernels still have their bran layer and germ intact, so they have a nutty, grainy character and are rich in complete proteins, minerals, and vitamins. The germ contains some oil, so to avoid rancidity, buy in small quantities and store it in the fridge.

Pasta method basics: Like pasta, the raw rice goes into a large pot of boiling water and cooks uncovered. When the grains reach the desired tenderness, the water gets poured off.

Basmati rice, the pilaf method

With its low starch content and long, slender grains, basmati rice takes beautifully to the pilaf method, which allows for maximum expansion of the grains as they cook up light and separate. Washing and soaking the grains before cooking makes the rice even less starchy, helping you achieve perfect single-grained and fluffy results.

Pilaf method basics: With the pilaf method, the rice is first sautéed in oil along with aromatics and spices. A measured amount of liquid is added, the mixture is brought to a simmer, and then it is covered and left to cook until the rice absorbs the liquid.

—RAGHAVAN IYER, *Fine Cooking* contributor

To rinse or not to rinse? ➤

—RAGHAVAN IYER,
Fine Cooking contributor

Rinsing isn't necessary with packaged brands of American-grown white rice. But if you are using basmati, if you buy your rice from a bulk bin, if it's imported from Asia, or if it came in a burlap-type bag, do rinse the rice before cooking. As long as the rice isn't fortified with minerals, you don't have to worry about washing away nutrients.

How to fluff pilaf ➤

—RIS LACOSTE,
Fine Cooking contributor

Without a doubt, a fork is the best tool for fluffing rice pilaf. A spoon encourages clumping, but a fork's narrow tines gently separate the grains without breaking them, which helps preserve the perfect texture you've taken pains to achieve. Use a light hand, because vigorous stirring could break up the grains and encourage them to cling together.

Here's my fork-fluffing technique: Slip the tines down into the rice alongside the edge of the pan. Gently lift and toss the rice toward the center of the pan. Continue this process as you work your way around the perimeter. Then add your finishing-touch ingredients and gently fold them in with the fork, using a similar gentle fluffing motion.

Risotto, ➤
it's all in the rice

—LAURA GIANNATEMPO,
Fine Cooking contributor

Well, maybe not entirely—the cooking method is important too. But technique alone won't give you the rich, creamy texture of authentic risotto. You have to use the right kind of rice. Many of us have come to identify risotto with arborio, but other varieties, such as carnaroli, baldo, and vialone nano, make excellent risotto as well.

A stickier risotto, a less forgiving risotto. Compared to carnaroli and vialone nano, arborio and baldo have a higher starch content and tend to absorb less liquid, resulting in a stickier, more compact risotto. They're also less forgiving, going from just right to overcooked in a heartbeat.

A creamier, looser risotto. Carnaroli and, even more so, vialone nano contain less starch and absorb lots of liquid, producing a creamier, fluid risotto. Vialone nano is especially suited to seafood risottos, which are traditionally looser. Some supermarkets carry carnaroli in addition to arborio, but the other two are more of a gourmet shop product.

A trick for making risotto ahead

—JENNIFER ARMENTROUT,
Fine Cooking contributor

➤ A fresh batch of risotto takes at least 30 minutes to prepare. How then does your favorite Italian restaurant manage to serve you a hot dish of perfectly cooked risotto in about 10 minutes? The answer is par-cooking.

If you try to make risotto ahead completely and then reheat it, it'll be overcooked and mushy. Instead, you can cook it until it's about halfway done—the rice should still be rather firm inside—and then spread it out on a baking sheet to stop cooking and cool. Cover the rice and set it aside at room temperature for up to 2 hours. When you're ready to serve the risotto, return it to the pot and resume adding hot liquid until it's perfectly al dente, a few minutes later.

SALT & SPICES

To measure salt easily, get rid of the box

—ELAINE HANNA JOHNSON, Richardson, Texas

➤ Measuring salt out of its original container can be difficult and messy. I keep salt on the countertop in covered sugar bowls. One contains sea salt and the other kosher salt. Whether I need a pinch or a teaspoon, I always get the correct amount with no waste. The salt also stays dry, so it doesn't clump.

The best time to salt

—KIMBERLY Y. MASIBAY,
Fine Cooking contributor

➤ For the best-tasting soups and braises, add salt gradually throughout the cooking process. That gives the salt time to disperse and interact with the molecules in the food. Sprinkling salt onto food just before you eat it does give you a big, up-front flavor bang but not necessarily the deep, subtle seasoning you'd get from adding the salt while cooking.

Grinding spices with salt

—ANN HUBER, West Lafayette, Indiana

➤ I love the burst of flavor that comes from freshly ground spices, and the best way to achieve this is with a heavy mortar and pestle *and* a pinch of kosher salt. Instead of popping out of the mortar, cardamom and coriander seeds, for instance, are quickly reduced to a powder by the sharp edges of the salt crystals. I simply reduce the salt in the recipe by a pinch and proceed with my fragrant ground spice and salt mixture. This method also works wonders with garlic and citrus zest.

· SALT MAKES EVERYTHING TASTE BETTER ·

1. Salt tastes good—and makes everything else taste good.

Why does salt taste good to us? According to the experts at the Monell Chemical Senses Center in Philadelphia, it boils down to biology. We like the taste because our bodies need sodium chloride. And sprinkling a bit of sodium chloride onto other foods ensures that we'll consume lots of other essential nutrients, too, because salt makes pretty much everything else taste better. Thanks to its chemical nature, salt has the amazing ability to intensify agreeable tastes and diminish disagreeable ones.

Perhaps you've heard the old saw about salt bringing out the flavor of a dish. The scientists at the Monell Center say it's absolutely true. The reason: Some flavor compounds are too subtle to detect, but when you add even just a teeny amount of salt, neurological magic happens: Suddenly, our taste receptors can detect flavors they weren't able to sense before. So, when you add salt to roasted squash, the squash doesn't merely become salty; rather, the myriad complex flavors of the vegetable come to the fore. And the salt in recipes for cakes, cookies, tarts, puddings, and other sweets isn't there to make these treats salty; it's there to ensure that they taste good.

2. Salt enhances sweetness and blocks bitterness.

In addition to being a general flavor amplifier, salt has a special ability to enhance sweetness in foods. Taste two chocolate puddings that are the same in every way except that one contains a bit of salt and the other none: The one with salt will taste sweeter. That's because sodium ions zero in on bitter flavor compounds and suppress them, making the sweet flavors seem stronger. For the same reason, salt makes bitter foods more palatable. So it's always a good idea to pair bitter foods or drinks with something salty, be it curls of Parmigiano-Reggiano atop grilled radicchio or a well-seasoned steak with a big, tannic Cabernet (the salt from the steak actually improves the flavor of the wine because it tones down the bitter tannins).

And if you ever find that some of your roast's pan drippings have become too deeply browned (though not burned), don't despair. If you season them generously you can still make a delicious pan sauce, because the salt will balance much of the bitterness.

3. Salt can make meat juicier.

I'm no culinary genius, but my friends think I am. Why? Because my roast chicken is always juicy.

My secret? Salt. Before I roast a chicken, I treat the bird to a leisurely soak in salty water (aka brine). Meats that tend to dry out during cooking—chicken, turkey, pork, and shrimp—stay juicy and delicious if you brine them first. When you soak meat in brine, the salt water flows in, and the salt goes to work on the protein cells, altering them by loosening and unwinding the strands of protein and allowing them to sop up the brine. If you weigh your meat before and after brining, it will weigh more afterward, thanks to the liquid it has absorbed. Of course, this extra moisture would be useless if it were lost during cooking. But therein lies the magic of brining: The moisture isn't lost during cooking. Well, some is—that's inevitable because heat causes proteins to shrink and squeeze out liquid—but much less than if the meat hadn't been brined. The result is moister meat that's more flavorful, too, because the salt water that the meat soaked up tastes good. For even better flavor, savvy chefs add other flavorings to their brine, like sugar, herbs, and spices; meat will also drink in those flavors.

—KIMBERLY Y. MASIBAY,
Fine Cooking contributor

· HOW TO TOAST DRY CHILES & SPICES ·

Here's the method recommended by *Fine Cooking* contributor Daniel Hoyer: Be prepared to work quickly and ventilate well, as chile smoke is irritating and may cause you to cough and sneeze.

Heat a heavy-duty skillet (such as cast iron) over medium-high heat until you can feel the heat radiate from the surface. Working with one type of spice or chile at a time, add it to the skillet. Flip or stir frequently for even toasting, until browned for spices or lightly charred—not scorched—for chiles. Immediately transfer to a cool container.

Wipe out the skillet before adding the next ingredient, or any particles remaining may burn and taint the flavor of the new ingredient being toasted. It helps to toast coarser items like whole chiles and seeds first, followed by herbs and leaves, and then ground spices, and then ground chiles last. The finer ingredients are done last because they're the most difficult to wipe completely from the skillet, and they're more likely to burn because they have more surface area exposed to heat.

—**Fine Cooking Test Kitchen**

Can this oversalted dish be saved?
—**Fine Cooking Test Kitchen**

➤ If a dish has too much salt, there are a few ways to rescue it.

1 If you know instantly that you've added too much, don't stir it in. Grab a large spoon and lift out the salt. You can often remove nearly all of the unwanted salt in this way if you work quickly.

2 If step 1 doesn't work, and you still find the dish too salty, if the recipe contains an acid—citrus juice, vinegar, wine, buttermilk—you can try adding a bit more to balance the salt. (Likewise, a dish with too much vinegar or other acid can be balanced by adding salt.)

3 If salt still dominates, you might consider adding more liquid and other ingredients to dilute. Otherwise, you'll probably have to chalk it up to experience and begin again.

Paper plate to funnel spices
—**MAGGIE DEFAZIO, Holbrook, New York**

➤ When I need to measure ground black pepper or other spices, it can be messy trying to grind directly into the spoon. Instead, I grind the spice onto a paper plate and then fold the plate in half, creating a funnel that neatly tips the spice into the measuring spoon.

Measuring ▶ ground pepper

—**MARTHA DESHONG, Honeoye Falls, New York**

For recipes that call for a specific amount of ground pepper, I've found an easy way to avoid grinding it and scooping it into measuring spoons, which is messy and time-consuming. Instead, I counted the number of turns my peppermill took to measure out ½ teaspoon, which was 10 turns. Knowing that, I can grind pepper directly into the saucepan or skillet, turning the grinder 20 times for 1 teaspoon or 5 times for ¼ teaspoon. It's helpful to note the number of turns on a piece of tape on the side of the mill for easy reference.

· PEPPER: BEYOND BASIC BLACK ·

Pepper is the ever-present seasoning for savory foods, providing a pungent punch of flavor to everything it touches. Black, white, and green peppercorns are the dried berries of the *Piper nigrum* plant. (Pink peppercorns are in a class of their own; see below.) Each peppercorn has its own flavor characteristics and thus its own special uses in the kitchen. Try to buy peppercorns from a source with good turnover, store them away from heat and light (like any spice), and use them within a year.

Black peppercorns come in many varieties with varying degrees of heat and flavor complexity. The largest black peppercorn is the Tellicherry, considered to be the best because it's left on the vine longer for more developed flavor. Other black peppercorns are Sarawak, Malabar, and Vietnamese, but unless you're buying from a specialty spice store, the packaging usually doesn't specify the origin.

White peppercorns are from the same berries as black pepper, but they're vine-ripened longer, and the black shell is stripped before drying. Their flavor is sharp, floral, almost winey, and hotter than black pepper. High heat coaxes out the flavor of white pepper, making it a good choice for grilled meats. Some cooks prefer white pepper in pale foods, such as white sauce or mashed potatoes, because it blends in.

Green peppercorns are young berries that are mildly tart and full of heat but lacking in complexity. Pair green peppercorns with lighter foods, such as vegetables, chicken, and fish. You'll also find green peppercorns packed in jars of brine; use these whole or chopped in sauces, salad dressings, potato salads, pastas, and spreads.

Pink peppercorns aren't actually peppercorns; they're the berries of an unrelated tree. Mildly sweet and aromatic, they don't contribute a lot of flavor. They're often added to peppercorn blends for color. Pink peppercorns should only be used in pepper mills as part of a blend because their soft interiors could clog the mill's grinding mechanism if ground solo.

—**MARYELLEN DRISCOLL, *Fine Cooking* contributor**

What to look for in a pepper mill

—MARYELLEN DRISCOLL, *Fine Cooking* contributor

► It's difficult to evaluate a pepper mill by looking at it. You really need to fill it with peppercorns and try it out. Here's what to notice:

Get a handle on the handle. A detour from the classic twist top might seem more intriguing, but we discovered a reason for this design's longevity: Few others, including crank styles, worked as efficiently to produce as much pepper with as little effort.

Verify its capacity. The height of a pepper mill isn't a reliable indicator of how much pepper it can hold. Even if you open the mill and visually check the storage area, it can be tricky to gauge its capacity.

Assess its grinding ability. It's impossible to know how fluidly and abundantly a pepper mill will work until you try it.

- -

When to adjust the grind

—MARYELLEN DRISCOLL, *Fine Cooking* contributor

► How coarsely or finely you grind your pepper is a matter of personal taste, but certain grinds are better suited to certain foods.

A fine, powdery grind is ideal when you want the pepper to blend inconspicuously, such as in a salad dressing (unless it's a creamy cracked peppercorn dressing), a purée, or an egg or potato salad.

A medium grind is a good all-purpose setting, whether you're making a pasta dish or seasoning pork chops, a salad, mashed potatoes, or slices of fresh tomato.

Coarsely ground or cracked pepper works best in spice rubs for fish or meat, steak au poivre, or Caesar salad, or any time you want the pepper to stand out rather than act as a backdrop to a dish.

- -

A neat place for a pepper mill

—PETER HYZAK, Ponte Vedra Beach, Florida

► When my pepper mill isn't in use, it stands in a ramekin, which keeps residual ground pepper from dirtying my counter.

- -

Use both ends of a pestle for crushing

—GLENN BAGLO, via email

► Here's a way to get the most out of this tool: I've found that when crushing hard spices like black peppercorns, it's easier to turn the pestle over and use the small end. This way, you can exert more pressure on the small peppercorns, and it's easier to break them.

CHILE POWDER PROFILES —TONY ROSENFELD, *Fine Cooking* contributor

	PASILLA	ANCHO	NEW MEXICO	CHIPOTLE	CAYENNE
Heat level	Moderate	Moderate	Moderate	Hot	Very hot
Flavor	Sweet, berry-like	Fruity, sweet	Earthy, fruity	Smoky, sweet	Intense, sharp
Use in	Mole sauce, chili, braised pork, beef stews	Black beans, mole sauce, spice rubs for grilled pork or shrimp	Enchiladas, sauces, ground beef taco filling	Barbecue sauce, grilling spice rubs, mayonnaise	Dips, soups, crab cakes, roasted potato wedges

Oil your board to mince red pepper flakes

—MARY ANN SCHELLATI, Yonkers, New York

► When I want to keep a small amount of red pepper flakes from jumping and flying while mincing them with a chef's knife, I apply a light coat of oil to the surface of my board. This keeps the flakes from straying too far.

Buying saffron: the redder, the better

—SARAH JAY, *Fine Cooking* contributor

► Saffron is indeed "the most expensive spice in the world" by weight, but you need so little when cooking that it's actually cheaper to use than many everyday flavorings—a single lemon often costs twice as much as a pinch of saffron. And a pinch, which is 20 to 25 threads, is all you need in most cases. When buying saffron, keep two rules in mind:

1 Buy saffron in threads only. Powdered saffron can contain other products, and it's difficult to know whether you're buying the pure spice.

2 Look for saffron that contains only short, deep red threads (they're actually the stigmas from the saffron crocus). Lesser grades of saffron include threads with some yellow areas (which is the style part of the flower). This isn't a bad thing, but the yellow part doesn't have the same coloring and flavoring power as the red stigmas, so the saffron isn't as potent.

Label spice caps

—Fine Cooking Test Kitchen

► If you keep your spice jars in a kitchen drawer below eye level, write the spice name on the bottle lid. That way, you can find what you need without lifting each item out of the drawer to read its label.

➤ I live in a condo with a small kitchen that suffers from lack of storage space. To store my spices in an accessible way, I used hook-and-loop tape to adhere a magnetic photo strip to the inside of my cupboard door. I transferred my spices to tin shaker containers with magnetic bottoms, labeled the lids, and stuck them onto the photo strip. It works beautifully, keeping my spices organized and easy to find when I am cooking.

· A GUIDE TO PAPRIKA ·

In American cooking, paprika seems to be used more as a food coloring than as a spice. Sprinkled over deviled eggs and potato salads, it looks pretty and doesn't taste like much. But heat it gently in oil and this shy spice blossoms, exuding a sweet flavor with rich, earthy undertones and a heat level that ranges from gentle to spicy hot, depending on the variety of paprika.

Ground from dried chiles, paprika plays an honored role in both Hungarian and Spanish cuisines. Each country has a distinctive style of paprika, both of which are generally better than the generic paprika found in supermarkets.

Hungarian paprika is produced around the southern cities of Szeged and Kalosca. Traditionally, the ripened chiles were strung up to dry in the sun, but they are now more commonly dried in commercial ovens. Hungarian paprika is available in several heat levels and grinds, including special, mild, *delikates*, semisweet, sweet, and hot, but only the latter two are commonly found in the United States. Used in foods like kielbasa, chicken paprikash, and goulash, Hungarian paprika is especially good in rich dishes with sour cream, potatoes, egg noodles, cabbage, or meat. It can be used generously—think tablespoons of it.

Spanish paprika or pimentón comes from western Spain's La Vera valley. It differs from Hungarian paprika in that the chiles are dried over smoldering oak logs, giving them a smoky flavor. It comes in three heat levels: *dulce, agridulce,* and *picante* (sweet, bittersweet, and hot). It's a key ingredient in paella, chorizo, and many tapas dishes. In the United States, pimentón isn't as commonly available as Hungarian paprika, but it's well worth seeking out. Add a little pimentón to scrambled eggs, black bean chili, or roasted potatoes. It's delicious wherever you'd like a smoky flavor, but remember that smokiness can easily overwhelm a dish, so start experimenting by using only ¼ to ½ teaspoon.

Buying and cooking tips • Look for paprika packaged in a tin with a tight-fitting lid, and store it away from light and heat. • Heating paprika in a little oil or butter helps bring out the flavor, but because of the high sugar content, it burns easily, so keep the heat low and the time short. It's usually best to add it off the heat at the end of sautéing, before adding liquids.

—ALLISON EHRI KREITLER, *Fine Cooking* contributor

Keeping spices fresh ➤

—FLOYD CARDOZ,
Fine Cooking contributor

HOW TO BUY AND STORE

I always buy whole spices (with the exception of turmeric) and grind only what I need for a recipe because spices begin to deteriorate the instant they're ground. The most fragrant spices come from stores with a high rate of turnover. Many grocery stores have a good selection of spices, and if you live near an Indian or Middle Eastern market, check out its spice section, which may have more variety. You can also order by mail. Air, light, and heat are the enemies of spices, so keep them in airtight containers in a drawer or cupboard, but never over the stove.

Grinding spices Grinding releases a spice's flavorful aromatic oils. A coarser grind adds textural interest and a mosaic of flavors to a dish. Here are some tips for grinding spices.

- Not all spices should be left coarse: Cinnamon, clove, mace, nutmeg, and green and black cardamom are so strongly flavored that biting into a big piece is not pleasant.

- Finer grinds tend to be subtler, with the flavors more evenly blended.

- If you use a mortar and pestle to grind spices, grind in a circular motion and hold a piece of plastic wrap over the bowl while you grind to keep the spices from sneaking out.

- Before grinding whole dried chiles or bay leaves, put them in a low oven for about 5 minutes to evaporate moisture and make them brittle.

Using spices If you toast spices, add them to the dish toward the end of cooking or sprinkle them on the food right before serving, because the toasting process has already released the spices' aromatic oils.

Spices stored in zip-top ➤ bags save space

—SHARON LIN, Maui, Hawaii

I found a convenient solution for keeping all my spices in one single container that can be stored just about anywhere. I empty each spice jar into individual pint-size zip-top bags, write the name of the spice on each, squeeze out the air, and then seal and roll them up (making sure the name shows clearly). This way, I can fit more than 20 spice bags in a 1 gallon-size zip-top bag or in a container of equivalent volume. And I can actually measure out a tablespoon of spice. (I could never fit anything bigger than a teaspoon in regular spice jars.)

Working with brown sugar

—Fine Cooking Test Kitchen

➤ Brown sugar isn't a practical substitute for granulated white sugar because white sugar crystals are relatively large and sharp, while brown sugar crystals are small and softer. As a result, brown sugar is less effective at creaming, or cutting through butter to create air pockets that make baked goods light and tender.

To get the best results when using brown sugar, press brown sugar into the cup when measuring. Also, store brown sugar tightly wrapped in a cool, dark place.

Keeping brown sugar moist

—ALLISON EHRI KREITLER,
Fine Cooking contributor

➤ It seems like every time I need brown sugar, the package in my pantry has completely dried out and become a rock-like mass.

My mom always put a slice of apple in with her brown sugar, but it would eventually shrivel up. I tried keeping a piece of bread in my sugar, but it got moldy. Next I tried a damp paper towel on top of the sugar, but that caused it to become soggy in some spots and crystallized in others. Call me a slow learner, but I finally found the solution.

I leave the sugar in its original bag and close the top loosely with tape, a rubber band, or a clip. Then I put it in a zip-top plastic bag and tuck in a damp paper towel. The paper towel doesn't touch the sugar and make it soggy, but it keeps the air around the bag of sugar humid enough that there's no rock formation. I change the towel every once in a while, and my brown sugar stays soft and moist for months.

Make your own superfine sugar

—ABIGAIL JOHNSON DODGE,
Fine Cooking contributor

➤ Some recipes call for superfine sugar because it dissolves faster than regular granulated. This quality makes it perfect for meringues and for desserts that don't get baked, like mousses, where you want sweetness but not a gritty texture. If your grocer doesn't stock superfine sugar (known as caster sugar in the United Kingdom; also called bar sugar because it dissolves quickly in drinks), it's easy to make your own. Process regular granulated sugar in a food processor until it's pulverized to a fine texture, which takes about a minute. Measure the sugar for the recipe only after processing.

· A COOK'S GUIDE TO THICKENERS ·

Flour is the most common thickener used in recipes, from turkey gravy to apple pie, and for good reason: It's versatile and, in most kitchens, it's always on hand. But flour isn't a pure starch (it contains protein and other components), so it has only about half the thickening power of other starches. The best flour to use as a thickener is all-purpose flour, because it's higher in starch than other wheat flours.

Appearance: The proteins in flour make flour-thickened sauces and pie fillings look cloudy.

When to use: Flour works best for foods that don't suffer visually from opacity: white sauces such as béchamel, simple pan gravies, beef stew, chicken fricassée, and apple or pear pies.

When not to use: Berry pies or sauces where clarity is important.

How to use: There are lots of ways to use flour as a thickener—that's the great thing about it:

- You can cook it with aromatic vegetables in the pot before adding a braising liquid.
- You can dredge stew meat in flour before browning it, and the flour will later thicken the stew.
- You can mix it with a little cool liquid to form a paste and then whisk it into a simmering pan sauce.

One thing you shouldn't do with flour is toss it directly into hot liquid—the dry granules will likely clump together. To achieve full thickening power and eliminate raw flour taste, flour-thickened mixtures must be brought to a boil and then cooked for about 3 minutes. But don't go overboard with the cooking, because flour thickens more as it cools; as a rule, stop cooking gravies and sauces when they're a bit thinner than their ideal consistency.

Cornstarch is a pure starch derived from corn. It can withstand a good amount of cooking and stirring before it begins to break down. That's why it's frequently used for thickening vanilla pastry cream and banana cream pie filling, as well as butterscotch and chocolate puddings, all of which are cooked on the stove and involve prolonged heating and stirring.

Appearance: Cornstarch-thickened sauces have a translucent shimmer.

When to use: Cornstarch is great for delicate sauces and gravies that you want to be translucent, like stir-fry sauces. It's also a good choice for berry and stone-fruit pies, because it won't cloud the jewel-like colors of the fruit juices. Since it can handle a good amount of heat, it's fine for stovetop puddings and sauces that will be reheated.

When not to use: Don't sprinkle it directly into hot pan juices for gravy because it will clump.

How to use: More than any other starch, cornstarch is prone to clumping when exposed to hot liquids. To avoid lumps, mix cornstarch with something that will help separate the granules from one another. For pies and custards, combine it with the sugar for better dispersion. For sauces, mix the cornstarch with a tablespoon or two of the liquid called for in the recipe—the liquid should be cool. Simmer the sauce for at least 1 minute to eliminate the pasty flavor of raw starch.

Tapioca is a pure starch derived from the root of the cassava plant, and it comes in many forms. The small granules of pearl tapioca, labeled instant or quick cooking (Kraft®'s Minute® Tapioca is a common brand), are widely available and work well as a thickener. There's also a powdered variety, which dissolves more smoothly than the granules but is hard to find; look for it at health-food stores.

Appearance: Tapioca-thickened fillings are crystal clear and have a more jelly-like consistency than those thickened with other starches. Instant tapioca granules don't completely dissolve; they may linger in pie fillings as soft, clear beads.

When to use: It thickens juices faster than flour or cornstarch, so tapioca is great for all fruit pies, especially berry, peach, and rhubarb, which throw off a lot of juice. It's also great for pies that will be frozen and reheated, because tapioca holds liquid, so the pie filling won't weep when frozen and thawed.

When not to use: Don't use instant tapioca for pies with open lattices or large steam vents because the granules will be exposed directly to the hot air of the oven and won't dissolve. It's also not ideal for pan sauces or stovetop custards because it can't withstand a lot of stirring and boiling.

How to use: For best results, let pearl tapioca sit with the fruit for 5 to 10 minutes before you bake the pie so that the fruit juices can begin to soften the granules. And before you remove a pie from the oven, make sure the juices at the center are bubbling, even if it seems the juices at the edge have been fully cooked for quite a while.

And 2 more . . .

Potato starch is most commonly called for in European recipes. It's easy to find in the baking ingredient aisle of East Coast markets, but in the rest of the country, look for it in the kosher section of the store. Potato starch thickens quickly without a pronounced flavor that needs to be cooked off, which makes it great as a last-minute fix for too-thin sauces.

Arrowroot powder comes from the root of a tropical plant of the same name. Look for it in gourmet or health-food stores. Arrowroot starch granules are very small and make sauces exceptionally smooth. Like flour and cornstarch, it can withstand long cooking and higher temperatures, and like tapioca, it is remarkable for its clarity. It's a great choice for stir-fry sauces and any kind of fruit pie filling.

Substituting one starch for another

2 Tbs. flour = 1 Tbs. cornstarch
1 Tbs. tapioca = 1 Tbs. + 1½ tsp.
arrowroot = 1½ tsp. potato starch

—NICOLE REES,
Fine Cooking **contributor**

Shopping for and storing vanilla

—ABIGAIL JOHNSON DODGE,
Fine Cooking contributor

EXTRACT

Buying: Always buy pure vanilla extract, never imitation.

Storing: Sealed and stored in a cool, dark spot, vanilla extract will last almost forever—the flavor may even improve with age. That's good news if you like to buy in large quantities. Many good brands are available in larger volumes at discounted rates.

BEANS

Buying: Selecting vanilla beans is much like choosing fruit—look for size, shape, feel, and smell. The perfect bean is 5 to 7 inches long, plump, and has very dark brown skin; it should feel moist and supple (not dry and brittle) when rolled between your fingers. And be sure it passes the sniff test: Even through heavy plastic, the aroma should be close to intoxicating.

Storing: Store vanilla beans in a sealed container in a cool, dark place. They should stay moist for up to 6 months. If they begin to dry out, add them to your vanilla extract or a jar of vodka. And don't discard the used beans: The seeded pods still have tons of flavor. Add them to your sugar container, coffee beans, or favorite liqueur.

Scraping seeds from a vanilla pod

—ABIGAIL JOHNSON DODGE,
Fine Cooking contributor

Hold the bean at one end and, using a paring knife, split the bean lengthwise in half (if only half a bean is called for, cut the whole bean in half crosswise before splitting just one of the halves). Then slide the back of the knife down the opened or cut end of the bean and scrape out the seeds.

Substituting extract for beans

—ABIGAIL JOHNSON DODGE,
Fine Cooking contributor

There's no exact rule for determining equivalent amounts of vanilla beans to extract. After all, beans can vary in size while extracts can vary in potency. Vanilla will also behave differently in different types of desserts. If you need an estimate, though, a good place to start is substituting 1 teaspoon pure vanilla extract for half a vanilla bean.

Using up scraped vanilla beans

—Fine Cooking Test Kitchen

► In the test kitchen, we stash empty vanilla bean halves (what's left after scraping the seeds) in a container of sugar to make vanilla sugar for coffee and other treats. But some of our favorite bakers have other good ideas:

Regan Daley: "I collect a lot of them and pop them into a custard base or a syrup that's heated on the stove. Five or six scraped vanilla bean halves add up to one whole bean and will infuse a custard or syrup just as well. I also put them in a bottle of vodka or brandy. I keep putting the beans in as I use them (I give the bottle a swirl every now and then), and the flavor just gets more intense. It makes a nice little after-dinner drink."

Carolyn Weil: "If I scrape out a vanilla bean and don't use it to infuse something else, like a custard—in other words, it's still 'clean'—I put it in a small jar of orange liqueur to flavor the liqueur for future baking. I actually store my whole vanilla beans in vanilla extract. It keeps them from drying out, and they stay nice and plump, so it's easy to scrape out the seeds."

Rose Levy Beranbaum: "I sometimes use the bean as a decoration for a dessert that features vanilla, such as a vanilla cheesecake. I simply lay the bean on the top—it has such a graceful curve."

A GUIDE TO FOOD STORAGE

These guidelines for safe storage times are based on USDA recommendations and on our own experiences with freezing food. Food frozen a little longer than these guidelines won't necessarily be unsafe, but its texture and flavor will suffer. Buy a couple of refrigerator/freezer thermometers so you can be sure that your refrigerator is always 33° to 40°F and that your freezer is 0°F or below.

	REFRIGERATED	FROZEN
Beef, pork, lamb, veal	3 to 5 days	4 to 6 months for steak, chops, and roasts
Chicken, turkey	2 days	6 months
Ground meat	1 to 2 days	3 to 4 months
Sausage, raw	1 to 2 days	1 to 2 months
Ham, whole, fully cooked	1 week	1 to 2 months
Bacon	1 week	2 months
Fish	1 to 2 days	3 months
Sliced deli meat	3 to 5 days	1 to 2 months
Bread, rolls, breadcrumbs	Not recommended	1 month
Casseroles	3 to 4 days	2 to 3 months
Soups, stews	3 to 4 days	2 to 3 months
Broth, stock	1 to 2 days	2 to 3 months

Foods that don't freeze well
—LINDA J. HARRIS, PH.D.,
Fine Cooking contributor

- High-moisture vegetables like lettuce, celery, and cabbage become watery.
- Cream and custard fillings separate.
- Meringue toughens.
- Milk undergoes flavor changes.
- Sour cream and yogurt separate.
- Heavy cream won't whip after being frozen.

Help your freezer do its job
—LINDA J. HARRIS, PH.D.,
Fine Cooking contributor

- Set the freezer to 0°F or lower and monitor the temperature with a freezer thermometer (available at supermarkets and hardware stores).
- Store food in containers that provide a barrier to air and moisture. Well-sealed plastic freezer containers work, as do heavy-duty plastic freezer

bags or wrap, freezer paper, or heavy-duty foil. (Many foods expand upon freezing, so don't overfill, but don't leave too much air space either.)

- Small items freeze faster, so freeze food portions you normally use in recipes: 1 or 2 cups of stock, a cup of sliced bananas, a tablespoon of tomato paste.

- Arrange unfrozen packages in a single layer, slightly separated from one another, so they freeze faster.

- Try to place foods on the freezer's floor or near the walls.

- Don't overload the freezer with too much unfrozen food at once. And once food is frozen, keep the items stacked closely together. Freezers are most energy efficient when full. If your freezer is running low, consider freezing jugs or containers of water.

- Stick labels on the foods you freeze. Write the item's name (because, for example, sometimes chili and meat sauce are hard to tell apart) and the date. Use the guidelines on p. 159 to help calculate a use-by date.

Getting the air out of freezer bags
—MATT KASPAR, Austin, Texas

To prevent freezer burn, it's important to get all the air out of the freezer bag, but most of us don't have a vacuum sealer. Some people improvise by sucking the air out through a straw. I prefer to put the food in the bag and immerse the open bag up to the top edge in water. The water pressure forces all the air out of the bag. Then I zip the bag closed and take it out of the water.

Plastic bins keep the freezer organized
—JENNIFER GROBE, Burlington, Ontario, Canada

I use small plastic bins with lids (the relatively inexpensive ones you find at housewares stores) to organize my small freezer. I label each bin according to the food type it holds; for example, meat, fish, and doughs. I never have to dig around for things in the freezer, and I can fit more in it.

Defrosted food can be refrozen
—LINDA J. HARRIS, PH.D., *Fine Cooking* contributor

Food can be safely refrozen within 48 hours of thawing if the thawing took place in the refrigerator or in cold water and the temperature of the thawed food has remained below 40°F. But the food's quality might suffer because fluids that seep from cells during refreezing and subsequent thawing can adversely affect texture and flavor.

Freezing meat efficiently

—DESIREE MENDOZA, Veradale, Washington

When I buy meat in bulk, I put small portions into plastic sandwich bags, labeling and dating each with a permanent marker. Then I put these small bags into a big freezer bag and label it chicken, beef, or whatever. When I need meat, I take out a small bag or two, but I leave the bigger bag in the freezer. Not only does this save me money on freezer bags, but my meats also get double protection from freezer burn.

Freezing soup

—LORI LONGBOTHAM, *Fine Cooking* contributor

- Chill soup thoroughly before freezing; this allows it to freeze faster. The ice crystals that form will be smaller, so your soup will have better texture and flavor.

- Freeze soup in plastic containers, leaving about a half inch at the top to allow for expansion. Or fill plastic freezer bags about three-quarters full and squeeze out as much air as possible.

- Freeze soups in large amounts or in smaller, portion-size containers that are ready to heat and serve. The smaller the container, the quicker it will freeze and defrost.

- Before freezing, cover, label, and date your soup. As a general rule, stocks and broths can be frozen for up to 6 months; vegetable soups, about 4 months; meat, fish, or chicken soups, about 3 months; and soups with egg and cream, about 2 months.

- If you're freezing a large quantity at once, turn the thermostat to its coldest setting until the soup freezes.

To thaw: Leave the soup in its container and defrost in the refrigerator or microwave oven or under cold running water. You can also remove it from the container and reheat the frozen soup in a saucepan over low heat. A microwave oven is better for small amounts of soup. Serve soup as soon as possible after defrosting.

Don't be alarmed if puréed soup separates after defrosting. To fix it, just whisk it back together. Be aware that soups containing cream, wine, or lemon juice (or those thickened with eggs or flour) don't always freeze well. When reheating, simmer gently and whisk constantly to prevent curdling. Or better yet, add these ingredients after reheating.

· FREEZING & THAWING 101 ·

The words *fresh* and *frozen* are often viewed as mutually exclusive. Yet for keeping foods tasting fresh, a freezer is often your best ally. Freezing is also a way for people who can't get to the market every day (which means most of us) to easily create fresh-feeling meals any night of the week. My own freezer holds everything I need—frozen tortillas and breads, an assortment of vegetables and meats—to make tasty meals within minutes of arriving home from work. And when time is on my side, I know I'll have chopped herbs, homemade stock, berries, pastry dough, and many other ingredients on hand to prepare more elaborate dishes.

How does the freezer make all this possible? Well, when you freeze food, a couple of important things happen. First, the pathogens that cause foodborne illness can't grow, which makes food-safety experts like me jump for joy. In fact, as long as food remains frozen, it's as safe as the day it was put in the freezer. (It's thawing that invites trouble, but we'll get to that later.) Second, freezing also preserves food's quality by slowing down the microbes and chemical reactions that degrade food. But some of these reactions do continue during frozen storage, so eventually, the flavor, color, and texture deteriorate to the point that the food just isn't appealing, even if it's still technically safe to eat.

How to freeze for freshest flavor and safety. It might seem like the only role you play in freezing is finding space in the freezer, but there's actually a lot you can do to streamline the freezing process and keep your food in optimum condition.

Faster is better. The packaged frozen foods you see at the supermarket were most likely "flash frozen" in a super-cold industrial freezer. The faster food freezes, the better—because freezing is a bit injurious to food. As the water in food freezes, ice crystals form and rupture cell walls. Rapid freezing keeps the ice crystals tiny and reduces the time for cells to leak fluids, which is good for the food's quality. Large ice crystals can damage meat or produce, leading

to texture and moisture loss when the food is thawed. Your home freezer can't mimic the efficacy of an industrial freezer that freezes food in minutes and stores it well below 0°F. But you can still get decent results at home by using these tactics.

Freezing isn't forever. Commercially frozen foods often have a "best if used by" date, which makes inventory control easy. But what about all the food you've frozen yourself: Can you eat that chili that's a year old? I don't think there's a simple answer. Storage guidelines, like those listed on p. 159, give wide estimates because they depend on many variables:

* How fresh was the food when it was frozen?

- How quickly did it freeze?
- What was the storage temperature, and was it consistent?
- How will the food ultimately be used?
- And, perhaps most important, how discriminating is your palate?

For the sake of flavor, I'd probably make a new batch of chili before consuming vintage chili, but some people wouldn't give it a second thought.

Use the kitchen refrigerator's freezer for fast turnover only.

There are two reasons for this. The temperature inside fluctuates over a broad range because it's opened often, and also because the self-defrost feature includes programmed heating and cooling to melt frost before it builds up. Those temperature fluctuations cause microscopic melting and refreezing in foods, which encourage ice crystal growth. Over time, this harms the food's texture. And as water moves from one area in the food to another, the surface of the food dries out—a condition known as freezer burn. Water

migration can also create visible ice crystals. If you've kept ice cream for longer than a couple of weeks, you know what I mean. So for long-term frozen storage (up to 12 months), stash food in a stand-alone freezer that won't be opened often and doesn't have a defrost feature.

Thawing foods safely. There's

one thing I don't like about frozen food: thawing it. From a food-safety perspective, that's when you court trouble. As food thaws, the outer surface warms up first. Cells that were damaged during freezing release nutrients and moisture. And in some foods, this can create ideal conditions for pathogens to grow and multiply.

Thaw food at the temperature you plan to store it. Baked

goods, breads, cakes, and cookies can be safely thawed and stored at room temperature. But meat, prepared entrées, fruits and vegetables, and raw dough should be thawed and stored in the refrigerator to minimize pathogen activity. Just like slow freezing, slow thawing can lead to mois-

ture loss, but food safety always trumps quality. Admittedly, doing things the right way can try one's patience.

To safely hasten thawing, seal the frozen item in a leak-proof container or plastic bag and immerse it in cold tap water. (Check the water every half hour to be sure it remains cold.) Once thawed, refrigerate the food and use it soon. Thawed frozen food spoils as fast as, or faster than, its never-frozen counterpart because cells ruptured during freezing and thawing release nutrients for microbes to consume. If you're in a real hurry to put something on the table, you can use your microwave's defrost feature to thaw food you plan to prepare and eat right away. Or, better yet, skip thawing entirely. Some frozen foods, such as vegetables, can go straight from the freezer to the stove. And you might try putting frozen fruit right into the blender for a quick—not to mention pleasingly cold—smoothie.

—LINDA J. HARRIS, PH.D.,
Fine Cooking contributor

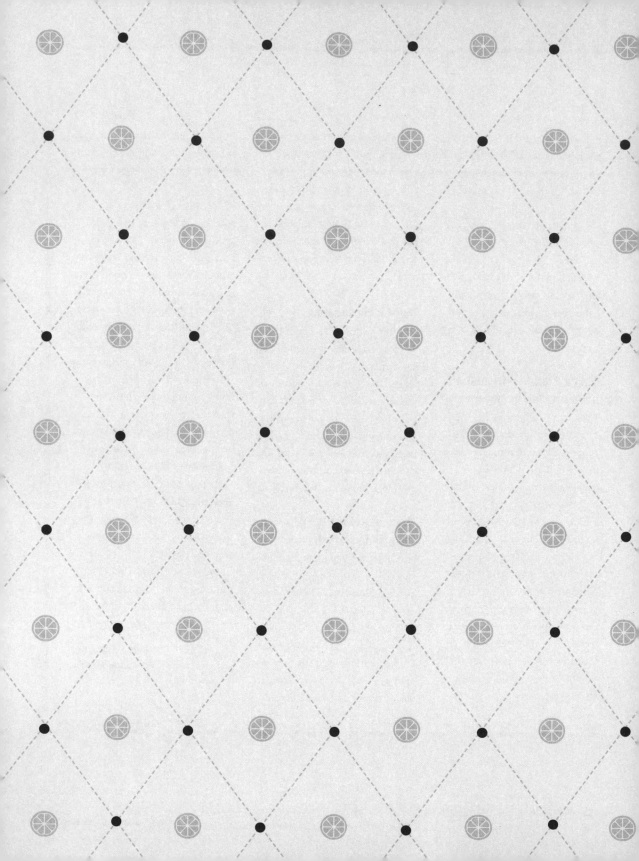

TECHNIQUES

BAKING

Keep melted butter from congealing in batter

—CINDY HUFLER, Atlanta, Georgia

▶ I separate my eggs and mix the yolks with slightly cooled melted butter. The butter and yolks emulsify, which seems to keep the butter from congealing when the mixture encounters the cool milk.

A little extra paper goes a long way

—DEBORAH TARENTINO, Pittsburgh, Pennsylvania

▶ Quick breads, brownies, and bar cookies come out of their baking pans with ease when you use a little extra paper to line the pans. I like to leave a 2-inch overhang of parchment on two sides of my baking pan so that I can lift the baked goods out of the pan in one big piece.

Measure now, bake later

—HELENE L. STONE, Highland Park, Illinois

▶ To get a head start on my holiday baking marathon, I measure out ingredients for my recipes a few weeks in advance. For every recipe on my baking list, I put the measured dry ingredients (flour, leavening, salt, and so on) into a plastic bag, the measured sugar into a second bag, and mix-ins like chocolate chips and nuts into a third bag. I store all three bags—along with the recipe—in a plastic container, and I repeat this process for every recipe I plan to bake.

Goop-free faucet handles

—ANNA VICTORIA REICH, Albuquerque, New Mexico

▶ Before I start any baking project, I wrap small sandwich bags around the handles of my kitchen faucet. This way, when I turn on the faucet to wash sticky batter or dough off my hands, I don't get goop all over the faucet handles.

Canning tongs have a slip-proof grip

—DONNA FERRIES, Wilton, Connecticut

▶ I remove hot ceramic ramekins or metal molds from a water bath with rubberized canning tongs. Their grip is much more secure than regular metal tongs.

A Popsicle stick measures batter level

—PATTY NIXON, Delphos, Ohio

▶ Whenever I make anything that requires filling ramekins, I use a Popsicle® stick marked off to the depth I need. For example, if I need 2 inches of filling, I use a ruler to mark 2 inches on the stick and then insert it into each ramekin while I fill it. This way, I have the same amount in each ramekin and don't have to worry about some being done before others.

Room temperature eggs and butter in a hurry

—Fine Cooking Test Kitchen

When a recipe calls for room temperature eggs or softened butter, it can stop some bakers short if they haven't planned ahead. But there's no need for that.

To warm cold eggs quickly, simply put them in a bowl of very warm water.

To soften cold butter quickly, you need to increase the area that's exposed to room temperature. Cut the butter into small cubes, separate the cubes into a single layer, and let them sit on the counter. They'll reach optimum creaming temperature (65° to 68°F) in about 30 minutes.

WHY SOFTENED BUTTER

Softened butter is called for in most cookie recipes, as well as in some cakes and pastries. Softened butter is best for baking when it's still somewhat cool. It should be pliable but not too soft. This is the temperature at which sugar crystals cut into the butter most effectively, creating the maximum amount of air pockets to lighten your batter. Too cold and firm and the sugar won't cut into the butter easily enough; too warm and the sugar will simply dissolve into the butter.

If you have an instant-read thermometer, you can check for the ideal temperature: 65° to 67°F, a little cooler than room temperature. Or you can press your finger into the butter to test it. It's perfect when your finger makes an indentation but can't go all the way through the butter. Also, if you can bend your stick of butter without it snapping or mashing, it's at the right temperature.

Use a slotted spatula when removing ramekins

—MARY VIERRA, Grants Pass, Oregon

I always found it tricky to remove crème brûlée ramekins from a hot water bath. I've tried tongs, with little success. Then I bought a flat, slotted spatula, which works like a charm. I just slide it under each ramekin, allow the water to drain, and transfer the ramekin to my work surface. It's easy and safe.

Avoid cracking by baking in a water bath

—NICOLE REES, Fine Cooking contributor

Baking in a water bath may seem like an unnecessary step, but this easy cooking method is your best insurance against curdled custards and cracked cheesecakes. These desserts are thickened primarily by egg proteins, which set well below 212°F. Unless these proteins are protected from the high heat of the oven, they'll overcook and tighten or shrink, causing your custard or cheesecake to crack or separate into curdled egg and liquid.

A water bath insulates custards from the direct heat of the oven because the water can't exceed 212°F, unlike the air in a 350°F oven. Without a water bath, the outside of your dessert would overcook before the center is done. And direct heat can take small custards from cooked to cracked within a minute. But if they're in a water bath, you have more time to catch them at the perfect degree of doneness.

Prevent pans from shifting in a water bath

—JOANNE NEIHEISEL, Edgewood, Kentucky

➤ Whenever I bake cheesecake or custards in a water bath, I start by laying a folded kitchen towel on the bottom of the water bath pan. Then I place it on the oven rack, put the cake pan or custard ramekins on the towel, and pour in hot water. The towel keeps the cake pan or ramekins from sliding when moving the water bath in and out of the oven.

Rubber bands give tongs more grip

—CASSIA SCHELL, Bay Village, Ohio

➤ I love making baked custards, but until recently I had trouble getting the hot ramekins out of the water bath and onto the rack to cool. Spatulas and oven mitts didn't work. Even metal tongs were hit-or-miss—as often as not, the ramekins would slip out of the tongs and splash back into the water. Now I wrap rubber bands around each of the tongs' gripping ends, and slipping ramekins are a thing of the past.

COOKIES & BROWNIES

Custom-cut parchment to fit cookie sheets

—ESTELLE TWOHEY, Peterborough, Ontario, Canada

➤ The rolls of parchment I buy are usually 15 inches wide, but my cookie sheets are only 12 inches. To avoid having to trim the excess to fit my sheets every time, I take a sharp serrated knife or a good pair of scissors and cut 3 inches off the end of the roll. I hold the excess together in a roll with a kitchen clip. This narrower roll is useful for lining the sides of a round cake pan or just for filling in where a narrow piece is needed. As for the remaining 12-inch roll, I'm left to make just one cut for each cookie sheet.

Keep your Silpat® in good condition

—DABNEY GOUGH, *Fine Cooking* contributor

If you bake lots of cookies, a couple of nonstick silicone baking liners are handy to have because they're reusable and they reduce the need for parchment. Often referred to generically by the name of the leading brand—Silpat—they rely on their silicone surface to maintain their nonstick quality, so it's important to treat them with care.

To clean a Silpat, wipe it down with a soft, damp sponge and let it air dry. I wash it last and drape it over everything else in the dish rack. You may use a diluted solution of mild dishwashing liquid if you like, but remember that an oily feeling on the mat even after cleaning is normal. Silpats are not dishwasher-safe.

Never use knives, scrapers, brushes, or scrubbers on the mats—they will damage the surface.

Store Silpats flat or rolled but not folded. Here are three ideas for safe storage:

- If you store your baking sheets flat, just lay your Silpats in one of them.
- Roll them up in paper towels and secure the roll with tape.
- Roll up each Silpat and store it inside an empty paper towel tube.

Use a sieve for small cookie cutters

—LAURA ROSE, Naugatuck, Connecticut

My small round cookie cutters often fell down the drain into the garbage disposal at cleaning time, until I came up with an easy solution. Since I already had my sieve out to sift flour for the recipe, I put the sieve in the sink and then put the cutters in the sieve as I was done with them. This also eased cleaning. After I scrubbed each cutter, I put it back in the sieve and rinsed them all at once.

Roll out delicate dough on parchment

—VERONIQUE VITT, Town & Country, Missouri

When I make sugar cookies from fragile or sticky dough, I roll out the dough on a sheet of parchment, and I leave it on the parchment while I cut shapes into the dough with a cookie cutter. Instead of transferring the cookies to a baking sheet with a spatula (which usually distorts the shapes), I cut the paper around each cookie, and lift the paper and cookie to the baking sheet.

Clearance for cookies

—MARYELLEN DRISCOLL, *Fine Cooking* contributor

Measure your oven and your cookie sheet. You'll get the best results if your sheet has 2 inches of space around it for heat to circulate.

DARK BROWN SUGAR FOR LIGHT BROWN SUGAR

A seemingly small substitution, switching from light brown sugar to dark brown sugar might increase cookie spread or cause your cookies to be softer because dark brown sugar contains more moisture from the added molasses. (Commercial brown sugar is made by blending a small amount of molasses with fine granulated sugar.) You'll probably also taste the difference.

MARGARINE OR VEGETABLE SHORTENING FOR BUTTER

In most well-written recipes, the fat was carefully chosen for the attributes it contributes to the finished cookie. So making a substitution might not be the best idea. But that doesn't mean it's impossible. For example, there's no substitute for the flavor of butter, but you can replace butter with stick margarine. Like butter, stick margarine is 6% to 10% water and performs similarly to butter in recipes. There's no water in vegetable shortening; it's pure fat, lightened with air. So if you replace butter with an equal amount of shortening, your cookies may not spread as much due to the lower water content and the fact that shortening melts at a higher temperature than butter, giving the cookies time to set in the oven and retain their height. Also, your cookies might look paler (not necessarily a bad thing—sugar cookies you'll decorate actually benefit from a blond color), because the milk solids present in butter contain protein and sugar, which help cause browning.

Scoop your macaroons ▶

— Fine Cooking Test Kitchen

To make perfectly round macaroons, use a small ice cream scoop and bake them right after they're shaped.

**Keep cookies longer ▶
with sugar**

—BARBARA ADAMS,
Howard Place, South Africa

When storing freshly baked cookies, I find that I can extend their keeping time by sprinkling 1 teaspoon of sugar on the bottom of the container. Then I line the container with parchment or paper towels, put the cookies on top, and close the lid. The sugar absorbs moisture and keeps the cookies crisp and fresh.

After baking many batches of cookies, we think we've broken the cookie code: To get the cookie you like, control the amount and temperature of key ingredients.

SUGAR

The relative amount of white vs. brown sugar has a great effect on chewiness because brown sugar is much wetter than white. Using more brown sugar will produce softer, chewier cookies, while using more white sugar will turn out cookies that are sandier in texture and crisper overall.

FLOUR

The way you measure flour makes a big difference, because too much flour makes cookies dry and tough, while too little causes cookies to spread too much and lose structure. If possible, use a scale to measure the flour so that your results are as consistent as possible.

BUTTER AND EGGS

The temperature of these ingredients helps control how much the dough spreads, so always follow a recipe's instructions.

Cool ingredients keep your dough cooler, which means it spreads more slowly in the oven, letting the oven's heat "set" the cookie while the dough is still thick and producing denser, chewier cookies.

Warm dough spreads more quickly in the oven, which makes the cookies thinner and crisper. A high proportion of butter to flour in the dough will also allow it to spread quickly.

KITCHEN TEMPERATURE

The temperature in your kitchen also affects dough temperature, as will dropping cookies onto a still-hot baking sheet: For chewy cookies, have cool sheets handy. And humid weather will soften even the crispest cookies in as little as a day, so store them well wrapped.

- -

Making cookie logs, ▶
perfectly square

—LORELEE KIMBLEY, Calgary, Alberta, Canada

To make logs of refrigerator cookies in a square shape, I line an aluminum foil or plastic wrap box with plastic wrap and then press the dough inside. I put the dough-filled box in the fridge to chill. The result is a uniform, precisely shaped log.

- Once your dough is mixed, make sure it's not too soft to shape. Stash it in the refrigerator for 20 to 30 minutes, until it's firm enough to handle. If it becomes too firm, let it stand at room temperature until it's malleable.

- When shaping dough into cylinders, sprinkling a thin dusting of flour (no more than 1 teaspoon) on the rolling surface can help make the logs easier to handle.

- Moistening your hands ever so slightly can make shaping easier.

- Put the cylinders of dough on plastic wrap at least 6 inches longer than the length of the log.

- As you wrap the log in plastic, roll tightly and tug on the ends to tighten the plastic and smooth any creases.

- To secure the plastic, twist the ends well, and then roll the dough back and forth to eliminate any air pockets.

- To compact the log, push the ends of the cylinder firmly toward the center.

- Take care not to roll the logs any longer than 10 inches. Dough that you'll roll in nuts or other coatings will lengthen when coated, so start them off slightly shorter.

To keep your perfectly shaped round dough log from flattening out on the bottom while it chills, try these ideas:

TURN FREQUENTLY

Put the logs on a level shelf or flat baking sheet in the refrigerator or freezer and turn each log every 15 minutes for the first hour. As the logs chill, the bottoms will flatten from the weight of the dough. To correct this, remold the logs by rolling them back and forth a few times on the countertop.

USE A CRADLE

If you happen to have a baguette pan, it makes a perfect cradle for chilling logs of dough. If you don't, save a few empty paper towel rolls, cut each in half lengthwise to make two cardboard troughs with rounded bottoms, and then place a log in each half for chilling. For both of these methods, after the logs have chilled for 15 to 20 minutes, turn them over once and chill until firm.

USE A SHARP KNIFE AND A RULER FOR EVEN SLICES

To cut even slices of cookie dough, lay a ruler alongside the log of dough. Use your sharpest thin-bladed knife and a continuous slicing motion if the log is uncoated. If it's coated with nuts or other garnishes, use a small serrated knife and a gentle sawing motion for the cleanest cut.

Tips for evenly baked cookies

—JOANNE CHANG, *Fine Cooking* contributor

- Be sure that unbaked cookies are all about the same size or rolled to an even thickness; that way, they'll all finish baking around the same time.
- Use cookie sheets, not rimmed baking pans. Unrimmed sheets allow better air circulation around the cookies while they're in the oven.
- Be sure to use heavy-duty cookie sheets that won't warp. If the sheets warp, your cookies will slide around and bake unevenly.
- Bake cookies one sheet at a time, unless you're using a convection oven. If the dough doesn't fit onto one cookie sheet, drop the remaining batter onto a second sheet and bake it after the first batch comes out of the oven. If you're reusing cookie sheets, be sure to let them cool down before putting more dough on them.

Freshly baked cookies times two

—KAREN ROLFE, Toronto, Ontario, Canada

When I'm making cookies, I portion and bake only as many cookies as my family will eat in the next day or two. Then I refrigerate the dough for later in the week or freeze it for baking another time. This way, we have freshly baked cookies at least twice from one recipe's worth of dough.

Keep homemade cookies soft for days

—ANNE PARK, Blacklick, Ohio

To preserve the softness of freshly baked cookies and brownies, I put a slice of bread in the storage container. The moisture from the bread keeps the cookies soft and makes them taste fresh from the oven—even after several days. When the bread becomes dry, just toss it and replace it with another slice.

Leftover cookies today; crumb crusts tomorrow

—ADELE DEETER, West Chester, Ohio

I put leftover undecorated molasses, chocolate, and sugar cookies in the food processor to make cookie crumbs. I store the crumbs in the freezer and use them instead of graham cracker crumbs when I make desserts with crumb crusts.

Brownies are chewy when they're high in sugar, fat, and eggs but low in flour. The last variable in determining their texture is the nature of the fat used in the recipe—specifically, how hard the fat is at the temperature the brownies are to be served. Butter is soft at room temperature, so brownies made with cocoa plus butter (or oil) have a noticeably soft, chewy texture. And the flavor is intensely chocolatey, with a wonderful lingering buttery flavor. By contrast, brownies made with chocolate plus butter are often firmer, almost fudgy, because cocoa butter is harder than butter at room temperature. The more chocolate the recipe contains, the fudgier the finished brownies.

When I was cutting a pan of brownies recently, the tops stuck to my knife, damaging the brownies and making a mess. My 11-year-old son suggested we use a pizza cutter. The cutter glided smoothly through the rest of the brownies with no mess.

MUFFINS

ROOM TEMPERATURE INGREDIENTS ARE KEY

If the batter uses melted butter and the other wet ingredients are too cold, the butter will solidify and won't blend in well. Also, whisk the wet ingredients together before adding them to the dry; combining them thoroughly helps them mix evenly into the dry ingredients.

DON'T OVERMIX THE BATTER

Add the fruit and other flavorings before the batter is fully mixed. This way, the wet ingredients, dry ingredients, and add-ins come together at the same time, so you avoid overmixing. This results in a more tender crumb—overmixing will make the muffins tough.

OVERFILL THE CUPS

The batter should mound higher than the rims of the cups by about ¾ inch; this makes the batter bake up into those great big bakery-style muffin tops. The tops might meld together while baking, but that's okay—once they've cooled, just cut them apart with a table knife.

Shoehorn muffins out of the pan

—SANDY EVY, Martinsburg, West Virginia

▶ I found my latest kitchen helper in an unlikely place—my closet. I had an unused shoehorn that turned out to be just the right shape for lifting muffins out of their tins. The horn works gently and doesn't mangle even the most delicate muffins.

A plastic knife for muffin removal

—PATTIE MITCHELL, Nanaimo, British Columbia, Canada

▶ I use a plastic knife to remove delicate baked goods from muffin or tart tins. Plastic knives are thin and flexible, and they don't scratch the finish on my bakeware.

CAKES

Prep baking pans to prevent sticking

—Fine Cooking Test Kitchen

▶ If you've ever experienced the heartbreak of a cake sticking to its baking pan, chances are you didn't prepare the pan well enough. Here are two tips to ensure your cakes slide out flawlessly.

- Grease the pan liberally with a visible coating of vegetable shortening, soft butter, or vegetable oil spray. Too little grease is the most common cause of sticking cakes.
- If your recipe calls for flouring the pan, spoon a generous amount of flour into the pan and tilt it so the flour slides over all the inside surfaces of the pan. Dump out any extra and then give the pan a few hard knocks over a trash can to get rid of any excess.

Line pans with butter wrappers

—M. H., via email

▶ I save waxed paper butter wrappers and reuse them to line cake or brownie pans instead of parchment. I always place the printed side down, away from the food. This method is ecofriendly and is a good backup option when you're out of parchment.

Prevent flour specks on chocolate cakes

—DEBORAH PASCUZZI, Placitas, New Mexico

▶ When greasing and flouring a cake pan for a chocolate cake, I mix cocoa with the flour. This prevents the white dusting that sometimes shows on the bottom and sides of the cake if you use only flour.

A better way to grease a bundt pan
—Fine Cooking Test Kitchen

Fancy fluted tube pans, popularly called bundt pans, turn out gorgeous cakes—as long as the cake doesn't stick to it, that is. To make sure your bundt cakes never stick, try greasing the pan with melted butter and a pastry brush instead of softened butter. The pastry brush lets you get the butter down into the crevices of the pan. Softened butter, on the other hand, tends to coat these pans unevenly—thickly in some spots and not at all in others. For extra anti-stick insurance, flour the pan after buttering it.

Use parchment to pour flour
—NIKKI ELKINS, New York, New York

Whenever I made layer cakes that called for adding dry and wet ingredients alternately, I ended up with a mess. Now, I mix my liquid ingredients in a measuring cup, which makes pouring a cinch, and I sift my dry ingredients onto a sheet of parchment. Then I fold up the ends to create a chute that makes it easy to pour flour into the mixing bowl. It saves me from washing an extra bowl, and I can reuse the parchment.

Flour matters
—FLO BRAKER, *Fine Cooking* contributor

Using cake flour in place of all-purpose flour can often result in a more tender cake with a finer crumb, although some cakes aren't suited to this substitution, such as pound or bundt cakes. The only way to know if a cake recipe can be improved upon with cake flour is to give it a try. If you're substituting cake flour for all-purpose flour and measuring by weight, the two flours are interchangeable. If you're measuring by volume, use 1 cup plus 2 tablespoons cake flour for every 1 cup all-purpose flour in the recipe. (This is because cake flour is less dense than all-purpose flour, so you need to add more of it by volume to compensate.) Whichever way you measure, be sure to briefly whisk the cake flour first to aerate it a bit and break up any lumps. If measuring by volume, spoon the aerated flour into the measuring cup (don't tap or tamp) and sweep a metal spatula across the cup to level it off.

Cool cake layers on stockpot pasta inserts
—CHRISTIN ELLINGSWORTH, via email

If you bake a lot of layer cakes and you don't have enough cooling racks, you'll find this tip helpful. I invert the pasta inserts from two stockpots and rest the cake layers on top. The colander-type holes allow for air circulation, and the sturdy metal keeps the layers from sagging.

Eggs can break your batter

—ABIGAIL JOHNSON DODGE,
Fine Cooking contributor

➤ You'll often see the directive in a cake recipe to add the eggs slowly or one at a time. The reason for this is that it helps keep the batter emulsified, which is important for the cake's final texture. If you add all the eggs at once, the batter could break and look curdled. This could cause it to lose volume (that is, air pockets would collapse), and the baked cake would not be as light.

A spoonful of flour keeps raisins from sinking

—LAURA ROSE, Waterbury, Connecticut

➤ I've found that dusting raisins with flour keeps them from sinking in cake batter. Before adding raisins to a batter, I simply toss them in a couple of tablespoons of flour until they're coated. This technique also works for chocolate chips in cake or quick-bread batters.

---

7 tips for cake success

—JENNIFER ARMENTROUT & SAMANTHA
SENEVIRATNE, *Fine Cooking* contributors

➤ **DON'T USE COLD INGREDIENTS**

Butter, eggs, and other dairy ingredients will blend better if they're not refrigerator-cold. Unless your recipe specifically calls for cold ingredients, let them sit at room temperature until they've warmed or softened a bit. Don't let your butter get too warm, though—the ideal temperature is around 65°F, just shy of room temperature.

CREAM THOROUGHLY

Beating butter and sugar together for 3 to 5 minutes may seem excessive when they appear combined much sooner, but proper creaming is key to a light cake. A lengthy creaming time ensures that enough air bubbles are created to lift the cake. If you're using a hand mixer, add an extra minute to your creaming time.

START SLOWLY

To keep dry ingredients from flying out of the bowl as you mix them into wet ingredients, run the mixer on low speed at first just until they're moistened, and then ramp it up to the speed recommended in the recipe.

SCRAPE OFTEN

Even if the recipe doesn't say to do so, stop the mixer and scrape down the bowl and beater whenever it looks like your batter is blending unevenly.

USE A SCALE

Not only is a scale great for measuring your ingredients, but it also makes dividing batter between cake pans faster and easier. Start by weighing your mixing bowl. When your batter is ready, weigh it in the bowl, subtract the bowl's weight, and divide by the number of pans you have to fill. Then simply weigh that amount of batter into each pan—no messing around with measuring and scraping cups of batter into each pan.

MAKE SURE YOUR TOOLS ARE CLEAN

When beating egg whites for a meringue or foam cake, make sure your bowl and whisk are spotless. Even a trace of fat on your equipment can slow down foaming and decrease the overall volume.

USE STRAIGHT-SIDED CAKE PANS

Some cake pans are made with slightly slanted sides—not ideal for layered cakes. Before you begin, make sure your cake pans are straight sided so that your finished cake will stack neatly.

For the smoothest cheesecake, don't overwhip

—Fine Cooking Test Kitchen

It's important to avoid overwhipping the filling for cheesecake so that you don't end up with a puffed, cracked cake. Take these precautions:

- Start with the cream cheese at room temperature (about 70°F).
- Use the paddle attachment of a stand mixer to cream the cheese without aerating it.
- Don't add the eggs until you're sure that the cream cheese is super-smooth and that the other ingredients are well combined. Add the eggs one at a time and beat on low speed until just blended.

Splash-guard your cheesecake

—SHARON RICHARDSON, Corinth, Texas

Whenever I make cheesecake (or anything else that requires baking in a water bath), I set the pan of batter into a large baking pan and add the water after the pan is on the oven rack. Despite these precautions, I'd invariably wind up splashing water into the cheesecake mixture when pouring the water into the pan. Now I've learned to hold a small saucer or salad plate vertically, like a shield, at the cheesecake pan's edge as I'm pouring. Splashes are no longer a problem.

· EVEN A BEGINNER CAN FROST LIKE A PRO ·

A layer cake can be homey, but it shouldn't be messy. Follow these tips for a frosted cake that stands tall and beautiful.

- Let the cake layers cool completely before frosting them so the frosting doesn't melt and make the cake slip and slide.
- Brush stray crumbs from all cake layers.
- Set the first (bottom) layer, flat side down, on a serving plate or a piece of cardboard; cover the top evenly with 2/3 cup of the frosting.
- Set the second cake layer on top, flat side up; cover the top evenly with another 2/3 cup of frosting.
- If the frosting is very soft and the cake layers start to slide, refrigerate the cake for about 20 minutes.
- Before frosting the sides, slide 4 wide strips of waxed paper under the cake to keep the serving platter clean.
- When ready to frost, spread a very thin layer of frosting all over the top and sides of the cake just to cover and smooth the cracks and secure loose cake crumbs (this is called a crumb coat). As you work, be sure to keep cake crumbs from getting into the frosting bowl.
- To spread the rest of the frosting lavishly over the cake, smooth it with a spatula and then create texture with a cake comb, a serrated knife, or the back of a spoon.

—Fine Cooking Test Kitchen

Inverting cakes with streusel toppings
—CAROLE WALTER, *Fine Cooking* contributor

➤ How do you keep the streusel topping from falling off when you invert a cake baked in a large tube pan? Here's the solution:

1 Gently lift up the center tube while carefully pushing the bottom upward with your opposite hand. If the cake doesn't release easily from the sides, run a thin knife between the cake and the tube and between the cake and the outer wall of the pan. Once the cake is out, run the knife under the bottom, too.

2 Fold a 12-inch square of aluminum foil into quarters. Measure 1¼ inches from the inside tip of the foil and cut an arc (this will become a hole for the tube when you unfold the foil). Unfold the foil and place over the cake, pressing gently onto the top of the cake and molding the foil around its sides to hold in the streusel.

3 Invert the cake onto a plate and remove the center tube.

4 Invert the cake again, so it's right side up, onto a rack. Remove the foil and let cool.

What to do if a cake sticks

—PETER BARHAM, *Fine Cooking* contributor

➤ If you've greased and floured properly, a cake should release from the pan when you invert it onto a plate. If it doesn't, the best thing to do is to turn the tin and plate right side up and leave the cake to cool completely. The cake will be stronger when cool, so there's less risk of it breaking when you try to extract it. To get the cooled cake out, gently slide a thin knife around the sides of the pan to free it. This, we hope, will be enough.

If the cake has stuck to the bottom of the pan, you'll have to try something more drastic. If you have time, freeze the cake in the pan overnight, so that the cake becomes hard (and quite strong). Then put the base of the pan in hot water for a minute or so to soften a thin layer at the bottom. Now invert the pan onto a plate and firmly strike the bottom with your hand, or if it's that sort of day, any available blunt instrument. This should release the bottom so the frozen cake can come out in a single piece.

Putting the "roll" in roulade

—Fine Cooking Test Kitchen

➤ The cake for a roulade needs to flexible; follow these 3 steps to be sure your cake doesn't split when you roll it:

1 Invert the warm baked cake onto a clean dishtowel and pull away the parchment. The paper may pull off a thin layer of cake, but that's okay.

2 Gently but firmly roll the towel and cake together into a spiral. Letting the cake cool like this will help it hold the spiral shape once you fill it. If you tried to roll the cake after cooling it flat, it would simply crack too much.

3 Carefully unroll the cake, remove the towel, spread with filling, and then roll the cake a final time. Try to roll evenly so that your cake slices look pretty. Don't worry if the ends are messy—you'll trim those off anyway.

How to split cake layers

—DABNEY GOUGH, *Fine Cooking* contributor

➤ If your recipe calls for split cake layers, use a long serrated knife to gently draw a line all the way around the side of the cake at the center point. Turn the stand slowly, with your knife exerting gentle pressure on the cake. (If you aren't using a rotating stand, use a gentle sawing motion, giving the cake quarter turns as you go.)

When you get back to where you started the cut, begin to cut horizontally through the cake, using the cut line as a guide. Focus on keeping the handle end of the knife in place; if you do this, the far end will follow naturally.

Cutting even cake layers ▶

—SONIA GIBBS, Clemmons, North Carolina

My six-layer banana-nut cake may never taste quite as good as my grandmother's version, but my layers always look great, thanks to the foolproof cutting technique she taught me. Just take a long piece of thread and wrap it around the circumference of the cake layer, crossing the two ends and tightening until you see a slight impression in the "waist" of the cake layer. At this point, adjust the thread if it's not level, and then keep tugging the thread until it slices through the layer. I've found that this cutting method works for all types of layer cakes, not just banana.

- -

Keep cake layers intact when moving ▶

—MARY WANG, Allendale, New Jersey

Cake layers will often break when you try to lift them after splitting them in half horizontally. I was taught to slide cardboard rounds in between to make it easier, but I don't always have a supply on hand. Now I use the bottoms from my tart pans. They are so thin that they slide easily between the layers and work perfectly to lift the cake and move it to a rack or onto a frosted layer.

- -

Aligning cake layers ▶

—BETSY SCHWARTZ, Greenwich, Connecticut

When making a layer cake, I cut a single cake into two layers and spread filling in between them before icing the entire cake. Here's a simple method for realigning the cut layers so the cake ends up level. Before I cut, I insert one toothpick horizontally into the side of the cake near the top and insert another one near the bottom, directly underneath the first one. I cut the cake, spread the filling on the first layer, and then set the top back, realigning the toothpicks. This method ensures a level cake but doesn't require a perfectly level cut.

- -

Improvise a cake platter ▶

—IRENE ONG, Madison, Wisconsin

When I bake a cake to bring to a friend's house, I want to be able to leave without bothering the host to claim my cake platter. So I create one from cardboard and foil. While the cake is cooling on the rack, I invert a platter that fits the cake size onto a piece of cardboard—usually cut from a box—and trace a circle around it. Then I cut out the cardboard circle and wrap it in foil to get a perfectly functional "silver" platter for my cake.

Ganache is a mixture of cream and chocolate, which, when poured warm over cakes, makes the ultimate rich chocolate glaze. Ganache naturally loses its shiny appearance as it cools and sets and even more so when refrigerated, but there are several simple tricks you can use to preserve its attractive sheen.

- If your cake requires refrigeration, be sure that it's refrigerator-cold (not frozen) before you glaze it, and return it immediately to the refrigerator (not the freezer) to set. Do this even if you plan to remove the cake from the fridge before serving to soften the texture.

- For the best sheen, let the ganache cool to a tepid temperature—90° to 100°F—and stir it before pouring it on the cake. If the ganache is too thick to pour at this temperature, thin it with warm cream.

- Once the ganache is poured over the cake, use as few spatula strokes as possible to spread the glaze; too much spatula work will dull the ganache.

- For 1 to 1½ cups ganache, add 2 to 3 teaspoons corn syrup to the glaze.

- Remove the dessert from the fridge 30 to 60 minutes before serving to bring back some of the sheen.

- And as a desperate measure, you can temporarily make a dull glaze shiny again with the help of a hair dryer set on low heat. Very carefully, starting from a conservative distance of at least 3 feet, aim the warm air at the glaze, moving the dryer constantly to avoid melting the glaze in a single spot and moving closer to the cake as necessary. Stop when the cake looks shiny, and don't overdo it. Serve the dessert shortly there-after, since there's no telling how the ganache will look later, when it hardens again.

One last note: If the dessert doesn't require refrigeration, don't chill it. Glaze it and let it sit at room temperature. This will give you the best-looking ganache of all.

When glazing a bundt cake, I put the cake on a wire rack set over a sheet of waxed paper. After I pour on the glaze, I quickly move the rack to another sheet of waxed paper, pick up the first sheet (which now holds a lot of excess glaze), and pour that glaze over the cake. This gives the cake an extra coating of yum.

Cake decorating without mistakes

—TIFFANY HALBERG, Anaheim, California

If I want to write a message such as *Happy Birthday* on a cake without making a mess, I first write the message on the cake itself with the sharp end of a toothpick. Then, I trace over the message with icing or melted chocolate using a decorating tip and a pastry bag. This helps with the spacing and uniformity of the letters, and it helps avoid potential mistakes.

To slice a dense cake, heat the knife first

—JENNIFER ARMENTROUT,
Fine Cooking contributor

I use this trick for any sticky cake. To heat your cake-slicing knife, either dip it in a tall container of very hot water or hold it under hot running water for a few seconds. Then wipe it dry before cutting the cake. The knife will cool quickly and the cake will start sticking, so expect to rinse and repeat several times. If you have a crème brûlée torch, that's also handy for heating up a knife.

A cheese knife makes a clean cut on cheesecakes

—JENNIFER GOLDBECK, Cedarburg, Wisconsin

I was recently slicing a cheesecake using the technique of heating a knife under hot water and wiping it dry after every slice or two, but I found it laborious. It occurred to me to try my cheese knife, which has holes meant to prevent cheese from sticking. It made clean cuts and did not require any wiping between slices.

Cut a cake in small portions

—LILIA DVARIONAS, Kanata, Ontario, Canada

At a dessert party, guests may wish to sample many tarts and cakes, so they may want only a small serving of each. A good way to deal with this is a traditional Scandinavian technique: Cut a cylinder from the center of a round cake, using a small pot lid or saucer as a guide. Cut the outside ring into wedges about 1½ inches wide. When the outside of the cake is gone, you're left with a smaller round cake for teatime, another use, or more small pieces.

Baking liner keeps cupcakes from sliding

—DONNA BRIDGER, Olympia Fields, Illinois

Having broken my cupcake carrier, I was in a quandary about how to transport 2 dozen cupcakes from my home to my grandsons'. All I had handy was my sheet-cake carrier, so I put a silicone baking mat on the bottom and filled it with cupcakes. It held them securely and safely, with no sliding around, so not a bit of frosting was smudged when I reached my destination.

The pie baker's ➤
tip sheet

—**Fine Cooking Test Kitchen**

COLD BUTTER

For flaky piecrust, it's important to start with very cold butter, so that it doesn't melt while you work it into the flour. When this happens, butter becomes too thoroughly mixed with the flour, resulting in a mealy, crumbly crust rather than a flaky one. Freeze butter briefly if you have warm hands, live in a warm climate, or are making a very large batch of pie dough. It's also a good idea to chill the bowl and even the flour when making pie in warm weather.

JUST ENOUGH WATER

For a tender piecrust, don't add too much water. Water contributes to the development of gluten proteins. If you add more than necessary, the resulting crust may still be flaky, but it will be tough rather than tender. For these reasons, trust your fingertips over your eyes: The dough should hold together when pressed between your fingers, although it will still look pretty shaggy.

EASY ROLLING

Take the time before chilling the dough to form an even, circular disk with clean, smooth edges. This will make rolling out the dough much easier because the edges are less likely to crack.

CRISP CRUST

Bake filled pies on a heated, rimmed baking sheet in a lightweight metal pie dish. Both will help set the crust quickly, preventing it from getting soggy. Baking on a sheet is also handy for catching bubbling juices.

Rolling pin ruler ➤

—**NANCY BRODERICK, via email**

Many recipes call for rolling out dough to certain dimensions. To make this easier, I marked off the center on my wooden 18-inch rolling pin, and then I marked various increments of inches. This means I don't need any other instrument to make the perfect-size crust or pastry sheet.

I've always made pie dough the old-fashioned way, cutting the fat into the flour by hand rather than with a food processor. For a long time, however, I had trouble mixing in the ice water: Trickling it off a spoon invariably left me with a few wet clumps of dough sitting in a bowl of dry crumbs.

I had to find a better way. So one day, I filled a clean spray bottle with ice water and spritzed the dry ingredients while tossing them with a fork. The ice water dispersed evenly, and my pie dough quickly came together into a workable mass that didn't crumble when I rolled it out. I now consider a spray bottle an essential pie-making tool.

There's no denying it: Piecrusts are one of the hardest things for a home cook to master. When it comes to rolling them out, experience counts for a lot, but good techniques are also crucial. Here are some of my best pointers for rolling out lovely, even rounds of dough.

START WITH DOUGH AT THE RIGHT TEMPERATURE

If it's too warm and soft, it'll stick like crazy to the rolling pin and the work surface, forcing you to add too much flour as you work it. Dough that's too cold and hard resists rolling and cracks if you try to force it. Press the dough lightly to check its rolling readiness—your fingertips should leave an imprint but shouldn't easily sink into the dough.

GO EASY ON THE FLOUR

Even dough that's at the perfect temperature needs a little extra flour to keep it from sticking, but try not to use more than you really need—the more extra flour you work into the dough as you roll it, the drier and tougher the crust will be.

TRY AN ALTERNATIVE ROLLING SURFACE

Beyond the usual lightly floured countertop, other options for rolling surfaces include a pastry cloth (our current favorite, especially when paired with a cloth rolling pin cover), a silicone rolling mat, and sheets of parchment, waxed paper, or plastic wrap. Choose whichever one you like best.

USE THE FEWEST POSSIBLE PASSES OF THE ROLLING PIN

Overworked dough equals a tough crust, so the less you have to work it during rolling, the better.

ROLL AROUND THE CLOCK

Start with the rolling pin in the center of your dough disk. Roll toward 12 o'clock, easing up on the pressure as you near the edge (this keeps the edge from getting too thin). Pick up the pin and return it to center. Roll toward 6 o'clock. Repeat this motion toward 3 and then 9 o'clock, always easing up on the pressure near the edges and then picking up the pin rather than rolling it back to center. Continue to roll around the clock, aiming for different "times" (like 1, 7, 4, 10) on each round until the dough is the right width and thickness. Turn the dough and check often for sticking. After each round of the clock, run a bench knife underneath the dough to make sure it's not sticking, and re-flour the surface if necessary. When you do this, give the dough a quarter turn—most people inevitably use uneven pressure when rolling in one direction versus another, so the occasional turn helps average it out for a more even thickness.

A chilled rolling pin keeps pie dough cold
—KATHY DEERING, Burns Lake, British Columbia, Canada

I put my rolling pin in the freezer for about 20 minutes before rolling piecrust. It helps the dough stay cold while I'm rolling. This is especially useful if your kitchen gets very warm.

Give pie dough a soft, cold pillow
—MARIE P. AFFA, Saint James, New York

My technique for rolling out pie dough is a bit unusual: Instead of chilling the dough for a long time before rolling it, I refrigerate it for just 10 minutes and then roll it between sheets of plastic wrap. To cool the dough while rolling, I half-fill a zip-top bag with ice and water. This makes a soft, cold "pillow," which I periodically lay over the dough being rolled out. (Be sure that the outside of the bag is completely dry, of course.) I also rest my stainless-steel rolling pin on the ice pillow.

Flattening crumb crusts with a film canister
—HELENE STONE, Highland Park, Illinois

Getting crumb crusts or pastry dough to fit in a mini muffin tin can be a challenge. I've found that a 35-mm film case makes a great tool to fit the crusts smoothly and evenly and works better than my fingers.

Perfect piecrust overhang
—ALLISON EHRI KREITLER,
Fine Cooking contributor

When measuring the overhang on a piecrust (before you fold it under and crimp it), press the piecrust against the end of the ruler just enough to mark the correct measurement in the dough. Do this at intervals all the way around, and then follow the marks to cut the crust evenly with kitchen scissors to the correct overhang. That way the crust will be an even thickness when you fold it under and crimp it.

Cut steam vents for a crisp, pretty crust
—CAROLE WALTER,
Fine Cooking contributor

Cutting steam vents in the top crust of a pie allows for the release of excess moisture while the pie bakes. The vents help the juices evaporate, preventing a soggy bottom crust. Venting also keeps the top crust from cracking by allowing air that builds up under the crust to escape. You can make steam vents by cutting 6 to 8 slashes in the top of the pastry using the blade of a knife or a dough scraper.

Pricking the pastry 12 to 15 times with the prongs of a fork is another venting method that works well. Or, for a more ornamental look, you can cut several holes in the dough with a tiny cookie cutter or canapé cutter. It's natural for steam vents to close somewhat during baking. If they close completely, make them a little larger next time.

Blind bake without spilling the beans
—MARY HOOTEN, Austin, Texas

When prebaking or blind baking a pastry shell, I keep the crust from slipping by anchoring it with dried beans sealed in a heat-resistant nylon oven bag. The bag removes easily, without tearing the delicate crust or spilling the beans, and it can be used to store the beans for reuse.

Easy blind baking
—CAROL WEBB, Kelowna,
British Columbia, Canada

When prebaking a pie shell, instead of filling the unbaked pie with pie weights, beans, or rice (which can often make a mess), I line the unbaked shell with aluminum foil and then nest another pie plate of the same size inside and bake for the desired time. I get perfect pie shells every time.

Crumple parchment for a just-right fit
—JENNIFER ARMENTROUT,
Fine Cooking contributor

A crisp, new sheet of parchment doesn't snuggle into a pie or tart shell very well when you need to blind bake, but if you first crumple the sheet into a ball and then unfold it, it'll fit easily.

· BLIND-BAKING BASICS ·

Blind baking means baking an empty piecrust before adding a filling. This gives the crust a head start, allowing it to firm up before the filling is added and preventing sogginess. Here are a few tips for getting the best results.

Remember to chill. Chill the pie shell before blind baking it. Piecrusts baked right after shaping are warm enough for the butter to melt quickly in the oven, causing the edge to sink or even slump over the edge of the pie pan.

Weight it down. Dried beans or pie weights will help the crust keep its shape. Without them, the crust will rise and puff on the bottom or slide down the sides under the weight of the crimped edge.

Bake it right. In recipes where the filling doesn't need further cooking or cooks for a short period of time, such as cream pies or fruit tarts, the crust is usually blind baked until cooked through and golden brown. But in recipes where the pie cooks for a while after adding the filling, it's best to blind bake the crust just partway so that it won't overcook as it continues to bake with the filling.

—NICOLE REES,
Fine Cooking contributor

Prevent soggy tart shells
—MARY BENDAYAN,
North Woodmere, New York

➤ It isn't always possible to fill fruit tarts just before serving, and I used to be disappointed at how soggy the tart shell would get. I discovered that a thin layer of chocolate between the shell and the filling solves the problem. After baking and cooling the tart shell, I use a pastry brush to paint the inside of the shell with dark, milk, or white chocolate. Once the chocolate hardens, I add the pastry cream or other filling and then decorate it with the fruit. The chocolate acts as a barrier, preventing the cream from penetrating the crust, and, of course, it adds a chocolate flavor.

Perfect lattice strips for pies
—JEAN BRAYMAN, Fremont, Michigan

➤ To cut even strips of dough for a lattice-top pie, I use my rasp-style grater (without a handle) as a guide. The long sides have curved, raw edges that are perfect for cutting through the dough. I lay the grater on the rolled-out dough and press down to cut a strip. Then I move the grater so that the bottom edge is in the center of the strip. I just cut and press down again, creating a strip that's half as wide as the grater. I continue this pattern over the entire pie round.

A foil shield for piecrusts

—CAROL SPIER, via email

To keep the edges of a piecrust from browning too quickly, I used to wrap little strips of foil around the rim of the pie, a tedious process. Now, I simply take a square of foil somewhat larger than the pie, cut a big X through the center, and place it over the pie. Then I fold back the quadrants from the center and secure the edges of the foil around the pie pan.

Keeping your custard pie together

—CAROLE WALTER,
Fine Cooking contributor

A custard pie filling separates from the crust because of shrinkage, which is a normal part of the cooling process. The fact is, all baked goods shrink as they cool due to the evaporation of moisture during baking; with a pie, the filling and crust are shrinking in opposite directions, which often results in separation. There are ways to reduce the chance of this happening, though.

- Avoid extreme changes in temperature, choose a spot to cool your pie that is free of drafts, and do not put the pie in the refrigerator until it has cooled completely.

- Prebake the pastry crust for pumpkin and other custard pies to give the crust a chance to shrink before the filling is added. Even though the filling will still shrink upon cooling, separation will be minimized.

If you still have separation, your best bet is to disguise it. I like to sprinkle chopped toasted pecans or almonds around the edge of the filling before serving. I've also used crushed gingersnaps or biscotti. If you like, you can pipe whipped cream decoratively around the edge.

➤ Fruit pie or tart fillings thickened with quick-cooking or instant tapioca have a bright appearance and a clean taste, with no floury or starchy mouth-feel or aftertaste as can happen with flour or cornstarch. The disadvantage is that, if not properly handled, quick-cooking tapioca's tiny granules can leave behind a slightly grainy, almost bead-like texture in the fruit juices. (Don't confuse this form of tapioca with pearl tapioca, which is primarily used in puddings.) To avoid a granular texture and uneven thickening, follow these tips:

- Thoroughly mix the tapioca into the fruit filling, making sure it's evenly distributed.
- Set the filling aside for 15 minutes to let the granules absorb moisture from the fruit and expand properly.
- Just before scraping the filling into the crust, give it one last gentle toss.

These tips will help ensure that the tapioca gets well incorporated (for even thickening) and that all the granules have plumped and swelled.

➤ To remove a tart from the pan, set the pan on a wide can and let the outside ring fall away. If it's stubborn, grip the ring with your fingers to coax it off. Slide a long, thin metal spatula between the pan base and the crust and ease the tart onto a flat serving plate.

GRILLING

The top 11 tips for successful grilling

—Fine Cooking Test Kitchen

Stick by these laws of the grill and you'll have success every time.

- **Do all your prep and gather your tools in advance.** You don't want to leave your steak unattended or miss the window of a perfect-temperature fire because you're looking for your tongs or slicing a mountain of vegetables.

- **Keep a spare gas tank on hand.** If you have a gas grill and use it often, it makes sense to have a full spare tank on hand in case yours runs out at an inconvenient time (like right in the middle of grilling dinner).

- **Make sure your grates are really clean** (see "The Best Way to Keep Grill Grates Clean," p. 196).

- **Be patient.** Don't start grilling until your coals are ready or your gas grill is heated. That way you will get a good sear and food is less likely to stick.

- **Don't crowd the grill.** Leave enough room around each piece of food for air to circulate so that the food sears properly and your fire has the air it needs to fuel it.

- **Don't move the food too often.** It's tempting to check on something by turning it over, but if you can be patient and let the food sit long enough to really sear, you won't have as many sticking problems (see "Why Foods Stick to the Grill," p. 198).

- **Pay attention.** Unless you're cooking with indirect heat, you'll have the best results if you keep a close eye on how fast your food is cooking.

- **Learn to manage flare-ups.** You can prevent flare-ups by letting excess marinade or oil drain or drip off before putting food on the fire. When flare-ups do happen, move food to a cooler spot on the grill or temporarily cut off the air to the grill by covering it or shutting the air vents.

- **Check for doneness early.** You can always put food back on the grill, but once it's overcooked, there's no going back. Use an instant-read thermometer to check on meat temperatures (see the chart on p. 203).

- **Brush on barbecue sauces and sweet glazes toward the end of cooking.** They'll burn if they're put on too early.

- **Let it rest.** Let grilled foods, especially meats, rest off the heat for at least 5 and up to 15 minutes before slicing and serving. This allows the juices to redistribute for more tender, tasty results.

- -

Nutshells create flavorful smoke

—SHARON R. HOWARD, Eugene, Oregon

We save our nutshells and toss them onto hot charcoal briquettes in our grill. The smoldering shells give a uniquely smoky flavor to anything grilled or barbecued.

· A GUIDE TO TAMING & TENDING YOUR FIRE ·

Pick your fuel: gas vs. charcoal

There are pros and cons to grilling with gas and grilling over coals. Gas is quick and easy. Charcoal takes a little longer but adds great smoky flavor.

If you grill with gas, all the fuel you need is a tank of propane gas (an accurate gauge is good to have, too).

The best fuel for charcoal grills is natural hardwood charcoal. It burns cleaner and hotter than briquettes (which often contain fillers) and has the added benefit of providing that wonderful campfire aroma while you're grilling. Natural hardwood charcoal is now available in some supermarkets, gourmet specialty stores, and by mail. If you can only find charcoal briquettes, try to use those labeled "hardwood briquettes," and steer away from the self-lighting kind, which are saturated with petroleum. You can also try grilling over real hardwood like oak or hickory, but the logs need 1 to 2 hours to burn down to coals, and the heat is less consistent.

Heat the grill. No matter which fuel you use, you need to give the grill time to heat up.

For a gas grill: Be sure to give a gas grill plenty of heating time so that the grill and the grates are really hot when you start cooking. Unless you have a super-powerful gas grill (burners with lots of BTUs), you'll want to crank all the burners up to the highest setting to heat (you can always adjust one or more burners later). Use an oven thermometer to determine how hot your grill is (keeping the cover down, of course).

For a charcoal grill: The easiest way to start a charcoal fire is with a chimney starter. Load the top of the metal canister with charcoal, stuff newspaper in the bottom, and light the paper with a match. Updraft spreads the fire from the paper to the charcoal, and in about 30 minutes, all your coals are glowing. Turn the starter over (beware: the handle will be hot) to dump the coals into the grill. Then rake the coals to spread them or bank them.

How to build a two-level fire.

A two-level fire, where one area is hotter than the other, is a good idea for almost every kind of grilling. With a two-level fire, you can easily move food around if it's cooking too quickly or too slowly. Even hamburgers, chicken breasts, and steaks—which should be grilled quickly over direct heat to stay juicy—can benefit from resting on a cooler part of the grill.

For a gas grill: Turn one or more burners to medium-high heat and one to low heat.

For a charcoal grill: Bank most of the hot coals to one side of the grill or on the outer edges of the grill. This gives you the option of direct grilling (putting the food right over the coals) or indirect grilling (putting the food on the cooler side of the grill, farthest from the hot coals, and covering the grill to create an oven-like atmosphere).

How to set up a grill for low and slow cooking. Some foods, like large roasts and whole chickens, must be cooked entirely with indirect heat so that they don't burn on the outside before they're fully cooked inside.

For a gas grill: First, be sure you have a tank that's at least half full. After heating the grates, turn the gas down to medium-low if using two burners. If your grill has three burners, turn the center one off and keep the outside burners on medium-low. If you plan to add soaked chips for smoking, follow your manufacturer's guidelines. Or, see "2 Ways to

Add Smoke to a Gas Grill," p. 197. For a charcoal grill: Remove the cooking grate. Light about 50 hardwood charcoal briquettes in either a large chimney starter or in a pyramid-shaped mound over the electric starter on the charcoal grate. Once the coals are covered in a white-gray ash, pour or rake half of the briquettes to each side of the grate, and set a 13- by 9-inch disposable aluminum roasting pan between the two piles of coals. (The pan will catch fat and juices as the meat cooks.)

If you want a pronounced smoky flavor, set about 1 cup soaked chips onto the charcoal just before you're ready to cook. Replace the cooking grate. Set an oven thermometer directly on the cooking grate; when it reads 325° to 350°F, position the meat in the center of the grate directly over the pan, cover, and proceed with the recipe.

To maintain the cooking temperature, add about 10 briquettes to each pile of coals every hour or so, or when the temperature gets below 250°F. The best way to add briquettes to the fire is to light them 20 minutes before you need them (ideally with a chimney starter) so that they're already hot when you add them to the grill.

—Fine Cooking Test Kitchen

HOW HOT IS THE GRILL? —JENNIFER ARMENTROUT, *Fine Cooking* contributor

To test the heat of your grill fire, hold your outstretched palm an inch or two above the grill grate without burning yourself. The length of time you can stand the heat tells you the level of grill heat. You can use this test on gas grills as well as charcoal grills.

TIME HAND CAN BE HELD OVER GRILL	GRILL HEAT	TEMPERATURE RANGE (IN °F)
Less than 1 second	Very hot	Over 600°
1 to 2 seconds	Hot	400° to 500°
3 to 4 seconds	Medium	350° to 375°
5 to 7 seconds	Medium-low	325° to 350°

Visual Clues

- When the coals are all bright red and still flaming, they're very hot—too hot for most grilling.
- When the coals are red but covered with a light ash, the fire will be a little cooler.
- When the coals are thickly covered with a yellowish ash, the fire is medium-hot.

For best results, keep the grilling grate about 4 inches above the coals.

The best way to keep grill grates clean

—ELIZABETH KARMEL,
Fine Cooking contributor

▶ The trick to maintaining clean grill grates is to brush them when they're very hot.

For a gas grill, the best time to do this is just before grilling. Turn all the burners to high and let the grill heat with the lid down for 10 to 15 minutes, or until the internal grill temperature is higher than 500°F. This burns off the residue from the last cookout, making it much easier to brush off with a brass-bristle grill brush (steel bristles are too hard and can damage enamel-coated grates). If you have a lot of accumulated buildup on your gas grill grates, you'll need to allow more time to burn off the residue, so let the grill heat up on high for a full hour before brushing.

For a charcoal grill, burn off any residue on the grates right after grilling. Just set the lid on the grill and, as the hot coals burn out, any residue should burn off. Then brush before the next use.

When you're brushing the grates, don't be afraid to use some elbow grease. You want the surface of the grates to be smooth and free from any food that may have stuck the last time. This prevents the buildup of charred food on the grates and helps ensure that the food you're about to cook won't stick.

Safety first: top tips for gas grillers

—JENNIFER ARMENTROUT,
Fine Cooking contributor

▶ Gas grills have made it so effortless to fire up the grill that it's sometimes easy to forget to handle the propane tank with care. To keep the grill action safe and fun, here are tips from the Propane Education & Research Council:

- Always follow the grill manufacturer's instructions for lighting the grill, and make sure the grill top is open. If a match or lighter is needed to light the grill, turn the gas on only after the lit match is inserted into the proper hole.
- Before lighting a propane gas grill for the first time or after it's been stored for the winter, use a leak-detection solution to check connections for tightness (check your owner's manual for details). Don't use matches or lighters to check for leaks.
- If you suspect a gas leak, call the fire department immediately.
- Never pour an accelerant such as lighter fluid or gasoline on the grill.
- Don't allow children to play with the cylinder or the grill.
- Don't smoke while handling a propane cylinder.

- When the cylinder is refilled, have the supplier check for dents, damage, rust, and leaks.
- After filling or exchanging a cylinder, take it home immediately. Keep the vehicle ventilated and the cylinder valve closed and capped.
- Always use or store cylinders outdoors in an upright (vertical) position. Don't use, store, or transport cylinders near high temperatures (this includes storing spare cylinders near the grill).
- When not in use, grill burner controls should be turned off and the cylinder valve closed.

2 ways to add smoke to a gas grill

—Fine Cooking Test Kitchen

It's hard to beat a gas grill when it comes to ease of use, but what you don't automatically get with a gas grill is the flavor of smoke that comes from grilling over wood or charcoal. Some gas grills come with a built-in smoker box to which you can add wood chips, but if your grill doesn't have one, you can improvise. You can:

- Get a small, rectangular disposable aluminum pan and cover the bottom of the pan with a layer of wood chips that have been soaked in water for about half an hour. Put the pan under the grill grate, directly on a burner in a corner of the grill. Turn the burner to the highest setting until the chips start to smoke.
- Fashion a homemade smoker pouch. Wrap a large handful of soaked wood chips in heavy-duty aluminum foil to make a pillow-shaped package. Poke holes on top to release smoke and set the pouch under the grill grate. Run your grill on high until you see smoke.

Whichever method you choose, once you've got smoke, adjust the burner settings as needed for whatever food you're grilling. If the chips stop smoking, you can crank the heat back up to get them going again as long as it won't cause the food on the grill to burn.

NOTE: Never throw wood chips directly on a burner, as this could clog the gas line.

- -

Microwave veggies before grilling

—GEOFF MAYO, Toronto, Ontario, Canada

We love to grill zucchini, carrots, and potatoes, but too often we find that the carrots and potatoes burn on the outside before fully cooking through. Now, before grilling, I par-cook potatoes, carrots, and other hard vegetables for a couple of minutes in the microwave on high to give them a head start.

Why foods stick to the grill

—SARAH JAY, *Fine Cooking* contributor

You can blame the proteins in meat or fish for your troubles with sticking. When proteins are heated, they first unfold into long strands and then they start to coil up again into new, tighter forms (a process called coagulation). Initially, these unfolded strands of proteins will bond with the metal grates. But as they continue to coagulate, the proteins interact and bond more with themselves than with the grill grate. That's the moment you're waiting for, because at that point, they'll more or less naturally release from the grill. So the bottom line is that beef, chicken, pork, and fish will always be prone to some sticking, but if you can resist the urge to flip or move them too soon, you'll get a cleaner release.

Also, be sure the grates are hot and clean, and don't be shy about oiling the food. Hot grates are key, because the heat seals microscopic pores in the metal where proteins would otherwise have a chance to bond. Cleaning the grates with a brush removes any cooked-on protein residue, which can also exacerbate sticking. And coating the food with oil inhibits sticking because oil acts as a lubricant (you can oil the grates if you want, but it's more efficient to coat the food).

Sugary sauces can also cause sticking due to the sugars caramelizing and bonding to the metal grates. If you're basting with a sweet sauce, try brushing it on toward the end of cooking to minimize the problem.

Brush vegetables with mayonnaise

—YVONNE CATTY, via email

Before grilling, I like to brush my vegetables with mayonnaise instead of olive oil. Whether plain or seasoned with garlic, herbs, or spices, the mayonnaise clings effectively and imparts great flavor to the vegetables. It also forms a protective coating, keeping the vegetables from drying out on the grill. If used judiciously, it won't add any more fat to your food than oil would.

3 tips for good kebab karma

—BRUCE AIDELLS, *Fine Cooking* contributor

- Pay attention to the recipe and cut your kebab ingredients the same size. Small cubes of meat tend to dry out, while large chunks take too long for the center to cook before the outside gets too charred.
- If the called-for ingredients cook at widely different rates, separate them and cook them on different skewers.

- Invest in sturdy metal skewers. I prefer these to disposable wooden ones. The best metal skewers are flat, or if rounded, double-pronged so that the food doesn't slip and twirl when you turn the skewers. If you do use wooden skewers, go for flat ones, soak them first to keep the exposed ends from burning (they usually do anyway), and use two parallel skewers per kebab to keep the food from spinning.

Use poultry lacers for perfect grilled onions
—SUE STRAUGHAN, Denver, Colorado

Sliced onions have a tendency to fall apart when you grill them. To keep grilled onion slices whole, I insert several metal poultry lacers through an uncut onion at regular intervals. Then I slice the onion between the lacers, so that each slice has a lacer in it, and grill the slices following my favorite recipe. I pull out the lacers before serving.

Slow roast summer tomatoes on the grill
—NANCY TYLER, Whittier, California

It's often too hot in the summer to leave the oven on for hours in order to dry fresh summer tomatoes. So I slow roast them on a sheet pan in my gas grill (covered), sometimes adding wood chips for some nice smoky flavor.

Plan ahead for weeknight grilling
—CAITLYN SASSAMAN, Victoria, British Columbia, Canada

I rarely have time to grill during the week unless I plan ahead. On weekends, I freeze several batches of beef, pork, or chicken in plastic zip-top bags in their marinades. Before going to work in the morning, I pull out a bag from the freezer and transfer it to the fridge to thaw. When I get home, the meat is ready for the grill.

Soak skewers in a vase
—ALLISON JOSEPH, Quincy, Massachusetts

Instead of soaking skewers laid flat in a baking dish, I put them upright in a tall flower vase filled with water (a tall pitcher also works). I set a saucer or small plate on top to keep the skewers from floating to the top.

· THE MYTHS (AND FACTS) OF MARINATING ·

Before firing up the grill, get the facts on what this technique can (and can't) accomplish.

Myth 1 A marinade will infuse a steak completely if you let it soak long enough. (Or if you vacuum seal it. Or if you inject the marinade into the steak.)

Fact: Whether you marinate for 3 minutes or 3 days, a marinade penetrates the meat by only a fraction of an inch. Here's an easy experiment you can do to prove this. Take a steak, plop it in a zip-top bag with some marinade, squeeze out as much of the air as possible, and put it in your refrigerator for 3 days. Take it out, cut the steak in half, and see where the meat is darker. You'll find the marinade has permeated about ⅛ inch.

Meat is made up of bundles of muscle fibers, which are packed densely together. That density blocks the marinade from getting through. Those vacuum sealers that claim to help the marinade drill down deeper and faster don't do anything to pull apart the cells and let in the marinade (or any other liquid). You could inject some marinade deeper into the meat using a syringe sold specifically for that purpose. This would give you pockets of flavor below the surface. The problem is that the syringe punctures the surface of the meat, creating little escape hatches for the juices during cooking. After all, what lets liquid in also lets it out, and while the steak is cooking and shrinking, the moisture is going to look for any way it can to get out. A dry steak is the opposite of what you're going for, so resist the temptation. Besides, you don't really want your entire steak to taste like the marinade. The goal is to enhance the flavor of the meat, not cover it up.

The lesson: Marinades may never penetrate deeply into a piece of meat, but they do flavor the surface.

Myth 2 A marinade will tenderize a tough piece of meat.

Fact: Not exactly. As I explained above, a marinade doesn't penetrate very deeply into a piece of meat, so it can't transform its makeup. Some chemical tenderizing does take place on the surface, because the acids in a marinade break down muscle tissue, a process called denaturing. Let it go too long, though, and the muscle tissue will coagulate, squeezing out water molecules and resulting in mushy yet tough meat.

How long is too long? It depends on what you're marinating and how strong an acid you're using. A relatively tough cut of meat like flank steak can handle a more acidic marinade (say one part acid to two parts oil) for a longer period than delicate shrimp (which would be better served with an acid-to-oil ratio of one to four). The acid in yogurt and buttermilk is far milder than that in wine, vinegar, and lemon juice. Yogurt and buttermilk also contain calcium, which activates enzymes in meat that break down muscle fibers. So dairy products are a better choice for delicate proteins.

But the only way to tenderize meat beyond the surface is through cooking slowly in a liquid (also known as braising) or through aging. In aging, natural enzymes in the meat break down the tough connective tissues all the way through the meat. Wet aging is done by sealing the meat airtight in the fridge; dry aging involves a controlled rotting in a cool, well-ventilated environment. It causes molds and yeasts to grow on the surface, which are cut off before cooking. In olden days, people left meats in an acidic marinade for days or weeks, and the acid in the marinade protected the surface of the meat from spoiling while the rest of the meat matured. (Of course, the surface texture of the meat suffered.) As a result, many people think it's the marinade that leads to tender meat, when it's really time that does the work.

The lesson: Aging, not marinating, is the key to tender meat.

Myth 3 Marinating always takes place before cooking.

Fact: Sometimes, a marinade can do the cooking. As explained in Myth 2, the acid in a marinade denatures a food's proteins. Heat does the same thing. So when a delicate protein like fish is bathed in an acid, such as lemon juice, the proteins will be denatured and then coagulate (technically, the acid is unraveling the molecules and altering their chemical and physical properties). This causes raw foods to firm up and appear more opaque, as in seviche.

The lesson: A marinade can take the place of cooking.

Myth 4 Some marinades can make grilled foods healthier.

Fact: This one is true, actually. If you cook red meat at a high enough temperature, you can create heterocyclic amines, or HCAs. HCAs are carcinogenic, so you'd be smart to avoid them. However, herbs in the mint family, such as sage, thyme, rosemary, and mint, contain phenolic compounds, which are impressive antioxidants. It's believed that the phenolic compounds keep the HCAs from forming, according to a study published by a team of food researchers at Kansas State University. A marinade with oil allows those herbs to stick to the surface of the meat and do their antioxidant best.

The lesson: Some myths are true.

Myth 5 A marinade adds flavor to meat.

Fact: This one is true as well. Restrained marinating adds a layer of flavor to meats and vegetables that can elevate a simple steak or chicken leg. Think about your last grilling adventure. An average steak is received with a chorus of "Great steak!" and promptly forgotten. A steak marinated briefly in a balanced mixture of wine, spices, and oil and then grilled perfectly haunts the eater, even when the days of summer have waned. The memory may have your guests digging out their grills in winter in an attempt to recapture that taste experience.

The lesson: A marinade is the secret to creating a steak of legend.

—**BRIAN GEIGER**, *Fine Cooking* contributor

Use a quick-soak method for skewers

—"CHIFFONADE," Port Richey, Florida

▶ It's easy to forget to soak bamboo skewers in water for 30 minutes before grilling. When that happens, I take a shortcut: I boil them for 5 or 10 minutes in a shallow frying pan. The hot water seems to penetrate the skewers more quickly, so they don't burn on the grill.

Use poultry lacers as skewers

—MICHAELA ROSENTHAL, Woodland Hills, California

▶ I love to make hors d'oeuvres like bacon-wrapped shrimp or chicken satay on the grill. Wooden skewers always seemed to char, no matter how long I soaked them in water. So, recently I bought a few dozen metal poultry lacers. They're the perfect size for skewering appetizers, and they don't burn.

Improvise a grill basket

—KAREN ANN BLAND, Gove, Kansas

▶ If your outdoor grill doesn't have a grill basket, do what I do. I use an ice pick to poke several small holes in the bottom of a disposable aluminum pan. I add cut-up vegetables to the pan and then grill, shaking the pan occasionally for even cooking. The disposable grill basket is easy to clean and can be reused several times if washed gently.

Make a customized grill caddy

—R. B. HIMES, Vienna, Ohio

▶ No matter how carefully I'd plan a session at the grill, I would always have to make a few trips back to the kitchen for this item or that. My solution: I bought a small plastic tool tote and stocked it with grilling staples—salt, pepper, olive oil, tongs, aluminum foil, paper towels, and so on. Now when I head for the grill, the tote goes with me.

Eliminate cleanup with a zip-top bag

—AMY CATTANACH, via email

▶ When preparing a marinade for grilling meats, I line a mixing bowl with a zip-top plastic bag and mix the marinade ingredients in the bag. The bowl provides the stability I need, and when I'm done mixing, I simply add the meat to the bag, seal it, and remove it from the bowl. No cleanup is necessary, and the bag is ready to be refrigerated or frozen.

Carry meat on a plastic-lined platter

—TOM SCHRAND, Philadelphia, Pennsylvania

➤ To cut back on having to tote plates and platters to the grill, I transport raw meat on a platter that I've completely covered with plastic wrap. Once the meat is on the grill, I crumple up the plastic and use the platter for serving. This prevents contamination and means fewer dishes to wash.

Supple basting brushes

—"TOPFOR," via email

➤ After washing a basting brush, I place it in a mug half-filled with coarse salt, such as kosher salt. The salt helps absorb excess moisture and oil and keeps the bristles separate and pliant. Before storing, I tap off any salt crystals that are clinging to the brush.

· IS IT DONE YET? ·

With experience, you can learn to judge how well done a piece of meat is by touching it—the firmer it is, the more done it is. And in a pinch, you can always make a cut to take a peek. But for large cuts of meat and bone-in pieces, an instant-read thermometer is still the best way to gauge doneness. An instant-read thermometer only gives an accurate reading if inserted at least a couple of inches deep, so you can't use it on the thinnest cuts (in such cases, use visual clues). The internal temperature tends to go up 5 to 10 degrees as meat rests off the heat, so pull your food off the grill a few degrees shy of the temperatures listed below.

TYPE OF MEAT	IDEAL INTERNAL TEMPERATURE (IN °F)
Chicken and turkey	Breast: 160° to 165° Thigh: 170° to 175°
Beef and lamb	Rare: 120° to 130° Medium rare: 130° to 135° Medium: 140° to 150° Medium well: 155° to 165°
Veal	Medium: 140° to 155°
Pork	Medium: 140° Medium well: 155° to 165°
Fish	Medium rare: 120° Medium: 135°

—Fine Cooking Test Kitchen

OTHER TECHNIQUES

Getting the right amount of liquid

—MOLLY STEVENS,
Fine Cooking contributor

By definition, *braising* means gently cooking ingredients in a covered pot in a small amount of liquid. As a general rule, the liquid should come less than one-third of the way up the sides of the main ingredient. This may look like a scant amount, but all foods release liquid as they braise and thereby increase the amount of liquid in the pot. The goal is to have just enough to create a moist environment in which the liquid evaporates and then condenses on the underside of the lid and falls back into the pot to baste the food. This way, the main ingredient becomes irresistibly tender, and the braising liquid transforms into a concentrated, flavorful sauce. Adding too much liquid to start will result in a diluted sauce that lacks flavor and body.

One word of caution with long braises (anything over 3 hours): If the liquid threatens to dry up after a couple of hours, add a bit more. The one exception to this rule is a hybrid technique used by many chefs in which they braise uncovered. In this case, you'll need enough liquid to just barely cover the main ingredient to account for the evaporation that happens without a tightly sealed pot.

A pot lid can serve as a plate

—STEVE HUNTER,
Fine Cooking contributor

When cooking a braised dish, you often have to brown the meat first and set it aside on a plate while you cook the aromatics. Instead of dirtying a plate, I use the lid of the braising pot and set it upside down on a burner or inside another pot so it sits level. A bonus: You get every last bit of juice back into the braise.

Home cooks and chefs alike have taken to brining—and for good reason. Brining can make meat moist and tender.

HOW IT WORKS

Think of a piece of meat as a mass of tightly entwined protein strands. When you submerge the meat in a saltwater brine, the salt causes the tightly wound protein strands to loosen and unwind. Like a sponge, the loosened strands take up and trap additional water. The meat has gone from being a dense, taut mass of protein to being a soft, fluid web of protein and saltwater. This extra moisture can make all the difference when you're grilling, roasting, or sautéing small, lean cuts—such as boneless chicken or turkey breasts, pork chops or cutlets, or even sea-food—that dry out easily if overcooked.

BROWNING AND BRINING

People sometimes gripe that brined meat doesn't brown well, but this is a result of surface moisture rather than the brining process. And it's a problem easily solved: Simply pat the meat dry before cooking so that moisture won't interfere with browning, and be sure to use high heat. Another thing you can do to boost browning is to add a little sugar to the brine.

Typically, brines contain 1 cup salt, more or less, to 1 gallon of water.

Never put meat into warm brine, which can encourage bacterial growth and can also draw out the meat's natural juices. It's safest if the brine is refrigerator-cold before you add the meat.

Brining time depends on the type and size of the meat, as well as on how much salt is in the brine. Generally, the smaller the item, the less time it needs to soak in the brine: Shrimp need just 30 minutes, chicken breasts and pork chops 4 to 8 hours, and a whole turkey 12 to 24 hours.

A good recipe will tell you exactly how much salt to use and how long to soak the meat; it's best to follow the directions, because oversalting ruins more than just flavor; the meat can become spongy, rather like lunch meat. Also, at high levels, salt interacts with myoglobin, the protein that gives meat its color. Light meat, especially near the bone, sometimes turns pink from the interaction of salt with myoglobin, so chicken or pork will look undercooked even though it's done, and no amount of cooking will make the pink coloration go away.

Rules for better brining ▶

—JENNIFER ARMENTROUT,
Fine Cooking contributor

Don't brine kosher meat. Kosher meat has already been treated with salt.

Don't overcook. Brining doesn't completely protect meat against dryness, but it will give you more leeway.

Jazz up your brine with other flavors. Add herbs and spices or a little of a flavorful sweetener (like honey or maple syrup), or replace some of the water with another liquid (like apple cider or coffee). Just remember that when you add sugar, foods tend to brown faster.

Keep it cold and rinse it well. Raw meat is still raw meat, whether it's in brine or not. Always keep foods below 40°F while brining and then rinse them to remove excess salt from the surface before cooking.

Be careful when adding more salt. The brine provides just about all the seasoning you need, so be judicious about adding more just before cooking. Always taste first when making sauces with pan drippings, which end to be quite salty already.

Making space to brine ▶

—ALLISON EHRI KREITLER,
Fine Cooking contributor

The hardest thing about brining meat is finding the space to store it in its brine; particularly around Thanksgiving time, you might be challenged to fit a large pot in the refrigerator. Here are a couple of alternative space-saving approaches to brining.

USE ROASTING OR BRINING BAGS

Brining the turkey in a jumbo plastic bag uses less space and less brine than a pot does. Look in kitchen shops for turkey brining bags, and follow the instructions on the package. Or use the plastic turkey-cooking bags found in the plastic wrap and foil section of the supermarket. Just double up the bags (for leak protection) and add the turkey, breast side down. Put the bagged turkey in a roasting pan or bowl (again, for leak protection) and add enough brine to fill the inner bag about halfway up the turkey. Then tightly close the opening of each bag with a twist tie, eliminating as much air as possible from the inner bag to force the brine to surround the turkey, and refrigerate.

BRINE IN A COOLER

Using a clean cooler means the turkey won't be in the fridge at all—nice if you're really crunched for space. The challenge here is that you need to add ice to keep the turkey cold, but you don't want the melting ice to dilute your brine too much. To offset the ice melt, use an additional ½ cup kosher salt in your brine. Make sure the brine is refrigerator-cold before pouring it over the turkey in the cooler. Add enough ice to submerge the turkey in brine—you'll need 5 to 10 pounds, depending on the cooler. Store the cooler in the coldest location you can think of. If that happens to be outdoors, put it in a place where animals can't get to it, like a screened porch or your car.

- -

**Brine and defrost ►
at the same time**

—JENNIFER MACH, Chicago, Illinois

Whenever I have frozen meat that I want to brine, I put the meat in a resealable plastic freezer bag with the brine while it's still frozen. The salt in the brine helps defrost the meat quickly, and the flavor begins to penetrate right away. This works best for thinner pieces of meat, such as pork chops, steaks, and chicken parts.

**Broiling: ➤
door open or closed?**

—Fine Cooking Test Kitchen

Many of use learned to broil with the oven door open. But times change, and so do appliances. If your oven is less than 10 years old, chances are you should be broiling with the door closed. Most ovens sold today are built as closed-door broilers, for reasons of safety and smoke control. We learned this the hard way in the test kitchen when one of our ovens shut down after we broiled with the door open, and we had to call in a technician to reset the electronic controls. To find out if your oven is a closed-door or an open-door broiler, consult your manual or call the manufacturer. If your broiler is gas powered, you should always broil with the door closed.

3 tips for better broiling ➤

—LORI LONGBOTHAM,
Fine Cooking contributor

1 No preheating is necessary. Not only does the broiler cook food quickly, but it also heats up in just a few minutes, unlike the oven, which can take 15 to 20 minutes to reach the desired temperature. So just turn it on and get ready to cook.

2 Be ready to move the pan around. Take a close look at your broiler and see how it releases its heat. If the heat is concentrated right down the center of the oven, arrange the food right down the center of the broiler pan. Most broilers have hot and cool spots, so be ready to move the broiler pan around to compensate.

3 Some pieces may cook faster than others. The pieces you're broiling won't be exactly the same size, so they won't cook in the same amount of time; remove what's done and continue to cook anything that needs more time.

**An ad-hoc rack ➤
for broiling**

—ALISON BUHLER, Sacramento, California

I always forget to move my oven racks to the broiling position before the oven has heated, making the job more difficult and dangerous. When this happens, I invert my large cast-iron skillet onto the middle oven rack and set the item to be broiled on top of it. It provides a stable base and keeps my frustration to a minimum.

COOKING SUGAR

5 tips for perfect caramel
—TISH BOYLE,
Fine Cooking contributor

One of two things can go wrong when making caramel: The caramel burns; or sugar crystals form, which results in the caramel going from liquid and smooth to crystallized and solid. Here are a few pointers for making a properly cooked and perfectly smooth caramel every time:

- **Watch bubbling caramel like a hawk.** Caramel cooks quickly and will turn from golden amber to a smoking mahogany in seconds. Burnt caramel has an unpleasantly bitter taste.
- **Use clean utensils.** Sugar crystals tend to form around impurities and foreign particles.
- **Acid helps.** Adding lemon juice to the sugar and water helps break down the sucrose molecules and prevents sugar crystals from forming.
- **Swirl, don't stir.** Stirring tends to splash syrup onto the sides of the pan, where sugar crystals can form. So once the sugar is completely dissolved in water, just gently swirl the pan to caramelize the sugar evenly.
- **A pastry brush is your friend.** Keep a pastry brush and some water next to the stove; you'll need it to wash off any crystals that might form on the sides of the pan.

Quick caramel cleanup
—Fine Cooking Test Kitchen

The easiest way to clean a caramel-coated pan is to boil water in it until the sugar has completely dissolved. Then you just pour out the water, let the pan cool, and wash with soap and water. For ramekins or other vessels that can't go directly on the stovetop, pour boiling water into the ramekins, let soak until cool, and repeat if necessary until all the caramel is gone.

FREEZING & CANNING

Keep your jars hot and pack them tight
—ANDREA CHESMAN,
Fine Cooking contributor

Whether you're using our pickle recipes or one of your own favorites, follow these guidelines for safe canning.

- Wash the jars and screw bands with hot, soapy water and rinse them well. Follow the manufacturer's directions for preparing the lids. The jars must be hot when you pack them; otherwise, the hot brine may cause them to shatter.

- Pack the jars tightly, and then pour in the hot brine to cover the vegetables, allowing the specified amount of headspace (the space between the rim of the jar and its contents).
- Remove air bubbles by slowly raising and lowering a chopstick or a plastic blade around the inside of the jars. This is crucial: A trapped air bubble may shatter a jar as it heats. Add more brine to cover the vegetables, if necessary.
- Wipe the jars' rims with a damp cloth before putting on the lids. Secure the lids with screw bands tightened by hand into place.
- Set the jars on a rack in a canner or pot that's half-filled with very hot water (but not boiling, which may cause the jars to break). Add more hot water, if necessary, to cover the jars with 2 inches of water. Cover the pot, turn the heat on high, and bring the water to a boil. When it starts to boil (you'll have to peek), begin timing—see your recipe for processing time.
- Remove the jars immediately when the time is up. Let them cool undisturbed for at least 12 hours. Never tighten the bands after the jars have been processed, as this could break the seal.
- Test the seals. After the jars have cooled, gently remove the screw bands and test the seals by lifting the jar by its lid. (Do this over a towel to catch the jar if it hasn't sealed properly.)
- Store sealed jars in a cool, dry place. Unsealed jars should be stored in the refrigerator and used quickly.

- -

Flat-freezing ➤ vegetables

—SUSAN ASANOVIC, Wilton, Connecticut

When you flat-freeze vegetables, they sometimes stick to the pan's surface. I line a jellyroll pan or baking sheet with a linen dishtowel and spread the produce on the towel in a single layer. I freeze the produce until hard and then transfer it to storage bags. The towel absorbs any excess water and prevents the fruits or vegetables from sticking to the pan.

· FREEZING THE HARVEST ·

If you have a vegetable garden in the backyard, or even if you're just a farmers' market junkie, you know you can't possibly use up the season's bounty of fruits and vegetables. It's just too much in too little time. If jams and preserves are not your thing, think about freezing, which is a great way to preserve the fresh flavors of fruits and vegetables at their peak. And it's easy—all you need is a baking sheet, heavy-duty freezer bags, and the best your summer garden has to offer. Here's a handy guide for freezing all the season's favorites.

How to freeze: 4 easy steps from fresh to frozen

1. Create a level area in your freezer to fit a rimmed baking sheet. If you're strapped for space, use something smaller—like a cake pan—and repeat the freezing steps below as needed.
2. Line the baking sheet with parchment, foil, or waxed paper. Arrange the prepared fruits or vegetables in a single layer, making sure they don't touch (see chart, on the facing page, for prep directions). Freeze until solid, 1 to 1½ hours depending on size and freezer temperature.
3. Transfer to heavy-duty freezer bags. Press out as much air from the bag as possible (if you have a vacuum sealer, use it), seal, and store in the back of the freezer (the coldest part) until ready to use.
4. To thaw, transfer the amount you need to a bowl or plate and thaw in the refrigerator.

From freezer to table
Freezing is a great way to preserve flavor, but don't expect fruits and vegetables that have been frozen to have the same texture as fresh ones. That's why it's better to cook with them than to eat them out of hand. Here's how:

Fruits

Frozen: Use in pie or galette fillings and in smoothies.
Partially frozen (5 to 10 minutes out of the freezer at room temperature): Use in sauces, smoothies, cake batters, and pancakes, and as garnishes.
Thawed: Use in sauces, smoothies, and jams.

Vegetables

Frozen: Use in soups, braises, and stews, and steamed.
Thawed: Use in sautés, stir-fries, and purées.
A couple of exceptions: Tomatoes should always be thawed and drained before using in soups, braises, stews, and sauces (don't use in sautés or stir-fries).

Corn on the cob can be steamed frozen but should be thawed before grilling.

Freezer basics

Freezer temperature: Set your freezer at 0°F or colder (use a freezer thermometer to check). Many home freezers are opened and closed frequently, causing the temperature to fluctuate. This makes fruits and vegetables thaw slightly and refreeze—not ideal for texture and taste. To prevent this, stash frozen fruits and vegetables as far from the door as possible.

Freezing time:

Stand-alone freezer (infrequently opened chest or upright): 10 to 12 months.
Frequently opened freezer compartment: 3 months.

Blanching Most vegetables benefit from blanching before freezing. The process stops the enzymes' aging action while slowing vitamin and nutrient loss. It also brightens and sets the vegetables' color. In general, fruits don't need blanching (unless it's to remove the peel).

Here's how to blanch:

1. Bring a large pot of water to a rolling boil (about 2 quarts per 2 to 3 cups of vegetables).

2. Working in small batches, add the vegetables. Allow the water to return to a boil and cook very briefly (see the chart below for blanching times).

3. Using a large slotted spoon, scoop out the vegetables and immediately immerse them in a large bowl of ice water to stop the cooking. Remove and dry thoroughly before freezing.

—ABIGAIL JOHNSON DODGE,
Fine Cooking contributor

HOW TO PREP 20 VEGETABLES & FRUITS FOR FREEZING —Fine Cooking Test Kitchen

VEGETABLES & FRUITS	PREP	BLANCH
Asparagus	Trim woody bottoms	1 to 2 minutes
Bell peppers	Trim stem and seeds; cut into 4 pieces or into strips or dice	No
Broccoli, cauliflower	Remove stems and cut florets into 1½-inch pieces	2 to 3 minutes
Corn	Remove husks and leave cob whole	3 to 5 minutes; cut kernels off after blanching, if you like
English peas	Shell peas	1 to 1½ minutes
Rhubarb	Cut into 2-inch chunks	Not necessary but can help retain vivid color
Snap peas, snow peas	Trim strings	1 to 1½ minutes
Spinach	Wash and trim	1 to 1½ minutes
Tomatoes	Peel (blanch first), seed, and cut into chunks	30 seconds, to loosen skin
Wax or green beans	Trim stem ends	1 to 2 minutes
Apricots	Remove pit; cut in half or in quarters if large	No
Cherries	Leave whole, wash, and dry well; remove pit, if you like	No
Peaches, nectarines	Peel (peel hardens during freezing) and remove pit; cut into 1-inch wedges	No
Raspberries, blackberries, blueberries	Leave whole, wash, and dry well	No
Strawberries	Wash, dry well, and hull	No

MEASURING

Give flour a shake before measuring ➤

Give flour a shake before measuring

—NAOMI KURKJIAN, Piedmont, California

Before spooning flour into a measuring cup, give the flour bag or canister a good shake. It aerates the flour for more accurate measuring.

How to measure well ➤

—Fine Cooking Test Kitchen

LIQUIDS

Always use *liquid measures* (spouted cups and beakers with fluid ounce and cup measurements) unless you're measuring tablespoons and teaspoons. Put the cup on a level surface and get yourself at eye level with the measure before assessing the amount of liquid.

DRY GOODS

Always use *dry measures* (measuring cups and spoons that hold the exact amount) for dry ingredients like flour, sugar, spices, grains, cornstarch, baking powder, and so on. Unless the recipe calls for a "heaping" measure, level it.

FLOUR

Weighing is the best way to measure flour. If you must measure by volume (cups), always stir the flour a little and then spoon it into the cup before leveling with the flat side of a knife. Scooping the cup directly into the flour compacts it, and you'll get too much. (It's also inconsistent.) If your recipe calls for sifting, be sure to sift at the right time. "1 cup flour, sifted" means you should sift after measuring; "1 cup sifted flour" means you should sift before.

SUGAR

It doesn't make much difference if you scoop or spoon granulated white sugar into the cup. But treat confectioners' sugar as you would flour. For brown sugar, measure by scooping the cup into the sugar and packing it in.

Measuring a reduction ▶

—KEN ERDMAN, Hydesville, California

When a recipe called for reducing a sauce or stock by a fraction, say by half, I always ended up measuring it with a cup several times and making a mess. To avoid this, I now prepare whatever I need to reduce in a straight-sided saucepan and dip a bamboo skewer straight into the sauce. I score the skewer with my knife at the height of the sauce, and then at the halfway mark (or whatever the recipe calls for) to note where my sauce should be when reduced. I continue to dip the skewer in every so often to see how much the sauce has reduced until I reach the amount I need.

A neat way to measure sticky items ▶

—JENNIFER ARMENTROUT,
Fine Cooking contributor

Sticky ingredients like honey and molasses can be a pain to measure because they stick in the measuring spoon or cup. But if you lightly coat that measuring cup or spoon with a little oil or cooking spray first, the sticky liquids will slide right back out.

And another way ▶

—KIM LE, via email

To speed your cleaning time and ensure that you'll use every last drop of sticky items like honey, corn syrup, and molasses, line your measuring cup or spoon with plastic wrap, making sure that you have a bit of overhang. Pour the amount you need, gather up the excess plastic wrap, and twist tight. You should have a bundle ready for use. Simply poke a small hole in the plastic with a paring knife and squeeze the ingredient out with your fingers.

ROASTING

No-mess carving ▶

—JANA WACHOWSKI,
Delta, British Columbia, Canada

When I make a roast for dinner, I put my cutting board in a jellyroll pan and carve the roast that way. The juices spill off the board and into the pan, not onto my table or kitchen counter. This also works for roast chicken.

Roast meats without a rack ▶

—R.B. HIMES, Vienna, Ohio

A tasty way to keep roasts off the bottom of the roasting pan without a rack is to set the meat atop several celery ribs or carrots cut lengthwise.

SEARING

Spatter-free searing ➤
—LAURA GIANNATEMPO,
Fine Cooking contributor

Whenever I'm going to sear meat or sauté ingredients in oil over moderately high heat, I cover the other burners of my stovetop with aluminum foil to keep the spatter to a minimum and my stove mess-free.

Show your best side ➤
—DABNEY GOUGH, *Fine Cooking* contributor

Whenever you sear meat or fish, always begin with the "presentation side," the side that will face up when plated. Although it doesn't make a huge flavor difference, the side that gets browned first usually ends up looking the best. As protein cooks, it stiffens, shrinks, and even changes its shape a bit. The first side to hit the pan is still completely raw and malleable, so much of its surface area will touch the pan directly. Once you flip it over, though, the partially cooked second side won't lie on the pan as evenly, and it'll also develop a spotty look due to the brown bits left in the pan from searing the first side.

So how do you know which side should be up and therefore cooked first? Sometimes the presentation side is obvious: For chicken, it's the side that has or had skin on it. For a skinless fish fillet, it's the side that was closest to the bone, which is more evenly colored than the skin side. On other proteins, like pork chops or steaks, the presentation side is not as obvious. In that case, just start with whichever side is most attractive.

STEAMING

Marbles warn when boiling water is too low ➤
—SUSAN BEDSOLE, via email

I'm prone to burning pots when steaming vegetables because I let the water completely evaporate. To prevent this, I place four or five glass marbles on the bottom of my stainless-steel pot. Then I add water, bring it to a boil, and steam my vegetables. When the water is low, the marbles start moving around on the bottom of the pot, making a racket, which tells me that I need to add more hot water.

Tie a cork to the steamer basket

—FAYE FIELD, Kihei, Hawaii

➤ When I use a steamer basket, the tiny metal piece in the center, which serves as the basket's handle, gets too hot to touch with bare fingers and is too small to grab easily with a potholder or an oven mitt. To solve the problem, I wrapped thin wire around a cork and threaded the wire through the small hole at the top of the basket's centerpiece. To remove the hot basket from a pot, I just grab the ends of the cork and lift—no more burned fingers.

STIR-FRYING & DEEP-FRYING

For the best stir-fries

—TONY ROSENFELD,
Fine Cooking contributor

➤ • Cut the ingredients uniformly so that they will cook evenly.

• Use a stir-fry pan if you have one. If not, use a heavy skillet with a large surface area, which will give the ingredients enough space to sear properly.

• Make sure your pan is hot before cooking so the ingredients will brown but not stick.

Car-care aisle yields deep-frying help

—MATTHEW CLEMENTE,
Kingston, Ontario, Canada

➤ When I deep-fry, I like to reuse the oil at least once. To strain it before storing, I use a funnel designed for car oil. (It's made of HDPE plastic, which is known not to leach chemicals and is used in many food-storage containers.) Available in the automotive section of department and hardware stores, these funnels are larger than most kitchen funnels and have built-in strainers. Some even have a handy on/off spout, which helps prevent overflow. Look for a funnel with the finest wire-mesh strainer, clean it thoroughly before use, and use it only for food.

Oils for deep-frying

—SUSIE MIDDLETON,
Fine Cooking contributor

➤ The best oils for deep-frying have a neutral flavor and a smoke point higher than the temperature at which you'll be deep-frying (which is usually 375°F). Good choices include peanut oil, safflower oil, and corn oil, all of which have smoke points above 400°F.

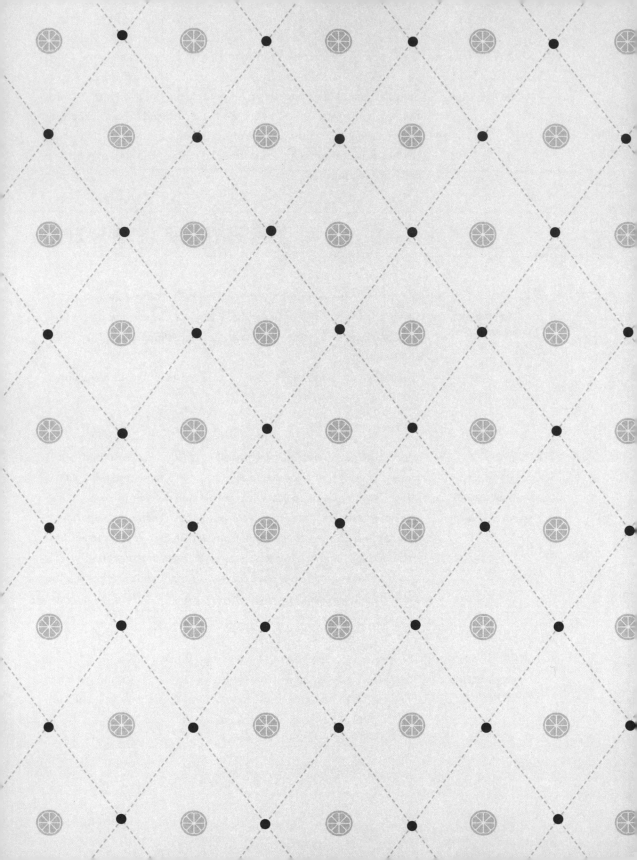

WINE & BEER

WINE

- About 95% of wine is meant to be consumed within the first year after release.
- The proper humidity for storing wine is between 60% and 70%.
- Store wine away from natural or ultraviolet light, which can interact with the sulfites in a bottle of wine to form mercaptans, foul-smelling aromas that make the wine undrinkable.
- If you break or lose a cork, you can store leftover wine by securing a piece of plastic wrap over the bottle opening with a tightly wound rubber band.

 I'VE HEARD THAT STORING SPARKLING WINE OR CHAMPAGNE IN THE REFRIGERATOR FOR MORE THAN A SHORT TIME WILL RUIN IT BECAUSE THE VIBRATION OF THE REFRIGERATOR MOTOR WILL SOMEHOW MAKE THE WINE GO FLAT. IS THIS TRUE?

Vibration is the enemy when it agitates the wine or produces too much heat, but most commercial refrigerators don't generate enough to worry about. More of an issue in storing wine in the refrigerator is how dry the air gets. This can dry out a cork, which would release all the bubbles in a sparkling wine. That's why it's best to keep a bottle of sparkling wine in a refrigerator for no more than 6 weeks.

—TIM GAISER, *Fine Cooking* contributor

· WINE LINGO, DEMYSTIFIED ·

Wine can be a very complex subject but it becomes a lot less intimidating once you're familiar with the basic jargon. Here's a glossary of many commonly used wine terms with easy-to-understand definitions.

Wine label jargon You'll frequently encounter these terms on a wine label or when reading about wine. They don't describe a wine's taste per se, but they offer details about the wine's origin and the way it was made, both of which affect the quality and character of the wine.

Appellation tells you where the grapes were grown and the wine was produced. The appellation is especially important for French wines, which are known by place names and rarely list grape varieties.

Cru is a French term denoting a vineyard or estate of exceptional merit. The concept of cru is especially important for Burgundy and Champagne, where the best vineyards are labeled "premier cru" and "grand cru."

Cuvée means *blend*; a wine labeled "cuvée" is a blend of many different base wines, which may themselves be blends.

Estate-bottled wines come from grapes grown on a winery's own vineyards.

Meritage is a marketing term developed to describe California Cabernet Sauvignon blends that are modeled after the great reds of Bordeaux.

Reserve is the most abused term in the world of wine. Theoretically, it should be used by a winemaker only to designate his best product, but you'll see the term slapped on the labels of cheap, mass-produced wines.

Varietal wines are made from a single grape variety and bear the grape's name on the label. To bear a varietal name, such as Merlot, Riesling, or Chardonnay, on the label, the wine must contain at least 75% of that grape, according to United States law.

Vintage denotes the year the grapes were harvested and the wine made. Most wines state a vintage year on the label, but there are also nonvintage (NV) wines, which are blends of wines from several years.

Barrels and bottles

Barrel- or stainless-steel-fermented are the winemaker's two fermentation options. The choice depends on the style of wine and the specific grape variety. Stainless-steel-fermented wines emphasize bright, youthful fruit; barrel-fermented wines offer rich, creamy aromas and flavors.

Barrel- or bottle-aged tells you whether wine is aged in oak barrels or in the bottle. Oak aging adds aromas or flavors of vanilla, baking spices, and toast to the wine. Bottle aging (also called bottle maturation) implies aging in a cellar, which should increase the complexity of the wine and make it smoother.

Tasting terms These words are used to describe how wine tastes. Understanding them will help you make sense of the descriptions you read in reviews and wine-buying guides. They'll also help you evaluate the wines you drink by giving you specific aspects to focus on and words to describe what you taste.

Acidity refers to the tartness of a wine. A wine can be described as crisp or soft, depending on the amount of acidity. High-acidity wines might be described as crisp or racy, while those with low acidity are called soft, and wines with too little acidity are often described as flat. In addition to balancing and enlivening wine's flavor, acidity is a key element in successful food-and-wine pairing. Generally, the most food-friendly wines have moderate alcohol balanced by crisp acidity.

Alcohol refers to the amount of alcohol in a wine, which for table wines usually ranges between 13% and 15%. The amount of alcohol determines a wine's richness, body, and, to a great extent, intensity of flavor. Wines with low alcohol feel light-bodied, while wines with too much alcohol often taste overripe and imbalanced.

Balance describes the harmony (or lack thereof) among all the elements in a wine. A balanced wine is a seamless progression of fruit, acids, alcohol, and tannins, with nothing too prominent.

Body describes how weighty a wine feels in the mouth. Wines that feel heavy and rich are full-bodied (the word *big* is often used to describe these types of wines). Feathery wines with little weight are light-bodied. Medium-bodied wines fall in between.

Complexity refers to the aromas and flavors in a wine and how they interact with each other. The more layers of flavor and aroma, the more complex the wine and the higher its quality.

Corkiness, the most common flaw in wine, is caused by a tainted cork. Corked wines smell and taste of wet, musty, or mildewed cardboard.

Finish describes a wine's aftertaste, be it fruit, acidity, oak, or tannins. Generally, the longer the flavor lasts after you swallow, the better quality the wine. However, there are also bad wines with regrettably long finishes.

Legs (or tears) are the trickles of wine that run down the inside of a glass after you swirl it. The legs are clues to how much alcohol or residual sugar the wine contains; thicker, slower legs indicate a wine with more alcohol or residual sugar.

Malolactic fermentation is a process by which some of the sharp malic acid in a young wine is converted to softer, smoother lactic acids. The process also causes the wine to develop a buttery flavor compound, which you'll find in many Chardonnays.

Sweetness or dryness levels refer to the presence or lack of sugar in wine. Wines range from bone dry, with no residual sugar, all the way to dessert sweet in style. Off-dry wines have just a hint of sweetness. Most table wines are dry to off-dry.

Tannins, which come from the skins, seeds, and stems of the grapes and also from the barrels, are usually found in red wine. Tannins taste bitter and make your palate feel fuzzy, velvety, puckery, or even dry if they are present in large amounts. Wines high in tannins are often described as firm or chewy, and those without a lot of tannins are called soft or supple.

Texture refers to a wine's mouthfeel. The texture of a wine may be described as silky or astringent or dense.

Name that style

Brawny/muscular wines are big, robust reds with lots of tannins.

Earthy describes a wine whose aromas and flavors are either minerally or evocative of rich soil. European wines tend to be earthier than their New World counterparts. Earthy wines are often described as having a sense of terroir (pronounced teh-rwahr), a French term that refers to the specific region or vineyard where the wine was made. A sense of terroir lends complexity and interest to any wine.

Fruit-forward wines are dominated by the flavors of fresh fruit—berries, apples, cherries, and so on.

Jammy wines taste of very ripe, almost overripe berries. Zinfandels are often described as jammy.

Oaky wines have a toasty, vanilla flavor that comes from aging in oak barrels. It can be wonderful, but too much oak can throw a wine out of balance.

—TIM GAISER, *Fine Cooking* contributor

How to safely open a bottle of bubbly

—TIM GAISER, *Fine Cooking* contributor

Grand Prix auto racers may do it all the time, but don't try popping a cork at home. Not only is it a waste of wine, but a flying cork could really hurt someone. Here's the safe way to do it:

1 Cut the foil below the wire cage and remove the foil.

2 Place a cloth napkin over the top of the bottle and press on the cork (in case it's ready to pop on its own) as you loosen—but don't remove—the wire cage.

3 Lean the bottle against your hip at a 45-degree angle. Grip the cork while you gently turn the bottle (not the cork) and allow the cork to come out slowly.

Wines hot for the grill

—TIM GAISER, *Fine Cooking* contributor

White wines with pronounced oak, which usually pose a challenge to food pairing because they dominate, are ideal mates for lots of grilled foods.

Here, an oaked wine's powerful flavors and smoky notes can be just the thing. Chardonnay, for example, is a natural with richer grilled fish and grilled chicken. Oak-aged Fumé Blanc (Sauvignon Blanc that has been oaked, and sometimes blended Sémillon) and Viognier are good bets as well.

Red wines are a natural with many grilled foods. The combination of luscious cherry-berry fruit, bright acidity, and tannin is a perfect complement to the grill's robust flavors, especially when it comes to grilled meats. Red wine is usually aged in small oak barrels, which add flavor, structure, and tannins of their own. My favorite grill wines include Zinfandel from California, Shiraz from Australia, and Rhône-style blends with Syrah. Richer Merlots also work well.

· SOLVING THE WINE & SALAD PUZZLE ·

Pairing wine with salad can be tricky—vinaigrette posing the main issue—but this needn't mean forgoing a glass of something good with your dinner salad. You just need to know about potential clashes to watch out for, and then learn some clever ways around them.

THE CHALLENGES

Vinegar Most vinaigrettes contain vinegar and thus have very high levels of acidity. A vinegar's sour flavor comes from acetic acid, which plays havoc with a wine's balance, making wine taste dull and flat.

What happens: When a vinegar-based vinaigrette meets a perfectly delicious wine, the wine will taste unbalanced and unappealing. Acetic acid flattens the fruit flavors in a wine, rendering it one-dimensional. It can also make the oak in a wine taste much too pronounced, and this can translate to bitter flavors. All of this detracts from the wine you've spent time selecting and the salad you've spent time preparing.

Sweetness Some vinaigrettes contain sweetness in the form of honey, added sugar, or balsamic vinegar. Ingredients like fresh or dried fruit or candied nuts also add sweetness.

What happens: When paired with a dry table wine, sweet elements clobber the wine's fruit flavors and make it taste thin, overly dry, and bitter.

THE SOLUTIONS

Choose the right wines

- High-acid sparkling wines or white wines with little or no oak are the best choices for most salads. The crispness or bright acidity in these wines can step up to a vinaigrette without getting kicked out of balance. Look for nonvintage sparkling wines and Champagnes as well as unoaked Sauvignon Blanc, dry Riesling, and lighter Chardonnay with little or no oak. Other dry whites such as Albariño and Pinot Grigio also work well.
- Youthful dry rosés also work well with vinaigrettes and salads, thanks to their combination of juicy fruit and crisp acidity. Look for rosés and other blush wines made from Grenache, Pinot Noir, and Cabernet Franc.
- Light red wines with youthful fruit, crisp acidity, moderate tannins, and light oak can work with a salad containing poultry, meat, or cheeses rich in butterfat because the wine's tannins and acidity marry with the protein and the fat. Try a lighter Pinot Noir, a Barbera, or a Gamay.

Tweak the salad elements

- Include poultry, seafood, meat, cheese, or a combination. The protein and the fat will buffer the acidity in the vinaigrette. They'll match nicely with the acidity and soft tannins in red wine.
- Use a milder vinegar (like rice vinegar) in the dressing. The lower acidity in rice vinegar is much easier on the balance of a wine.
- Substitute fresh citrus juice, such as orange, lemon, lime, tangerine, or grapefruit, for some or all of the vinegar in the dressing. This does wonders for wine pairing. Citric acid is a much better match for wine than acetic acid because the flavors are much closer to the flavors in wine.
- Throw a splash of wine into the vinaigrette. I've found that this results in salads that taste much better with wine.

—TIM GAISER, *Fine Cooking* contributor

BEER

· TYPES OF BEER ·

Most beers fall into one of two categories—ales and lagers—based on the kind of yeast used for fermentation.

Ales are made with top-fermenting yeasts, strains of yeast that rise to the surface during fermentation, creating a thick yeast head. Ales have a distinctive fruitiness, which is offset by the addition of bitter hops, and they are produced in a wide range of colors and styles. Here are some of the most common:

Pale ales and India pale ales (or IPA): Made with lightly roasted malt, these beers are golden to copper in color and relatively mild, with a distinctive bitter finish. India pale ales have a higher alcohol content and more hops, giving them a pronounced bitterness.

What to pair them with: The crisp, citrusy notes of pale ales and IPAs pair well with a range of foods, from pizza, buffalo wings, and hamburgers to spicy Thai cuisine and Indian curries.

Brown ales: Deep amber to brown in color, brown ales display flavors of chocolate and caramel due to the deeply roasted malts from which they're made.

What to pair them with: Try them with hearty stews and braises as well as with aged cheeses.

Porters: Made with well-roasted malt, porter ales are deeply colored, full bodied, richly flavored beers with bold, chocolatey notes.

What to pair them with: Porters' deep flavor and full body are best suited to the rich flavors of stews and other hearty fare rather than to the light, bright flavors of summer.

Stouts: Exceptionally rich and creamy, these extra-dark, almost black ales are made with long-roasted malt, which gives them a caramel-like flavor.

What to pair them with: Stouts pair well with braised meats and rich, meat-based soups or stews.

Pilsners are excellent all-purpose beers with a light body, a clean, crisp flavor, and a prominent hoppiness, or bitterness.

What to pair them with: Pilsners are perfect served as an apéritif or paired with shellfish, grilled fish, or grilled or roasted chicken. They're also a great match for spicy Asian, Indian, and Middle Eastern food.

Lagers The term lager denotes any beer made with bottom-fermenting yeasts, strains of yeast that ferment at cooler temperatures and settle to the bottom during fermentation. Lagers tend to be yellow-gold or amber in color, although there are deeper-colored versions, too. The most widespread types of lagers include:

American-style lagers and amber lagers: Pale, crisp American lagers are the most well-known and marketed beers in the United States. These clean, zesty brews have a light body and a mild flavor with just a touch of hoppy bitterness. Amber lagers are reddish brown in color with a medium body and a caramelly malt flavor.

What to pair them with: Both are versatile beers that pair with a range of foods, from hearty barbecue to spicy Mexican.

Bocks: Traditionally brewed in fall or early spring to coincide with festivities like Christmas and Easter, bock beers (now brewed year-round) are strong, wonderfully rich dark amber lagers.

What to pair them with: Bocks are natural partners for hearty grill fare, such as sausages and marinated meats.

—TIM GAISER, *Fine Cooking* contributor

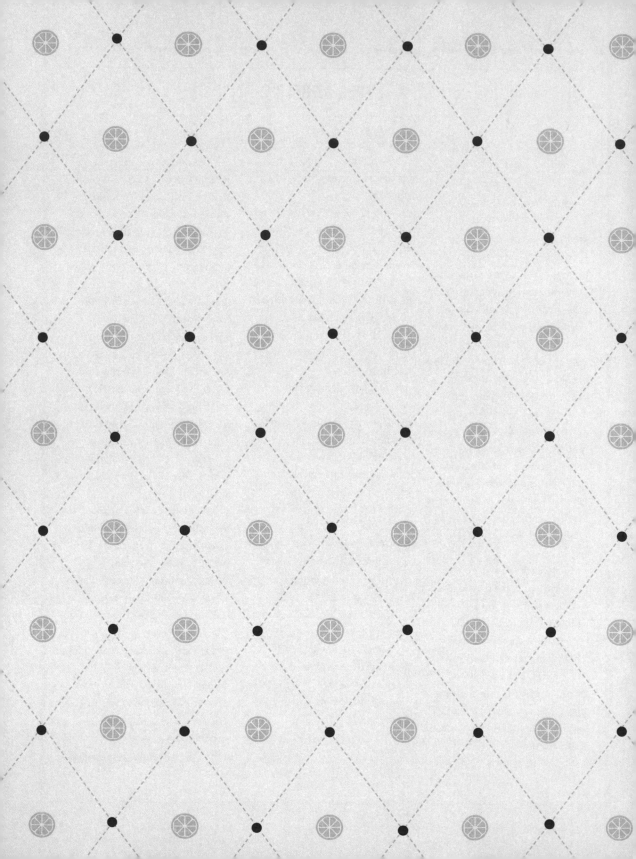

WHEN THINGS GO WRONG

A QUICK GUIDE TO SUBSTITUTIONS & EQUIVALENTS

CAKE CATASTROPHES, MUFFIN MISHAPS & BEFUDDLED BISCUITS

THE PROBLEM	POSSIBLE CAUSES	FIX-IT TIPS FOR NOW OR NEXT TIME
Cake batter looks curdled	Ingredients were either different temperatures or too cold. Eggs and/or liquids may have also been added too quickly.	Don't worry about a curdled-looking batter—the final height of the cake may be shorter, but it will turn out fine. Generally, all ingredients should be at same temperature for best volume, and adding eggs and liquids gradually creates a better and more stable emulsion.
Sponge or angel food cake falls	Though disturbing a foam cake during baking can make it fall, as will underbaking or overbaking it, the most likely culprit is overbeaten egg whites. Overbeaten whites are grainy and deflate easily; the egg proteins are overworked and no longer capable of expanding and holding air.	Next time, stop beating whites once they form stiff, shiny peaks. For extra-stable egg foams, beat a portion of recipe's sugar into the whites, beginning when they reach soft peak stage. If you moved the cake during baking or slammed the oven door last time, take it easy next time.
Layer cake or quick bread falls	Cakes fall for many reasons, but the most common is that the pan was overfilled: If the batter reaches the top of the pan and still needs to rise, it will collapse. Stale or the wrong type of leavening could also be at fault. Though atrocious mixing will do it, you'd have to really abuse the mixing method to make a cake fall.	Never fill cake pans more than half full, and leave an inch at top of loaf pans. Start with fresh leavening (6 months for baking soda and 1 year for baking powder) and don't make substitutions. Measure carefully and don't skip steps in mixing method.
Cake, muffin, or quick bread has poor volume	Poor volume is a result of temperature (ingredients were too cold) and improper mixing (fat and sugar were insufficiently creamed or eggs were incorporated too quickly). Overmixing can develop gluten in batter, resulting in a tougher cake with poor volume. Using the wrong type of or expired leavening will do the same.	For maximum volume, start with room-temperature ingredients. To best incorporate air, cream fat and sugar for time specified and beat in eggs one at a time. Use fresh leavening and don't make substitutions. Don't beat batter for long once all the liquid has been added.
Muffin or pound cake doesn't peak	The amount of batter in the muffin cup or pound cake pan is important: Underfilled muffin cups or loaf pans won't bake up with a nice peak. Too low a baking temperature will cause batter to spread outward rather than up, a problem seen in muffins especially. Insufficiently creamed or aerated batters also will not peak.	Fill muffin cups especially high, a little over three-quarters full, and loaf pans to within an inch of the top. Bake muffins at 375° to 425°F. Be sure to cream ingredients for the amount of time specified and add ingredients as indicated.

Muffins are dry and/or tough	Wrong flour may have been used. Also, overmixing after last ingredients are added can develop gluten in batter, resulting in toughness. (Muffin recipes typically contain less sugar and fat than other cakes; both interfere with gluten development and contribute to tenderness.) Finally, muffins may simply be overbaked.	Next time, use a low-protein all-purpose or pastry flour. After liquids are added, mix quickly and gently, stopping when batter is just combined, and then let it rest in muffin pan for 10 minutes to relax the gluten before baking. Start checking for doneness at least 10 minutes before end time specified in recipe.
Fruit-filled muffins burn and stick to the tin	Tin was not adequately greased and floured, allowing sugary, ripe fruit to stick to pan.	Stubborn scraping to loosen the muffins is the only way to salvage them. Next time, generously grease pan, covering every nook at bottom and even around top edge. Also flour pan for best insurance against sticking. Turn muffins out of pan while warm, before juices from fruit solidify.
Biscuits, shortcakes, or scones are dense, with poor volume	These need a hearty kick of leavening since they have little or no eggs or a creaming phase for aeration—inadequate or stale leavening makes short biscuits. These foods also get their lift from cutting fat into the flour, and then folding the dough into layers before cutting: The pieces of fat melt and leave air holes behind, and then steam gives the air pockets a lift, creating layers. If fat is completely ground into dough or high-protein flour is used, the baked good will be dense.	Biscuits need about 1½ teaspoons leavening per 1 cup flour, including no more than ¼ teaspoon baking soda per cup. Use the right flour: all-purpose, pastry, or cake flour mixed with all-purpose. Cut in very cold fat and use the least amount of liquid needed to get dough to come together. Try folding dough to create layers and let dough rest for 15 minutes before cutting and baking in a hot (425°F) oven.
Rolled biscuits or scones are dry	Adding too much liquid will make them drier and cakey rather than moist and rich. Also, there may not be enough fat in recipe.	Next time, add liquids gradually, stopping when dough is still shaggy in places. Press dough into a disk to see if it has enough liquid, and then add more if necessary. Never skimp on fat when making biscuits or scones.
Cake texture is grainy; coarse crumb	Poor texture in a cake is usually attributable to either overmixing or undermixing the batter. The most frequent undermixing error is either not creaming the fat and sugar long enough or adding eggs too rapidly; both create poor structure. Overmixing usually occurs after flour goes in and remaining wet ingredients are added.	Follow recipe instructions: Creamed mixtures should look light and fluffy. And, if all the ingredients are at room temperature, when the eggs are added slowly, batter should not curdle. Add dry and wet ingredients alternately, always beginning with dry. The fat coats the flour first, preventing the liquid from developing too much gluten as it comes in contact with the flour.
Cake or quick bread has tunnels	Either batter was overmixed after wet ingredients were added or flour used was too high in protein. In both cases too much gluten developed, making batter tight and dense. Too much leavening may have also been used. Air bubbles created by mixing or by chemical leavening continue to expand after cake structure starts to firm, resulting in tunnels.	When last ingredients have been added and batter looks relatively homogenous, stop mixing. Be sure you are using cake flour if it's specified and avoid bread flour, with its high protein content. Be especially careful not to develop too much gluten in batters leavened with baking soda, since soda does most of its work in the batter stage before the cake or quick bread even reaches the oven. *continued*

Sides of cake collapse	All-purpose flour was substituted for cake flour or batter contained too much liquid. Cake flour is uniquely processed to hold more liquid, sugar, and fat than other flours, and caved-in sides are a sure sign that the flour can't hold the amount of liquid in the recipe. If proper flour was used, then too much liquid is the problem.	Don't substitute one type of flour for another in cake recipes. Be precise about measuring both flour and liquids.
Pound or bundt cake has thick, dark crust	Oven temperature was too hot and/or cake was overbaked or a dark metal or glass pan was used, both of which conduct heat more readily, which will cause edges to brown and form a thick crust.	Rich pound and bundt cakes take a long time to bake through to center. Next time, try reducing oven temperature by 25°F and, if you don't use a heavyweight or light-colored metal pan, consider dropping the temperature even further.
Quick bread, muffins, or cake is gummy overall or has rubbery layer at bottom	Buttermilk, fruit purée, sour cream, and yogurt can all make cake gummy when used in excess. Also, cake may not have had enough egg or flour. Inadequately drained carrots or zucchini will also make a cake heavy.	Don't improvise when measuring, as too much of something may not be a good thing. If recipe says to drain carrots, don't skip this step. If you repeat recipe and still get a gummy texture, either reduce the fruit or dairy products or add more egg and flour to compensate.
Jellyroll cake will not roll	Eggs were underbeaten or overbeaten and egg foam was deflated when folded into dry ingredients. Flexibility for these cakes comes from a higher egg to flour ratio, since egg proteins remain flexible even after they are cooked. If cake had too much flour from inaccurate measuring, cake will not stretch as easily. Also, if cake is not trained while still warm (see right), it will break when rolled.	If jellyroll is merely cracking, it is possible to cover cracks with frosting. For cakes that break, however, there's no quick fix. Next time, be precise when measuring flour and take care not to deflate egg foam. Also, while cake is still warm, roll it up in a towel and let it cool to set shape.
Layer cake is too fragile to cut or assemble	Cake is still too warm to cut. Delicate layer cakes are heavy in sugar, liquid, and fat and have less flour and eggs than sturdier cakes, like pound cakes. This makes them especially hard to handle.	A quick chill in the refrigerator will solve the problem, since cold cake is firmer and easier to slice and frost. For an easier cake to work with next time, you can add more flour or eggs to recipe, but the moist, delicate crumb will be compromised.
Cheesecake forms cracks on top	It is overcooked.	Next time, remove cheesecake from oven when just barely set. If this problem recurs, try baking cheesecake in a water bath (using waterproof cake pan, of course).

—NICOLE REES, *Fine Cooking* contributor

PIE PITFALLS & TART TRIBULATIONS

THE PROBLEM	POSSIBLE CAUSES	FIX-IT TIPS FOR NOW OR NEXT TIME
Pie dough is still dry even after adding all the cold water specified	Pieces of fat cut into flour were left too large. Dough needed to be kneaded briefly. Flour required more hydration due to type or seasonal variation.	First, try mixing the fat into the dough with your fingertips. If still dry and crumbly, add more cold water, 1 tablespoon at a time. When dough just starts to look like it's coming together, stop and knead briefly to form a cohesive mass. Small pieces of fat should be visible in dough.
Pie dough or short (sweet) dough is too sticky to form into disk	Ingredients, room, or dough is too warm. Also, too much liquid may have been added.	Chill sticky dough for 10 to 20 minutes before trying to form it with well-floured hands. Next time, start with cold butter and shortening. When making pie on hot days, grate frozen butter into the flour or freeze all ingredients briefly. Keep water ice cold in refrigerator until needed.
Chilled pie dough cracks when rolled out	Dough is too cold or wasn't kneaded enough, making edges of dough disk ragged and dry. Also, dough may not have rested enough to allow flour to hydrate evenly.	If there are many cracks and edges seem dry, gather dough into a ball. Chill for 20 minutes and try again: Rolling should be easier now that dough has been mixed more from handling. One or two cracks can be fixed by brushing with water and rolling edges together to seal. Next time, allow dough to warm up slightly if very cold and roll as evenly as possible near edges to prevent cracking.
Pie/sweet dough sticks to counter and tears	Dough or counter is too warm. Insufficient flour was used on rolling surface and pin. Dough was not rotated or flipped while being rolled.	Slide a long spatula under dough to loosen, and then slide dough onto a floured sheet of parchment paper or cutting board. Chill and try again. Next time, start with cold dough. Roll sweet dough between sheets of floured parchment. If necessary, chill with parchment until firmer. Remember to flour while rolling and rotate dough frequently.
Crumb crust is too mealy to press into pan	Crumb mixture doesn't have enough butter and/or sugar.	Drizzle in melted butter just until mixture clumps when squeezed, and then press into pan. Mixture may need more sugar: Sugar melts readily in the oven and helps set crust, so don't skimp on recipe requirements.
Baked piecrust is tough	Dough was kneaded too much after water was added, or dough was not relaxed after rolling.	Next time, stop mixing as soon as dough just begins to come together after water is added. Don't rush the process. Then, after rolling, let dough rest in refrigerator for at least 25 minutes to allow flour to hydrate and gluten structure to relax.
Baked piecrust is crumbly and mealy	Fat and flour were overmixed in dough: Visible pieces of fat should remain. When baked, these pieces will melt, leaving air pockets, making crust flaky. Also, dough may have had too much fat.	Next time, stop cutting in fat when most pieces are pea size. Some pieces may be smaller, but baked crust will resemble crumbly shortbread if fat is too thoroughly mixed in. If still crumbly, reduce amount of fat by 2 or 3 tablespoons for a double crust.

continued |

Blind-baked pie/tart shell is misshapen, puffed on bottom with sides that have caved in	Dough was not allowed to relax before being fitted into pan or was stretched when fitted into pan. Pie weights were not used to stabilize dough during initial baking.	Next time, let dough rest after rolling and before fitting into pan; this relaxes the gluten and prevents shrinking. Gently push dough into corners of pan—do not stretch dough or it will contract during baking. Line cold pie shell with parchment and fill with pie weights (or dried beans or rice) to give crust support until its structure sets.
Edge of blind-baked piecrust falls off during baking	Shaped dough was not chilled to firm before baking. Crimped dough edge extended too far over pan edge. Also, oven may not have been hot enough to set crust quickly.	Next time, freeze crust until firm before baking to set structure and prevent edges from collapsing. A hot oven performs much the same function: Start crust at 425°F, and then reduce temperature by 50°F after 15 minutes if crust is browning too rapidly.
Pie browns poorly	Crust was underbaked or contained bleached flour. Doughs that include an acid such as lemon juice or vinegar to make rolling easier brown less readily.	Next time, use unbleached flour. Add milk or sugar to facilitate browning if you use an acid in the dough.
Bottom crust is soggy and pale	Not enough heat was directed to bottom crust. Or cut fruit and sugar sat for too long before pie was assembled, causing fruit to release its juice before baking. For custard pies, shell was not adequately prebaked.	For crisp crusts, bake pies and tarts in a heated sheet pan situated near bottom of oven. Next time, don't let fruit-sugar mixture sit for more than 15 minutes before baking. Prebake crust for custard pies whenever possible.
Pie/tart is burning at edges before filling is cooked	Heat is not penetrating to center of pie or tart before edges are set. Also, filling may be very cold.	Cover edges of piecrust with foil to prevent burning. Next time, let ice-cold fillings warm a little before pouring into pie or tart shell.
Fruit in filling disintegrates and is mushy	Pie was overbaked, fruit was very ripe, or wrong apple variety was used.	Next time, be prepared to reduce baking time for ripe, juicy fruit. Don't use eating or sauce apples for pies.
Fruit filling is sour	Not enough sugar was used; fruit wasn't ripe.	Always taste fruit before adding sugar and adjust accordingly. If fruit is really unripe, consider adding extra juice and flavorings such as vanilla.
Fruit filling is too stiff even though correct amount of thickener was used	Fruit was not ripe and released little juice during baking.	Underripe fruit may require more sugar, added juice, and a longer baking time to allow it to soften. Always assess ripeness of fruit before you begin.

Fruit pie has cooled to room temperature but juices are thin and runny	Filling contained too much sugar. Fruit was juicier than anticipated, or insufficient thickener was used. Filling wasn't cooked to a high enough temperature to set the starch.	Next time, taste and assess sugar content of fruit. Very ripe fruit will produce runnier (but still delicious) pies that require more starch to set juices. To make checking progress of the filling easier, cut vents in top of pie. Pie is done when filling is bubbling at the center.
Tapioca granules don't dissolve, leaving hard lump behind	Either tapioca in filling was exposed to heat of oven in a lattice or open-top pie or pie was underbaked.	Tapioca needs to be covered to dissolve and thicken effectively—double-crust pies are the best use for this starch. Or purchase it in gel form.
Custard pie, like pumpkin, cracks while cooking	Filling was overbaked or contained more starch than needed to set custard.	Next time, remove pie from oven when custard is just barely set. If it still cracks, reduce starch in recipe by one-quarter.
Cooked custard pudding or curd filling seems thick in baked shell but is thin and runny the next day	Filling was not sufficiently cooked: An enzyme in eggs will slowly break down the starches in the gel if not denatured by cooking.	Completely cook custards going into baked shells: Stir custard often, making sure heat penetrates evenly throughout pan, and cook until it bubbles gently at sides.
Quiche is watery instead of creamy and set	Most likely cause is the vegetables in the filling. Vegetables release water as they cook, which destroys the perfect creaminess of an egg custard. However, if quiche also seems tough, then it is overcooked.	Next time, thoroughly sauté or precook vegetables to be used in quiche, draining them on paper towels if necessary.
Meringue topping pulls away from side of pie during baking	Meringue was not pressed or spread carefully against crust. Meringue shrinks slightly as it bakes and will pull away from an edge if not firmly adhered.	Next time, spread meringue along edge of piecrust first before piling remainder high onto center of pie.
Meringue topping weeps underneath	Meringue failed to cook through because pie wasn't hot when it was applied.	Next time, place meringue directly on hot filling for even heat penetration from all sides.
Meringue topping forms beads on exterior	Meringue is overcooked: The egg proteins are no longer capable of holding liquid and have squeezed out sugar and water.	No quick fix here; just bake meringue more carefully next time. In general, higher heat for a shorter period is better for a meringue topping.

—NICOLE REES, *Fine Cooking* contributor

THE PROBLEM	POSSIBLE CAUSES	FIX-IT TIPS FOR NOW OR NEXT TIME
Cookie dough is sticky and difficult to work with	Dough probably became too warm. In particular, doughs rich in butter and eggs are especially difficult to handle if not kept very, very cold.	A quick chill in the refrigerator or freezer will make most doughs behave—butter solidifies quickly. For ease of handling, roll dough between sheets of parchment, and then chill. You can add more flour as a last resort if chilling doesn't do the trick.
Dough sticks to springerle mold, tears, and won't stay together when turned out of mold	Dough is too warm.	Keep dough as cool as possible, leaving portion you aren't working with in the refrigerator. Use a fine-mesh sieve to dust flour over mold or, even better, dust dough that will be pressed against it.
Slice-and-bake cookies are not perfectly round	Refrigerating a quickly hand-formed log often creates imperfections. Also, pressure of slicing can flatten bottom of log.	Roll log a couple of times throughout chilling process to work out inconsistencies of shape. Rotate log while you are working to prevent an uneven shape. If dough feels uneven and bumpy when you begin, let it soften for a few minutes and then roll it against counter until it evens out. Refrigerate once more, and then begin slicing and baking.
Cookies are unappealingly white and pallid	Recipes that contain mostly white ingredients (bleached flour, cake flour, shortening, granulated and confectioner's sugar) will make lighter cookies. Cookies containing baking powder will brown less than those made with baking soda, so be sure not to confuse the two. Also, your oven may not be hot enough.	Try increasing the oven temperature by 25°F to see if you get better results. Using unbleached flour in your next batch will darken your cookies a shade; substituting a little butter, margarine, or butter-flavored shortening for some of the white shortening will impart a golden hue. (But watch the spread! See next tip.)
Rolled cutouts spread, blurring shape	Dough was too warm going into oven—edges of cold dough will firm and set in oven before center of dough warms, which inhibits spread and creates defined edges on cutouts. Cookies rich in butter, molasses, honey, and a lot of leavening may not be suitable for detailed cutouts, so beware when adapting recipe to a new use.	A quick chill before baking is an easy fix: Just pop cookie sheet, with cutout dough and all, into refrigerator or freezer if you have room. If this doesn't solve the problem, knead a small amount of flour into dough. Flour is a guaranteed fix, but use it as a last resort, since finished texture and flavor will change.

Cookies brown too much but are not overbaked	An overly hot oven can make cookies brown before they are baked through, but browning is often an ingredient issue as well. Molasses, honey, corn syrup, dark brown sugar, milk products, and baking powder all encourage browning. Substituting dark brown sugar for light can dramatically change the color of your cookie.	For a quick fix, try reducing oven temperature by 25°F. If you don't see better results, next time substitute some lighter ingredients, like bleached flour or granulated sugar, or reduce amount of liquid sugars (molasses, honey, corn syrup) in recipe.
Cookies are pale on top and burnt on bottom	An oven that runs too hot; use of dark, heavy baking sheets; placement of baking sheets on bottom rack of oven; or any combination of these three things will cause cookies to burn only on the bottom.	If you don't bake often, get an oven thermometer. It will save you lots of guesswork. Choose lighter baking sheets for your cookie baking or a doubled pan (stack an extra pan underneath) to better insulate the dough. If oven has hot spots, always rotate pans from top to bottom rack (and back to front) midway through baking for even color and texture.
Cookies don't spread enough	Recipes high in shortening and flour but lean on sugar are more resistant to spread in the oven. A change in flour type or brand can cause this—both cake and bread flours absorb more liquid than other flours. A too-cool oven is another possible culprit. Leaving out or using expired leavening makes for leaden cookies, as does adding too many nuts or chips.	Before you start next time, scrutinize your flour and leavening, making sure you have the appropriate fresh ingredients on hand. Try holding back 2 tablespoons to ¼ cup of flour at end of mixing. Before adding last of flour, bake a test cookie to check texture. This will also help you decide whether to increase heat a little. Adding extra chips is fine, but don't double the amount.
Gingerbread ornaments/ house cutouts too soft and cakey	Many gingerbread cookie recipes have generous amounts of molasses, which keeps baked cookies soft and contributes to a cakey texture. They are delicious to eat but tend to be too delicate to handle if not thoroughly baked.	For firmer cookies that will stand up to being frosted, hung, or assembled into a house, return cookies to oven and bake until well done to compensate for softening effect of the molasses. Next time add more flour to accomplish the same thing, or reduce amount of molasses slightly.
Chocolate chip cookies spread too much	Recipes based on the Toll House® recipe are rich in butter, sugar, and eggs, all of which contribute to spread. Even just a brand change in flour can alter spread. A too-hot oven or too-warm dough is a secondary cause. If a recipe calls for lots of chips and nuts, but you leave out the nuts, your cookies will be flatter and wider.	Chilling the dough before baking might fix the cookies. If not, stir a small amount of flour into dough. Flour is a guaranteed fix but also a last resort, since texture and flavor will change. Adjust oven temperature, if necessary, and be sure you've added amount of chips and nuts specified.
Chocolate chip cookies are too crisp and thin	Recipes generous in butter and sugar create crisper cookies. Was leavening left out or flour mismeasured? Did you use smaller eggs than specified?	First, try chilling dough to firm up butter and slow down spread. If this doesn't do the trick, beat in half an egg (or a whole one if recipe contains no egg and calls for at least 2 cups flour) and 2 tablespoons flour. Bake a test cookie before adding more flour.

continued

Chocolate chip cookies are too cakey and/or dry	The most common cause is using a different flour than usual, such as cake flour, and measuring flour with too heavy a hand. Using larger eggs than called for can make cookies cakey, as will the addition of milk or more milk or other liquids than specified.	Next time, try holding back 2 tablespoons to ¼ cup of flour at the end of mixing. Before adding last of flour, bake a test cookie to check texture. Make sure eggs are the right size and omit the milk if you prefer denser cookies.
Oatmeal cookies are crumbly and dry	Classic oatmeal cookies have a lot of oats, which can be drying to the finished cookie and make them more susceptible to overbaking. Mismeasuring flour can also tip the balance from crisp-chewy to dry. Using all granulated sugar for the brown sugar will create a drier cookie, too, since the molasses in brown sugar provides moisture.	Try removing cookies from oven before centers are set—you'll be surprised at how much the cookies will firm as they cool. Next time, hold back ¼ cup of flour and/or ½ cup of oats and bake a test cookie; add more if necessary. Most oatmeal cookies call for some brown sugar—be sure to add the right amount and type.
Peanut butter cookies are too crumbly	Flour is likely at issue here, but changing brands of peanut butter will also affect texture.	Next time, try holding back 2 tablespoons to ¼ cup of flour at the end of mixing. Before adding last of flour, bake a test cookie to check texture. Be sure to use type of peanut butter called for, since added sugar and salt will affect texture and flavor of your cookies.
Biscotti are hard and tough instead of crisp	Biscotti that are cut while too soft will compress and have a tougher bite. Adding too much flour for ease of handling can also toughen these cookies. Using the wrong, too little, or expired leavening will have the same effect.	For a quick fix, try drying out your sliced baked cookies further in a 300°F oven—this will minimize toughness. Next time, cool baked cookie log longer before slicing to prevent compressing, and use a sharp, serrated knife. Avoid kneading in more flour when shaping cookies, and do not use leavening more than a year old.
Drop sugar cookies or gingersnaps do not have cracked tops	Baking powder and soda give these cookies their characteristic cracks, so stale leavening is probably at fault. Also, the right amount of flour is necessary to allow dough to expand, crack, and set at just the right time—too much flour will prevent this from happening. Check oven temperature, too, since a hotter oven is sometimes better for these cookies.	Next time, make sure you have fresh leavening on hand—baking soda is not usually tightly sealed and loses its power faster than baking powder from exposure to warm, humid air. Hold back 2 tablespoons of flour and bake a test cookie before deciding to add it to dough. This will also let you know if you need to boost heat in oven.

Shortbread tastes pasty instead of buttery	It may be underbaked, or oven temperature may be too low. Another possibility is that you added too much cornstarch or confectioners' sugar.	Return underbaked shortbread to a 350°F oven until it begins to turn golden. Flour and starch need to be cooked thoroughly to lose their cereal flavor and let the toasty flavor of the butter shine.
Shortbread crumbles when cut	The shortbread is no longer warm. Shortbread is prized for its sandy, crumbly texture, but this makes it difficult to cut when cool.	Use a serrated knife to gently saw shortbread into pieces. Next time, score shortbread before baking or when it first comes out of the oven, and cut through while it is still warm.
Blondies or brownies are dry and hard	Assuming all ingredients that create chewiness (butter, eggs, and sugar) were measured correctly, overbaking is the danger with bar cookies. Too much flour or changing types of flour can make them dry as well.	Next time, start checking for doneness 10 minutes before you expect them to be done. For chewy bar cookies, a skewer inserted two-thirds of the way to the center should come out clean, but center should be barely set. Be precise with flour measuring.
Brownies are too cakey	Some recipes are more cakey than fudgy, but if your brownies seem both cakey and a little dry, then they are also overbaked. Cakey brownies tend to have more flour than other types, and any mistakes in measuring flour will be evident as dryness. Cakey brownies often contain leavening, which provides a lighter texture. Using larger eggs than specified can create a dry, spongy texture in combination with too much flour.	Next time, start checking for doneness 10 minutes before you expect them to be done. For chewy bar cookies, a skewer inserted two-thirds of the way to the center should come out clean, but center should be barely set. Be precise with flour measuring. If your recipe contains leavening and you prefer fudgy brownies, try omitting it. Also try reducing flour by 2 tablespoons to ¼ cup for a moister, fudgier brownie. Be sure to use the right size eggs.
Baked hard meringue cookies or dessert shells are chewy and slightly soft	Either meringues were undercooked and remaining moisture caused them to lose their crunch or meringues picked up moisture from air due to improper storage. Rainy weather could also be at fault, since humidity quickly softens even the most perfectly crisp meringues.	Spread meringues on a parchment-lined baking sheet and bake in a 225°F oven until dry and crisp, at least 20 minutes. On rainy days, let meringues cool in oven after heat is turned off—you can even let them sit overnight. Place in airtight containers when completely cool.

—NICOLE REES, *Fine Cooking* contributor

BAD BREAD BLUES

THE PROBLEM	POSSIBLE CAUSES	FIX-IT TIPS FOR NOW OR NEXT TIME
Dough will not come together in mixer and appears soupy or shaggy	Salt was omitted. Salt tightens the structure of dough, and without it dough with a large amount of water may not come together. Also, dough may require more mixing (kneading)—when dough looks shaggy, this is usually the problem. If too much liquid or not enough flour was added, dough may look soupy and will need more flour.	Taste dough to see if salt was omitted—if so, add now and continue kneading. A dough high in water may form a ball when mixer is running, then slump when mixer is stopped. That's OK—if it is shiny, glossy, and elastic, it's done. Otherwise, keep kneading or mixing, adding more flour after a minute or two if necessary. Let dough rest for 10 minutes and try kneading again. Next time, if recipe gives weights for ingredients, use scale for best results.
Dough looks good, then loses cohesiveness	This problem usually occurs only when making bread in a stand mixer. Dough is kneaded for too long at too high a speed and overheats, and the nice gluten structure that was developed breaks down.	Overmixed or overheated dough looks rough, loses elasticity, and can rarely be salvaged. Next time, check dough frequently during mixing for a good gluten window. When dough can be stretched to form a transparent thin sheet, stop kneading. In general, knead on medium speed rather than high unless recipe specifies otherwise.
Dough will not form gluten window	A gluten window, the thin sheet of transparent dough formed by stretching a small portion of dough between the fingers, is a sure sign that the dough has been mixed enough. Not all doughs will make one, though, including rye and whole-grain breads. For other doughs, however, lack of a gluten window usually indicates dough has not been kneaded long enough or that flour may have poor protein quality.	First, try increasing speed of mixer for 1 minute. Check to see if dough feels stretchier and more elastic; if so, knead for another minute or two to finish up. Just watch carefully to make sure you don't overmix. If you don't see any sign of improvement, add small amounts of flour while continuing to mix, checking for a gluten window frequently. Next time, make sure to use bread flour or a high-protein flour.
Dough is taking too long to rise or doesn't rise very much	If dough is still rising, albeit slowly, the water and/or room temperature were on the cool side. If dough isn't moving or stopped rising before it doubled in size, yeast was insufficient or starter wasn't active enough. Also, yeast may have been killed if very hot water was used in dough.	Move dough to a warm, humid location, such as near stove's pilot light or on a baking sheet placed over a bowl of warm water. Be patient with breads using sponges or starters: They rise over a longer time period at a lower temperature than breads using commercial yeast. Next time, use water between 110° and 120°F, but do not exceed 140°F, which will kill yeast.

Dough overflows baking pan either during second rise or during baking	The most common cause is that too much dough was placed in pan. Another possibility is that time simply got away from you or the day was very warm and the loaf rose too long and expanded beyond its ability to either hold its shape or stay in pan. Finally, perhaps too much yeast was added—conversions between different types of yeast can be tricky.	Divide dough in half, reshape for two smaller pans, and let it rise again. Be aware that texture and flavor may be compromised. Next time, fill pan only half full to ensure maximum rise and stability. Keep a close eye on bread during second rise; it should increase from 1½ to 2 times in size and hold a dent when pressed lightly with a finger, but have enough spring to bounce back slightly without collapsing or tearing. Also, double-check any yeast conversions for accuracy: 2 teaspoons fresh (cake) yeast = 1 teaspoon active dry yeast = ¾ teaspoon instant yeast.
Dough is too springy to shape	Springy or "bucky" dough has not been allowed to rest long enough after kneading. Not only is it difficult to form, but it may also contract dramatically—a real problem for something like a pizza.	If dough is very resistant to being shaped, shape roughly, cover, and walk away for 5 to 10 minutes before finishing. The dough will be much easier to handle upon your return.
Dough is too slack to shape or shaped loaf loses form during rise or baking	Slackness is when dough just won't do what you want it to. There are several possible culprits. Dough may contain too much liquid. It may not have been kneaded sufficiently. It may have risen too long or loaves may require a pan or support (rising basket or linen couche) while rising and/or baking.	For now, gently knead in enough flour so dough stiffens up a bit, reshape loaf, and transfer to an appropriate pan for the second rise. After dividing, form into roughly the desired shape and let rest for 10 minutes. Finally, next time, try reducing amount of liquid added to dough and/or temperature of first rise.
Shaped or baked loaf lacks volume and crumb is dense	These related problems can be caused by either too much (or the wrong type of) flour or not enough water. The amount of water is very important—only a fully hydrated dough will expand easily and have a crumb structure that is relatively open. Another suspect may be a lack of yeast or starter. Finally, only a hot oven will allow bread to expand, or "spring," to its maximum volume.	Next time, increase water by at least ½ cup and try using a higher-protein flour if available. Increase yeast or starter amount slightly if first loaf was dense but didn't taste yeasty. Increase oven temperature 25° to 50°F for first 10 minutes of baking time to achieve maximum oven spring, then reduce temperature and bake through.
Shaped loaf falls during final rise, or loaf caves in while baking or right after it comes out of oven	Nothing is more disappointing than a collapsed loaf of bread. Loaf may have gone too long during second rise, or too much yeast may have been used.	Sorry, not even the shaped loaf is salvageable. Next time, adjust proofing environment as needed: Either let loaf rise at a lower temperature or over a shorter period of time. Check loaf more frequently during final rise. It should increase from 1½ to 2 times in size and hold a dent when pressed lightly with a finger but have enough spring to bounce back slightly. *continued*

Free-form artisan loaf explodes or is otherwise unsightly	Loaves that are not slashed on top may explode out the side, top, or bottom. Loaves slashed too roughly or too tentatively may sprawl or close back up in the oven. If no steam was created in the first stage of baking, the bread developed a crust before it expanded fully, forcing the loaf to burst.	Next time, use a razor blade or serrated knife to slice tops of free-form loaves just before baking: A swift, decisive motion is best, rather than a slow, hesitant dragging motion. Use a spray bottle to create steam in oven during first 10 minutes of baking.
Baked loaf is done but crust is still pale	Bread was baked for too long at too low a temperature. Caramelization and Maillard reactions, which contribute to bread's flavor and color, require relatively high heat.	Next time, increase oven temperature 50°F for first 10 minutes of baking time. Bread will bake through in less time, so monitor closely.
Baked loaf's crust is too dark	Oven temperature was too high, or perhaps amount of sugar in bread was excessive for that baking temperature.	Next time, reduce oven temperature and bake longer. If it still browns too much and contains a fair amount of sugar, try reducing amount (including honey or molasses) by one-quarter.
Baked artisan loaf's crust is too soft	Adequate heat and steam are needed for a crisp yet chewy artisan crust. Using steam during first 5 to 10 minutes of baking not only helps bread expand without breaking but also develops the crust: During baking minerals are precipitated out of the bread as steam. As they condense and settle back on the crust, they increase crispness and flavor.	Use a baking stone for a crisp crust, or bake near bottom of oven. Be sure to heat stone with oven and start bread at a high temperature (425° to 500°F) for first 10 minutes. Use a spray bottle filled with water to create steam in oven during initial 5 to 10 minutes of baking time.
Crust is too thick	Loaves were not covered while rising, or bread was baked too hot or for too long.	Next time, cover loaves with flour-dusted cloth or sheet of oiled plastic wrap to prevent drying. Reduce oven temperature by at least 25°F and use thumping test to see if bread is baked through (it will sound hollow when tapped on bottom).
Bread tastes bland	Dough was allowed to rise too quickly at too high a temperature, or it contains insufficient salt.	Next time, refrigerate shaped loaves overnight—this allows lactic acids to develop in dough, which contribute greatly to flavor—or increase salt by at least ½ teaspoon per loaf.
Bread stales quickly	Dough was allowed to rise too quickly at too high a temperature, or bread was baked for too long. Also, if baked loaf is stored improperly, it will deteriorate rapidly.	Next time, increase amount of water (up to ½ cup) and rise cooler over long period of time. Reduce baking time. Cool baked loaves on a rack. Store in a paper bag, placed inside a loosely closed plastic bag, to best maintain freshness.
Baked sweet bread (stollen, cinnamon rolls) texture is dense, gummy, or doughy and has poor volume	Most likely it is underbaked, or dough was not given enough time to rise. Doughs rich in fat and sugar take longer to rise and may require more yeast to get the job done. Also, dough may contain too much sour cream, buttermilk, yogurt, or fruit purée.	Be sure to give sweet dough plenty of time to rise, and increase amount of yeast by 25% to make sure dough at least increases to 1½ times if not double its original size. Make sure rolls or bread are baked through. Use an even hand when measuring rich dairy products—too much is not a good thing.

| Sweet dough crust is too brown, but sides and bottom are still pale | Amount of sugar or milk in dough was too great for baking temperature and/or length of bake. | Next time, either reduce amount of milk and/or sugar or drop oven temperature by 25°F. If top browning is still an issue, try making two smaller loaves, which will bake through in a shorter time. |
| Pizza or focaccia crust is not crisp | Oven temperature was too low or toppings were too high in moisture. | Heat a baking sheet or baking stone at 450°F and reheat pizza for 5 to 10 minutes to crisp up bottom. Next time, bake at 425° or 450°F. If you don't have a baking stone, bake flatbread nearly through, slide off pan onto bottom oven rack, and finish baking there for last 5 to 10 minutes. Prebake pizza crusts halfway before adding toppings to prevent sogginess, especially if adding vegetables. |

—NICOLE REES, *Fine Cooking* contributor

CANDY CALAMITIES

THE PROBLEM	POSSIBLE CAUSES	FIX-IT TIPS FOR NOW OR NEXT TIME
Candied citrus peel is bitter	Undercooking is the likely culprit, since raw citrus peels are bitter. If you removed peel with its white pith still attached, that can also result in bitterness.	If you have not yet dusted cooled peel in sugar, you can boil it in one or two changes of water until it is tender and no longer bitter. If pith is the culprit, there's nothing you can do.
Candy (any type) has lumps	These are sugar crystals that have resisted melting due to uneven or rushed heating in beginning of candymaking process. The melted sugar may have also crystallized accidentally from too much stirring, the introduction of crystals from side of pan, or contact with a spoon carrying sugar crystals.	Cooled candy cannot be saved. However, if lumps are detected in pot, just add a little water to encourage the lumps to melt. Cooking time will be extended since the extra water will have to boil off. Wash down any crystals that form on side of pan with a wet pastry brush, or cover pot briefly to allow steam to do the job. Avoid stirring after sugar is melted and smooth.
Candy (any type) does not set up properly and/or is sticky	Warm, humid, and rainy days wreak havoc on candymaking. Under heat, sugar or sucrose breaks down into glucose and fructose. Fructose is hygroscopic, attracting moisture from humid air and potentially making candy sticky.	If you are determined to make candy on a rainy day, cook candy a little more than directed, at least 5°F more. Keep windows closed and cool candy in driest place in house. Store in airtight containers as soon as completely cooled.

continued

Fudge or fondant is grainy	Sugar may not have been thoroughly melted initially. Fudge may have been disturbed before it was cool enough to beat, or it may not have been beaten long enough.	Generally, grainy candy is difficult to save. The determined cook can start over, returning it to the pot and heating slowly back to the soft ball stage. If the candy contains milk, however, it may curdle or break if this is done. Next time, wash down crystals that form on side of pan with a wet pastry brush or cover pot briefly to let steam do the job. Avoid stirring after sugar is melted and smooth.
Fudge becomes overly stiff when beaten	Fudge may have cooled too much during beating.	Stir in warm cream or half-and-half a few drops at a time until desired consistency is reached.
Fudge does not set up	Fudge was beaten before it had cooled sufficiently or was not adequately beaten.	Next time, cool fudge to 120°F before beating, and then beat vigorously until it is no longer glossy.
Divinity is too soft to hold shape when dropped from a spoon	Divinity was not cooked enough.	Place soft divinity in a bowl set over simmering water. Cook, beating constantly, until it holds its shape when dropped from a spoon.
Divinity is too stiff	Sugar syrup poured into beaten eggs was cooked past appropriate stage, or not enough syrup was added.	Add drops of hot water to the divinity, beating constantly, until it softens.
Caramel is too grainy	Sugar may not have been thoroughly melted initially. Melted sugar may also have crystallized accidentally from too much stirring, the introduction of crystals from side of pan, or contact with a spoon carrying crystals.	See advice above for fudge or fondant that is grainy.
Taffy is too stiff to pull and shape	Taffy was cooked to too high a temperature or has cooled too much to work with easily.	Butter your hands and work surface to prevent sticking. Try gently warming taffy under a hot lamp or in microwave at 10-second intervals on low power to soften. If it still won't budge, it is unsalvageable.
Peanut brittle is too thick	Peanuts added to candy were cold, causing the brittle to set up too quickly.	Next time, warm peanuts in oven for a few minutes before stirring into candy. Buttering the sheet will also facilitate spreading the brittle as thinly as possible.

Toffee is grainy and doesn't set up	Sugar may not have been thoroughly melted initially. Melted sugar may also have crystallized accidentally from too much stirring, the introduction of crystals from side of pan, or contact with a spoon carrying crystals.	Break candy into small bits and reheat slowly to temperature specified in recipe—even 5° to 10°F higher in humid conditions. Although this may actually take longer than making a new batch of candy, you will have at least not wasted your ingredients. Next time, wash down crystals that form on side of pan with a wet pastry brush, or cover pot briefly to let steam do the job. Avoid stirring after sugar is melted and smooth.
Toffee or peanut brittle is sticky when cooled, bends before it breaks, and sticks unpleasantly to teeth	Toffee or brittle was not cooked to proper temperature. Also, rain and humidity are the enemy of candies that start off crisp and crunchy, causing them to absorb moisture from the air and soften.	Break candy into small bits and reheat slowly to temperature specified in recipe—even 5° to 10°F higher in humid conditions. Although this may actually take longer than making a new batch of candy, you will have at least not wasted your ingredients.
Caramel sauce is too thick to pour when cold	Sauce needs more liquid.	Warm sauce over low heat. Slowly stir in heavy cream until desired consistency is reached.
Caramel sauce is too thin	Sauce contains too much liquid.	Place sauce over medium heat and reduce slowly to desired consistency. Caution: If sauce contains milk, not heavy cream, it may break if held at a high heat for too long.
Caramel sauce lacks flavor and is too sweet	The caramel was not allowed to darken sufficiently. Sugars break down during caramelization process, making candy more flavorful as it darkens and less sweet.	Next time, cook caramel until deep amber in color, rather than golden. The darker color is essential for a deepness of flavor that will stand up to the addition of cream and butter.

—NICOLE REES, *Fine Cooking* **contributor**

CHOCOLATE CONUNDRUMS

THE PROBLEM	POSSIBLE CAUSES	FIX-IT TIPS FOR NOW OR NEXT TIME
Chocolate forms hard, grainy lumps during melting process	If chocolate is improperly melted (over too high a heat or left in microwave for too long on high power), it may burn, forming small, hard lumps that float in the melted chocolate.	Taste smooth portion of chocolate. If it doesn't taste burnt, strain chocolate to remove lumps and proceed with recipe. Next time, be sure to finely chop chocolate for more even melting, monitor your heat level, and stir often, whether you use the microwave or stovetop.
Chocolate seizes suddenly, forming a single, grainy mass	If even a small amount of water gets into melting chocolate, it will seize. Steam created from melting chocolate over hot water could be the source.	If you needed pure chocolate for a recipe, you will have to start over, but the seized chocolate can be saved for another use. Ironically, though a little liquid will make chocolate seize, larger amounts of liquid are fine: Melt cream or another liquid into seized chocolate to create a delicious dessert sauce.
Chocolate ganache breaks or appears curdled	Though chocolate ganache can break (the cocoa butter separates out) if it is agitated or stirred too vigorously, the problem most likely lies with the ratio of chocolate to cream. Intense chocolates, such as bittersweet with its high percentage of cocoa solids, require more cream or a touch of sugar before they smooth out.	To bring ganache back into a stable emulsion, pour 1 to 3 teaspoons warm heavy cream on top of it, right in the saucepan. With a whisk, stir cream into uppermost layer of ganache. Start with very small circles, and then move outward and deeper once cream has formed a smooth ganache in the center.
Whipped chocolate ganache becomes hard and grainy	Overbeaten ganache will harden and seize easily. Often the ganache seems pliable at first but within a few minutes will become stiff and unworkable.	Melt a portion of hardened ganache and stir it into remaining seized ganache until smooth, adding a little warm heavy cream if necessary. Let ganache rest in refrigerator or a cool room for at least 6 hours. Whip briefly with an electric mixer until fluffy. For perfect whipped ganache, stop beating once it forms soft peaks; it will continue to firm up as it sits.
Chocolate mousse mixture seizes when melted chocolate is folded in	Seizing can occur when warm chocolate comes into contact with cold ingredients, like cold whipped cream.	Next time, try stirring melted chocolate into a small portion of the mousse and then folding in remaining mousse. Or melt chocolate with an equal amount of cream from the recipe. Let this cool, and then incorporate it into the mousse.

Unable to form sizeable chocolate curls using vegetable peeler	Using a peeler to shave delicate chocolate curls is hard work if the bar of chocolate is too cool—good chocolate that is well tempered may seem brittle at temperatures under 70°F.	To make chocolate more pliable, set bar under a warm lamp or heat it gently in microwave (5- to 10-second bursts). Just soften it enough to glide a peeler across it with minimal pressure.
Chocolate on chocolate-dipped fruit won't set up or softens if not kept cold	Chocolate was not tempered if it won't set up. If fruit was cold to begin with, or dipped fruit was placed in fridge to force it to harden, the coating will soften as soon as it is removed from refrigerator.	For best results, temper chocolate to ensure it will crystallize properly. If you don't have time for tempering, add 1 tablespoon vegetable shortening to the melted chocolate to stabilize it. Use clean, dry—not cold—fruit pieces.
Cocoa butter separates from chocolate during tempering	Chocolate was heated too harshly: Beyond 130°F, cocoa butter will separate from the chocolate liquor.	You'll have to start over. Next time, check temperature of melting chocolate with a chocolate or instant-read thermometer (don't use a candy thermometer—it's meant for measuring a higher range of temperatures).
Tempered chocolate is streaky instead of shiny, or tempered chocolate did not set up	There are four major crystal formations in chocolate, and the goal of tempering is to allow only one of those forms to dominate the chocolate's structure—otherwise the chocolate won't be shiny and hard when it cools. If the thermometer is not precisely accurate or if the room is unusually hot or cold, chocolate may not set properly.	Tempering requires patience and precision. Chocolate must be melted to near 120°F (but not over) and then cooled to 80°F. Milk and white chocolate must be heated back up to 85° to 87°F and bittersweet chocolate to 87° to 90°F. For nearly foolproof tempering, if the chocolate you begin with is in temper (shiny, with a nice snap when it breaks), save a portion and stir it into the melted chocolate. This acts as the seed, encouraging formation of the right crystals. Work in a draft-free environment that is moderate in temperature.

—NICOLE REES, *Fine Cooking* contributor

SAUCY SITUATIONS

THE PROBLEM	POSSIBLE CAUSES	FIX-IT TIPS FOR NOW OR NEXT TIME
Cream will not form peaks after whipping	Cream cannot be beaten into a stable foam unless it's cold. If room is hot, it will be more difficult to whip cream. Cream that is cold but will not hold air may not have a high enough fat content.	Place mixing bowl, cream, and beaters in refrigerator and try beating again in 15 minutes. Next time, chill bowl and beaters or whisk ahead of time. Be sure label says heavy cream for reliable results—it should have a fat content of at least 36%.

continued

Whipped cream is grainy	Whipped cream beaten beyond the stiff peak stage quickly becomes overmixed and grainy. If beaten even further, small hard lumps of butter will begin to form.	If cream is merely grainy, pour in more heavy cream (at least one-quarter of the total amount) and beat only until soft, smooth peaks form. Once hard lumps of butter have formed, the cream cannot be saved.
Crème anglaise has small lumps	See "Egg-ravations," p. 250.	
Sauce or gravy is too thin	If it is a cornstarch-thickened sauce, it may have been boiled for too long, causing the starch to lose its thickening capacity. A roux made with flour will weaken as it browns in the pan, reducing its ability to gel.	For every cup of sauce, mix 1 teaspoon cornstarch with 1 to 2 tablespoons water and quickly stir into warm sauce. Bring to a boil to cook the starch, and then let it simmer for 30 to 60 seconds to eliminate flavor of uncooked starch. For the same amount of flour-thickened sauce, knead 1 teaspoon butter into 2 teaspoons flour and follow same procedure, letting it simmer for at least a minute or two after it reaches a boil.
Sauce tastes pasty	The starch, probably cornstarch or flour, has not been cooked adequately.	Simmer sauce for a few minutes longer to cook off raw taste of starch. Cook cornstarch sauces gently, reducing heat once they reach a boil. Flour-thickened sauces need to cook for a few minutes longer.
Pan gravy is lumpy	When cold liquid was added to a roux, the flour didn't dissolve properly. Inadequate whisking also lets lumps form.	If sauce is thick enough to use, strain it to remove lumps. For a too-thin yet lumpy sauce, thicken as directed for a sauce that is too thin (above), and then strain.
Pan gravy is bitter	Browned bits of flavor on bottom of pan were burnt.	Once you've made the gravy, there's nothing you can do. Next time, taste the browned bits before making the gravy. If most taste burned, scrape up some of the pleasant-tasting bits to add to a gravy made in a clean saucepan.
White pan gravy has a skin on it	Any sauce made with milk or other dairy products will form a skin—the result of the protein casein separating from the sauce.	If sauce is in the pan, first try gently reheating it to melt the skin. Transfer gravy to a serving container and place plastic wrap directly against surface of sauce to prevent a skin from forming.
Pan sauce of reduced wine has separated	Sauce doesn't have enough water—too much may have evaporated while sauce was kept warm.	Stir in a little warm water and see if sauce comes together. Adding cream, which is a stable emulsion already, may also do the trick.
Pan sauce of reduced wine is bitter	Either the flavorful bits on bottom of pan were burnt or wine was not good.	Sorry, but with charred flavor and bad wine, you'll have to start over. If sauce is pungent from too much wine but the wine is good, whisk in reduced stock or butter to mellow out the flavor.

Cheese sauce or fondue is stringy, grainy, or oily	High heat will cause a cheese sauce to break. Stringy sauces, in which the cheese refuses to smooth out, don't have enough flour or lemon juice, or the liquid in your recipe may have evaporated. Also, the cheese may have curdled from high heat or too much stirring.	Over medium-low heat, stir in a little lemon juice and/or flour to reduce stringiness. If sauce is simply too thick and gloppy, add more liquid, whether it be wine, milk, or cream. If sauce won't smooth out, you're out of luck and will have to start over. Next time, reduce the heat before gently stirring in the cheese.
Mayonnaise looks separated	The emulsion has broken. You may have added too much oil or added it too quickly. Another culprit is the oil itself: Unrefined oils are more resistant to emulsifying than refined ones.	If mayonnaise was made with unrefined oil, discard and begin again. If not, you can try to re-emulsify it. In a blender or food processor, process sauce to see if high-speed agitation will bring it back. If that doesn't work or you don't have the machinery, try this: Start with a whole new egg or an egg yolk mixed with 1 tablespoon water or lemon juice, and slowly whisk the broken mayonnaise into it.
Beurre blanc, béarnaise, or hollandaise sauce has oil accumulating around edge of pan	Sauce is about to break. Separation occurs when cooking temperature is too high.	Get the sauce off the heat immediately, and whisk gently until it cools a bit and comes back together.
Beurre blanc sauce congeals into a grainy mass while cooling in pan	If left for too long, sauce can form a crystal structure, making it grainy.	You'll have to re-emulsify the sauce: Start with 1 or 2 tablespoons warm cream and slowly whisk sauce into it over low heat.
Beurre blanc sauce looks broken	Heat was too high. Once beurre blanc passes 130°F, it will break.	Remove pan from heat. As sauce cools, whisk in a little heavy cream until sauce comes back together.
Béarnaise or hollandaise sauce is broken	After oil begins to accumulate around sides of pan, the emulsion will break if heat remains too high. Besides high heat, adding too much butter or adding the butter too quickly can cause curdling.	Remove sauce from heat. Stir in a little water, lemon juice, vinegar, or cream until sauce comes back together. Reheat very gently over low heat if necessary.
Hollandaise sauce is lumpy and thick	Heat was too high and sauce cooked too fast, causing egg proteins to scramble.	If sauce is otherwise thick and smooth, you can strain out the lumps, but a scrambled sauce cannot be saved.

—NICOLE REES, *Fine Cooking* contributor

EGG-RAVATIONS

THE PROBLEM	POSSIBLE CAUSES	FIX-IT TIPS FOR NOW OR NEXT TIME
Beaten egg whites are grainy and won't fold into batter	Egg whites are overbeaten, causing proteins to contract and squeeze out water.	Sorry, but once egg whites are overbeaten, they cannot expand and hold air any longer—dump them in the garbage and start again. Next time, beat whites just until they are shiny; overwhipped whites become visibly dull and grainy.
Egg whites won't form stiff peaks	If you can't get whites to form a stable foam, then there is fat present in the bowl or on the beaters, usually in the form of a small bit of yolk that broke into the white.	Start over with a squeaky clean bowl and yolk-free egg whites.
Beaten meringue is grainy	Sugar particles have not dissolved if meringue is grainy, which means that egg whites were too cold or that meringue was not beaten slowly enough to allow sugar granules to dissolve.	Set grainy meringue over—not in—another bowl filled with hot water; whisk vigorously until meringue feels smooth between your fingers. Set bowl on counter and beat for 30 to 60 seconds at high speed for maximum volume. Next time, add sugar to soft peak stage egg whites 1 tablespoon at a time so that sugar dissolves without deflating the egg foam.
Pie meringue weeps or forms beads	See "Pie Pitfalls & Tart Tribulations," p. 233.	
Cooked eggs are discolored	Eggs cooked in reactive metal pans will discolor; cast iron can impart a reddish tinge and aluminum (not anodized) will turn eggs gray.	Sorry, but there's nothing to do except use a stainless-steel, anodized aluminum, or other nonreactive pan the next time.
Hard-cooked egg cracks in water	Cold eggs placed in rapidly boiling water are prone to cracking; the pressure of the hot water causes existing fissures to expand.	Next time, start eggs in cool water. Bring water and eggs to a boil together for a more gentle cooking method.
Hard-cooked egg has green layer around yolk	Egg is overcooked. When an egg is heated for a prolonged period, a chemical reaction takes place between the yolk and white, causing green iron oxide to form.	Next time, watch the clock closely. Don't boil eggs longer than 20 minutes and be sure to cool them promptly by rinsing in cold water.
Scrambled eggs are watery and tough instead of creamy and fluffy	Eggs were overcooked, causing protein network to become tighter and squeeze out moisture.	Next time, cook eggs slowly over gently heat, stirring often but not too vigorously. Turn off heat when eggs are just barely set—the hot pan will finish cooking them through.

Omelet sticks to pan	Eggs stick to the pan if they are cooked at too high a temperature. Omelets require the right amount of fat to grease pan, the correct cooking temperature, and an effective swirling motion to distribute eggs evenly.	If one portion of omelet is stuck to pan, simply flip the other half onto the stuck portion and pry omelet loose with a spatula. Serve it torn side down to hide the damage. If omelet is stuck completely, stir eggs and pretend the intent was scrambled eggs. Garnish with chopped herbs or scallions or grated cheese to further the pretense.
Omelet is overcooked on outside but under-cooked on inside	Omelet contains too many eggs or too much filling. Another possibility is that eggs may not have been adequately swirled in pan and set before filling was added.	Next time, consider the pan to egg ratio before you begin, which is traditionally 2 eggs for an 8-inch pan. An omelet of this size will be easy to swirl and will cook quickly and evenly, preventing a tough exterior and runny interior.
Poached eggs are misshapen and uneven	Older eggs have runny whites and delicate yolks that break easily, making them a poor choice for poaching. Rapidly boiling water can also cause an egg to set in an irregular shape.	Next time, start with the freshest eggs possible. Use gently simmering water with a little added vinegar and salt, which will help set eggs even faster.
Crème anglaise has lumps	Eggs may not have been tempered before being added to hot cream mixture, or sauce was cooked over high heat or at too high a temperature.	If eggs are scrambled, sauce is not thick enough to use, so you'll need to start over. Next time, whisk about one-third of hot cream mixture into eggs before returning it to the pot to finish cooking. Cook over medium heat. Crème anglaise is set well below boiling: It is done when a path drawn across a sauce-coated spoon remains clear.
Pastry cream has lumps	Pastry cream can be lumpy from eggs scrambling over too high a heat, or it may have lumps of flour or cornstarch that didn't dissolve during cooking. Eggs may not have been tempered before being added to hot cream mixture.	If pastry cream has thickened properly and lumps are the only concern, press it through a wire mesh strainer to make it perfectly smooth. If it's completely scrambled, pitch it and start over. Next time, whisk about one-third of hot cream mixture into eggs before returning it to the pot to finish cooking.
Baked custard (flan, pots de crème, crème brûlée) cracks or curdles	These custards contain little or no starch and thus set at a lower temperature than pastry cream. As a result, they are easily overcooked. Baked custards continue to cook for a few minutes after being removed from the oven—they are considered done when the center is just barely wobbly.	Next time, be sure to bake custards in a water bath to better insulate them and allow for even, gradual heat penetration. Remove from oven and water bath when they are just barely set.

continued |

Soufflé falls immediately when pulled from oven	Though all soufflés are ephemeral, recipes with little or no starch are especially fragile. Also, the egg whites may have been overbeaten and thus were unable to set the structure of the soufflé.	Next time, make sure soufflé base is thickened properly. Adding 2 tablespoons of additional flour will strengthen the structure. Seek out recipes that include chocolate or cheese, as these ingredients also stabilize a soufflé's structure. If soufflé didn't rise much before it fell, then be careful not to overbeat egg whites next time: The whites should be glossy and firm, not grainy and dry looking.
Quiche is watery instead of creamy and set	See "Pie Pitfalls & Tart Tribulations," p. 233.	
Mayonnaise looks separated	See "Saucy Situations," p. 247.	

—NICOLE REES, *Fine Cooking* contributor

STOVETOP STRUGGLES: PAN-SEARING, SAUTÉING, STIR-FRYING & DEEP-FRYING

THE PROBLEM	POSSIBLE CAUSES	FIX-IT TIPS FOR NOW OR NEXT TIME
Pan-seared meat sticks to pan	Pan wasn't hot enough or meat wasn't ready to be turned. Insufficient fat in pan can also cause meat to stick.	If meat isn't overly browned, continue cooking—it will release much easier once it has seared. Next time, be sure to heat pan first and check that pan is evenly coated with a small amount of fat to prevent sticking.
Pan-seared meat isn't browned	Either pan wasn't hot enough when meat went in or meat was overcrowded in pan. Overcrowding will cause temperature of pan to drop, and meat will end up steaming rather than searing.	To avoid cooking meat beyond desired doneness, brown it fast by placing it under a hot broiler. Next time, heat pan for 3 to 5 minutes before searing, and don't crowd meat in pan for maximum browning.
Herb and spice coating on meat is now stuck to bottom of pan	Some coating always sticks to the bottom of the pan, but if you lose most of it, there was too much coating on the meat or not enough fat in the pan, or the heat was too low.	If you plan to make a pan sauce, the flavor will be recovered in the end. If not, sprinkle finished meat with herbs to replace what was lost. Next time, use more fat in pan and more heat, and tap excess spices from meat before you cook it. Sear, turning only once, and finish cooking meat in a 425°F oven.

Garlic is burned before rest of sauté is done cooking	Garlic was minced too small or heat was too high. Garlic cooks lightning fast, owing to its size and softness, and will become bitter if it browns.	Though the flavor of burned garlic may have infused the sauté, you may be able to pick out the darkest, most bitter pieces. Next time, use larger pieces of garlic over a lower initial heat; turn heat up only when other foods are added to pan. The best bet, however, is to ignore the directions and add garlic later in recipe. The volume of food in the pan will act as a buffer and cook the garlic more slowly.
Sautéed onions are cooking unevenly: some are crisp, some are too brown, and some remain nearly raw	Onions have not been stirred often enough. A pan full of raw onions will collapse into less than a third of its volume when cooked—the trick is cooking so they caramelize evenly.	If some are getting too dark, pour in a little water. This will deglaze pan, coating all the onions in flavor. Cover pan and continue cooking: Onions will soften and cook through without burning.
Sautéed mushrooms aren't browned	Pan wasn't hot enough and there were too many mushrooms in pan. Mushrooms release liquid as they cook, which will change cooking method from sautéing to steaming if pan is too crowded.	Pour off excess liquid (but reserve if you are making a sauce) and cook mushrooms over medium-high heat until brown. Next time, heat pan before starting, and cook mushrooms in batches to avoid overcrowding pan.
Stir-fried vegetables are sticking to pan and burning on bottom	Pan wasn't hot enough and/or there wasn't enough oil in pan. In addition, vegetables may not have been tossed or stirred well enough to be evenly coated with oil during initial stage of cooking.	You can't repair overcooked food, but you can add a little oil to pan to help prevent remainder of vegetables from sticking. Next time, heat pan, and then swirl in oil, and then add vegetables in small batches, removing and repeating as many times as needed to prevent overcrowding. Be sure to toss vegetables often.
Stir-fried vegetables are unevenly cooked: some are crisp, others too soft	Each food was not cut into uniform-size pieces. Also, vegetables that cook quickly were cooked with vegetables that cook slowly.	You'll have to live with this one. Next time, cut vegetables into same-size pieces and begin with longer-cooking foods (onions, potatoes, broccoli), adding quicker-cooking ones later (peas, zucchini, eggplant). Hurry slow-cooking vegetables along by adding 2 to 4 tablespoons water to hot pan once they have begun to color and soften. Cover pan, letting food steam and quickly soften over high heat. Water should evaporate within a minute.
Coating falls off fried food	Coating (flour or crumbs) was too thick.	Next time, tap off excess coating before frying and let food rest for a few minutes after it has been coated. *continued*

Fried food has tiny black specks	One of ingredients in coating, such as a spice or sugar, is burning, leaving charred particles in the oil.	Unless you want to heat a pan with fresh oil, there's nothing you can do except keep a close eye on the heat to make sure burning doesn't accelerate. Once particles begin to burn, the oil degrades and may impart off flavors to finished food.
Fried food browns on outside but is undercooked in middle	Frying oil is too hot, or food was cold when immersed in pan. Pan may also have been overcrowded, especially when frying chicken.	Hold off on frying the next batch until oil has cooled down and you've checked the temperature with a frying thermometer. Fat should not be heated above 375°F—many oils will degrade quickly and smoke at higher temperatures. Before cooking next batch, let food warm up a little if it is cold.
Fried food is soggy and greasy	Either frying oil wasn't hot enough or too much food was added to pan at once, thus cooling oil. When temperature is too far below 350°F, oil will enter food faster than steam (generated by the pressure of the heat on the food's moist interior) will escape, causing food to take in too much oil.	Sorry, but there's nothing to do besides discard the greasy batch. Next time, monitor the oil's temperature with a frying thermometer. Adjust heat accordingly on stovetop to maintain correct temperature, or consider investing in a batch fryer with an automatic temperature control.
Fried potatoes (french fries) or plantains (tostones) are not crisp enough	Temperature of oil may not have been high enough, or you didn't fry the potatoes twice. Also, you may have overcrowded pan, slowing the cooking process.	Using a frying thermometer, check to make sure oil is at proper temperature. Fry in small batches to ensure quick and even cooking. The best french fries and tostones are twice fried: Fry at 300° to 325°F until vegetables just soften the first time; drain and cool briefly, and then fry at 350° to 375°F until crisp and golden.

—**NICOLE REES,** *Fine Cooking* contributor

EMERGENCY SUBSTITUTIONS

Just because you don't have an ingredient doesn't mean you can't make the recipe. Here's a list of some ingredients that come pretty close to the real deal if you want to make substitutions. Watch out for baking recipes, though; they're less forgiving than other recipes, and hasty substitutions can easily throw things out of balance.

PANTRY ITEMS	SUBSTITUTION
Allspice, ground	2 parts ground cinnamon plus 1 part ground cloves
Aniseed	Fennel seed
Apple pie spice (1 teaspoon)	¾ teaspoon ground cinnamon, ¼ teaspoon ground nutmeg, and ⅛ teaspoon ground allspice
Arrowroot	Cornstarch (as long as chilling or freezing is not involved)
Baking powder (1 teaspoon)	¼ teaspoon baking soda and ½ teaspoon cream of tartar or ¼ teaspoon baking soda and ½ cup buttermilk, yogurt, applesauce, or mashed banana
Black pepper	White pepper, allspice, or savory
Brandy (2 tablespoons)	1¼ teaspoons brandy extract
Breadcrumbs, dry	Cracker crumbs, matzoh meal, or crushed corn flakes
Capers	Chopped green olives
Cayenne (⅛ teaspoon)	3 or 4 drops hot pepper sauce
Chile paste	Red pepper flakes, cayenne, or hot pepper sauce
Chinese egg noodles	Fresh or dried angel hair, spaghetti, or thin linguine
Chocolate, bittersweet	Semisweet chocolate
Chocolate, semisweet (1 oz.)	1 oz. unsweetened chocolate and 1 tablespoon sugar
Chocolate, unsweetened (1 oz.)	3 tablespoons natural cocoa powder and 1 tablespoon melted butter
Cornstarch (1 tablespoon)	2 tablespoons flour
Corn syrup, dark (1 cup)	¾ cup light corn syrup and ¼ cup molasses
Corn syrup, light (1 cup)	1 cup sugar and ¼ cup water
Currants	Dark raisins
Dates	Dark raisins
Fish sauce, Asian (1 tablespoon)	2 teaspoons soy sauce mixed with 1 teaspoon anchovy paste
Flour, cake (1 cup)	1 cup minus 2 tablespoons all-purpose flour
Flour, self-rising (1 cup)	1 cup all-purpose flour, 1½ teaspoons baking powder, and ½ teaspoon salt
Mushrooms, dried porcini	Dried shiitake mushrooms

Mustard, dry (1 teaspoon)	1 tablespoon prepared mustard
Mustard, prepared (1 tablespoon)	1 teaspoon dry mustard mixed with 2 tablespoons wine vinegar, white wine, or water
Orange liqueur (1 tablespoon)	1 teaspoon orange extract
Pine nuts	Slivered blanched almonds
Poultry seasoning (1 teaspoon)	¾ teaspoon ground sage and ¼ teaspoon ground thyme
Pumpkin pie spice (1 teaspoon)	½ teaspoon ground cinnamon, ¼ teaspoon ground ginger, and ⅛ teaspoon each ground cloves and nutmeg
Rice vinegar, seasoned (¼ cup)	¼ cup unseasoned rice vinegar mixed with 4 teaspoons sugar and ½ teaspoon kosher salt
Rice wine	Dry sherry
Salt, table (1 teaspoon)	1¼ to 1½ teaspoons kosher salt (you need more to achieve the same saltiness because of kosher salt's larger flakes)
Shortening, vegetable (1 cup)	1 cup plus 3 tablespoons butter; if using to bake cookies, you may want to add just a bit more flour to the dough to keep the cookies from flattening out, if that's important to you
Shrimp paste	Dried salted anchovies
Sugar, brown	Light and dark can be used interchangeably; to make your own, pulse in a food processor 1 cup white granulated sugar and 3 to 4 tablespoons molasses to yield 1 cup
Sugar, palm	Maple syrup or light brown sugar
Sugar, superfine	Grind regular granulated sugar in blender or food processor
Sugar, white granulated	For every 1¼ cups sugar, you can substitute 1 cup honey plus ½ teaspoon baking soda (to counteract its acidity and added weight). For every 1 cup honey used, you need to reduce the liquid in the recipe by ¼ cup and, if you are baking, reduce the oven temperature by 25°F to prevent excessive browning.
Vanilla bean (2-inch piece)	1 teaspoon vanilla extract
Vinegar, sherry	Balsamic vinegar
Yeast, active dry (1 packet; 2¼ teaspoons)	1 packet quick-rise yeast; three-quarters of a packet instant yeast; or a 0.6-oz. cube fresh yeast

MEAT & DAIRY	SUBSTITUTION
Bacon	Smoked ham or Canadian bacon
Buttermilk (1 cup)	1 cup plain low-fat yogurt or 1 cup minus 1 tablespoons milk plus 1 tablespoon lemon juice or white vinegar
Cheese, cottage	Ricotta or farmer cheese
Cheese, goat	Feta cheese

Cheese, mascarpone	Cream cheese
Cheese, Parmigiano-Reggiano	Domestic Parmesan, Grana Padano, aged Asiago, Pecorino Romano
Cream, heavy (1 cup)	For whipping, use 1 cup whipping cream; if not for whipping, use ¾ cup milk plus ¼ cup melted butter
Crème fraîche (1 cup)	½ cup sour cream mixed with ½ cup heavy cream
Eggs (1 large egg)	2 egg whites or ¼ cup egg product
Milk (1 cup)	½ cup evaporated milk mixed with ½ cup water or 1 cup water mixed with 3 tablespoons powdered milk
Pancetta	Blanched bacon
Sour cream	Plain yogurt

FRUITS, VEGETABLES & FRESH HERBS	SUBSTITUTION
Celery	Green bell pepper or fennel bulb
Chile, Scotch bonnet	Habanero chile
Chile, serrano	Jalapeño chile
Chives	Scallion greens
Fava beans	Lima beans
Fresh herbs	1 teaspoon dried for each 1 tablespoon chopped fresh
Garlic (1 medium clove)	¼ teaspoon garlic powder
Jicama	Water chestnuts or tart apple
Leeks	Shallots
Lemongrass	An equal amount of lemon zest
Lemon juice	White wine vinegar or lime juice (though if lemon juice is called for in quantity in a particular recipe, substituting could quite significantly affect the taste of the dish)
Lemon zest, grated (1 teaspoon)	1 teaspoon lemon extract
Lime leaves (kaffir or makrut)	An equal amount of lime zest
Mango, green	Granny Smith apple
Mushrooms, cremini or baby bella	White mushrooms
Orange juice, blood (1 cup)	½ cup lemon juice mixed with ½ cup lime juice
Orange zest, grated (1 teaspoon)	1 teaspoon orange extract

Shallots	Scallions, white part only
Snow peas	Sugar snap peas
Tomatillos	Fresh green tomatoes plus a little lemon juice
Tomatoes (1 lb. fresh)	One 14-oz. can whole peeled tomatoes with juice

—Fine Cooking Test Kitchen

BAKING PAN SUBSTITUTIONS

If you don't have the exact size baking pan called for in a recipe, in most cases you can substitute a pan with the same volume capacity. Just make sure your substitute pan has sides that are of a similar height. A pan with taller or shorter sides will affect the rate of cooking and could ruin something like a cake. Also, be careful about substituting for a tube pan. If it's a delicate cake, such as angel food, the tube in the center of the pan is critical for proper cooking. To measure any pan not found on this list, fill it with water to within ¼ inch of the rim and measure the volume of water.

CAPACITY OF STANDARD PANS

SQUARE PANS		ROUND PANS	
8 by 8 by 2 inches	8 cups	8 by 2 inches	7 cups
9 by 9 by 2 inches	10 cups	9 by 2 inches	8 cups
		9 by 3 inches	12 cups
RECTANGULAR PANS		10 by 2 inches	10 cups
11 by 7 by 2 inches	8 cups		
13 by 9 by 2 inches	10 cups	SPRINGFORM PANS	
		9 by 2½ inches	10 cups
LOAF PANS		10 by 2½ inches	15 cups
8½ by 4½ by 2½ inches	6 cups		
9 by 5 by 3 inches	8 cups	TUBE PANS	
		9 by 3 inches	10 cups
		9½ by 4 inches	16 cups

—Fine Cooking Test Kitchen

MEASUREMENT EQUIVALENTS

VOLUME EQUIVALENTS

To convert liters to cups, multiply the number of liters by 4.22675 (1 liter = about 4¼ cups; 2 liters = about 8½ cups). To convert cups to liters, multiply the number of cups by 0.2368.

1 Tbs.	= 3 tsp.	= ½ fluid oz.	= 14.8 ml		
¼ cup	= 4 Tbs.	= 2 fluid oz.	= 59.2 ml		
⅓ cup	= 5 Tbs. plus 1 tsp.	= 2⅔ fluid oz.	= 78.9 ml		
½ cup	= 8 Tbs.	= 4 fluid oz.	= 118.4 ml		
1 cup	= 16 Tbs.	= 8 fluid oz.	= 236.8 ml		
1 pint	= 2 cups	= 16 fluid oz.	= 473.6 ml		
1 quart	= 2 pints	= 4 cups	= 32 fluid oz.	= 947.2 ml	
1 gallon	= 4 quarts	= 8 pints	= 16 cups	= 64 fluid oz.	= 3.79 liters

WEIGHT EQUIVALENTS

To convert grams to ounces and pounds, divide grams by 28.35 for ounces; divide grams by 453.6 for pounds. To convert ounces and pounds to grams, multiply ounces by 28.35 and pounds by 453.6.

1 lb.	= 16 oz.	= 453.6 grams
2.2 lb.	= 1 kilogram	

OVEN TEMPERATURE EQUIVALENTS

To convert from degrees Fahrenheit to degrees Celsius, subtract 32 from the Fahrenheit temperature, and then multiply by 5 and divide by 9. To convert degrees Celsius to degrees Fahrenheit, multiply the Celsius temperature by 9, divide by 5, and then add 32.

FAHRENHEIT (°F)	CELSIUS (°C, ROUNDED)	GAS MARK
225	110	¼
250	120	½
275	140	1
300	150	2
325	170	3
350	180	4
375	190	5
400	200	6
425	220	7
450	230	8
475	240	9

—Fine Cooking Test Kitchen

INGREDIENT EQUIVALENTS

A common kitchen quandary—a recipe calls for mincing a large clove of garlic and all you have are what seem like small cloves. How much garlic do you need to mince? Or maybe you're making a pie that calls for 7 cups of sliced apples. How many apples do you need to buy at the store? This chart gives you the answers so you can be all the more prepared in the kitchen—and at the supermarket.

DRY GOODS	WEIGHT	VOLUME
Beans, dried black	6½ oz.	3 cups cooked; 1 cup uncooked
Beans, dried kidney and Great Northern	6½ oz.	2¾ cups cooked; 1 cup uncooked
Breadcrumbs, fresh from about 2½ slices sandwich bread with crust	2¼ oz.	1 cup
Couscous	6½ oz.	3½ cups cooked; 1 cup uncooked
Nuts (whole shelled almonds, hazelnuts, and peanuts), 1 cup	5 to 5½ oz.	1 cup coarsely chopped; 1 cup plus 2 tablespoons finely chopped; 1¼ cups ground
Nuts (pecan and walnut halves), 1 cup	4 oz.	¾ cup plus 2 tablespoons coarsely chopped; 1 cup finely chopped; 1 cup ground
Pasta (penne), uncooked	1 lb.	8 cups cooked
Pasta (spaghetti), uncooked	1 lb.	8¾ cups cooked
Rice, arborio	7 oz.	2⅔ cups cooked; 1 cup uncooked
Rice, long-grain	6½ oz.	3 cups cooked; 1 cup uncooked
Rice, medium-grain	6¾ oz.	3 cups cooked; 1 cup uncooked

DAIRY	WEIGHT	VOLUME
Cheese, Cheddar	2 oz.	½ cup lightly packed, coarsely grated
Cheese, Parmesan	½ oz.	¼ cup lightly packed, finely grated

VEGETABLES & FRUITS	WEIGHT	VOLUME
Bell pepper, 1 medium	7 oz.	1 cup fine (⅛-inch) dice; 1⅓ cups medium (½-inch) dice; 1½ cups thin (⅛-inch) slices
Carrot, 1 medium	2½ oz.	½ cup coarsely grated; ⅓ cup small (¼-inch) dice; ½ cup ¼-inch slices
Celery, 1 medium rib	2¼ oz.	⅔ cup small (¼-inch) dice; ⅔ cup ¼-inch slices
Garlic, 1 large clove	¼ oz.	1 teaspoon paste; 1½ teaspoons minced; 1 tablespoon coarsely chopped
Leek, 1 medium	6 oz. (3 oz. white and pale green parts only)	1 cup medium (½-inch) dice; 1½ cups ¼-inch slices
Mushrooms, white	8 oz.	3 cups thin (⅛-inch) slices
Onion, 1 medium	8 oz.	1⅓ cups minced; 1⅓ cups medium (½-inch) dice; 2⅓ cups thin (⅛-inch) slices
Parsley, flat-leaf, 1 small bunch	3 oz.	½ cup lightly packed, chopped
Potato, red, 1 medium	5 oz.	1 cup medium (½-inch) dice
Potato, russet, 1 medium	12 oz.	2¼ cups medium (½-inch) dice
Shallot, 1 large	¾ oz.	3 tablespoons minced
Tomato, 1 medium	5 oz.	1 cup medium (½-inch) dice
Apple, 1 medium	7 oz.	1⅓ cups medium (½-inch) dice; 1 cup thin (⅛-inch) slices
Lemon, 1 medium	5 oz.	4 to 5 tablespoons unstrained juice; 2 tablespoons zest grated with a rasp; 1 tablespoon zest grated on a box grater
Lime, 1 medium	4 oz.	3 to 4 tablespoons unstrained juice; 4 teaspoons zest grated with a rasp; 2 teaspoons zest grated on a box grater
Orange, navel, 1 medium	10 oz.	6 to 7 tablespoons unstrained juice; 2 tablespoons zest grated with a rasp; 1 tablespoon zest grated on a box grater
Olives, Kalamata, ½ cup whole	3 oz.	Scant ½ cup pitted and coarsely chopped

—Fine Cooking Test Kitchen

CONTRIBUTORS

BRUCE AIDELLS is the author of 10 cookbooks, including *The Complete Meat Cookbook*.

PAM ANDERSON is a contributing editor to *Fine Cooking* and the author of several books, including her latest, *Perfect One-Dish Dinners: All You Need for Easy Get-Togethers*. She blogs weekly about food and life on her Web site, www.threemany-cooks.com

JENNIFER ARMENTROUT is senior food editor at *Fine Cooking*.

JOHN ASH is the founder and chef of John Ash & Co., in Santa Rosa, California. He teaches at the Culinary Institute of America at Greystone and is the author of *John Ash: Cooking One on One*, which won a James Beard Award.

DAN BARBER is the executive chef and co-owner of Blue Hill at Stone Barns in Pocantico Hills, New York, and the co-owner of Blue Hill in New York City.

JESSICA BARD is a food stylist, food writer, and recipe tester who teaches cooking classes at Warren Kitchen and Cutlery in Rhinebeck, New York.

PETER BARHAM, the author of *The Science of Cooking*, is a professor of physics at the University of Bristol, UK, and visiting professor of molecular gastronomy at the University of Copenhagen, Denmark.

JOANNE BOUKNIGHT is the author of numerous books including *All New Kitchen Idea Book*.

TISH BOYLE is a baker and cookbook author. Her latest book is *The Cake Book* and she can be found online at her blog, Tish Boyle Sweet Dreams, at www.tishboyle.blogspot.com.

FLO BRAKER is the author of numerous cookbooks; her most recent book is *Baking for All Occasions*.

TIM BUCCIARELLI is a manager at Formaggio Kitchen in Cambridge, Massachusetts.

FLOYD CARDOZ is the executive chef/partner of Tabla restaurant in New York City and author of *One Spice, Two Spice: American Food, Indian Flavors*.

JOANNE CHANG is the pastry chef and owner of Flour Bakery + Café, which has two locations in Boston and one in Cambridge, and she is the chef/co-owner of Myers + Chang in Boston.

ANDREA CHESMAN is the author of numerous cookbooks, including *Serving Up the Harvest*.

TASHA DESERIO is a cooking teacher and food writer, and the co-owner of Olive Green Catering in Berkeley, California. She is the co-author of *Cooking from the Farmer's Market*.

A former pastry chef, **ABBY DODGE** is a widely respected baking expert as well as a popular food writer and instructor. She studied in Paris at La Varenne and is the author of seven cookbooks, including *Desserts 4 Today* and *The Weekend Baker*, an IACP Cookbook Award finalist. A contributing editor to *Fine Cooking* magazine, she's a regular guest on TV and radio and teaches cooking around the country. Visit Abby's Web site, www.abbydodge.com.

MARYELLEN DRISCOLL is a *Fine Cooking* contributing editor. She and her husband own Free Bird Farm, in upstate New York.

PAULA FIGONI, author of *How Baking Works*, is a food scientist and associate professor at the College of Culinary Arts at Johnson & Wales University in Providence, Rhode Island.

ROY FINAMORE is the James Beard Award–winning author of *Tasty: Get Great Food on the Table Every Day* and co-author with Rick Moonen of *Fish Without a Doubt* and with Molly Stevens of *One Potato, Two Potato*.

TIM GAISER is one of only 105 master sommeliers in North America and the current director of education for the Court of Master Sommeliers Americas. He teaches classes at the Culinary Institute of America at Greystone.

ANNE GARDINER and **SUE WILSON** teach classes on the chemistry of cooking. Together they wrote *The Inquisitive Cook* and have contributed to many publications.

BRIAN GEIGER is a robotics project manager by day and the Food Geek at night and on weekends. He blogs at FineCooking.com and you can also find him at www.TheFoodGeek.com.

LAURA GIANNATEMPO is the author of *A Ligurian Kitchen* and former associate editor at *Fine Cooking*.

DABNEY GOUGH is a frequent contributor to FineCooking.com and a former recipe tester for the magazine.

TED GRAVENHORST, JR. is the vice president of sales and marketing at John Boos & Co., a manufacturer of premium-quality butcher block products.

LINDA J. HARRIS, Ph.D., is a faculty member at the University of California, Davis, where she is associate director at the Western Institute for Food Safety and Security and a specialist in cooperative extension in the Department of Food Science and Technology.

SHANNON HAYES is the author of *The Grass-fed Gourmet*, *The Farmer and the Grill*, and *Radical Homemakers: Reclaiming Domesticity from a Consumer Culture*. She is also the host of www.grassfedcooking.com and www.radicalhomemakers.com. Hayes works with her family on Sap Bush Hollow Farm in upstate New York.

DANIEL HOYER is the author of numerous cookbooks, including *Culinary Vietnam* and *Tamales*.

RAGHAVAN IYER is the author of three cookbooks, most recently *660 Curries*.

SARAH JAY is a former executive editor of *Fine Cooking* and the proprietor of www.paellapans.com.

ELIZABETH KARMEL is a nationally known grilling and barbecue expert and cookbook author and teacher. Her latest book, *Soaked, Slathered and Seasoned: A Complete Guide to Flavoring Food for the Grill* was published by Wiley in April 2009.

EVA KATZ has worked as a chef, caterer, teacher, recipe developer and tester, food stylist, and food writer. She is a member of the Program Advisory Committee at the Cambridge School of Culinary Arts in Massachusetts.

DENNIS KIHLSTADIUS is a technical consultant to the California Tomato Commission and the Florida Tomato Committee.

ALLISON EHRI KREITLER is a *Fine Cooking* contributing editor. She has also worked as a freelance food stylist, recipe tester, developer, and writer for several national food magazines and the Food Network.

RIS LACOSTE has been an award-winning chef for 25 years, including 10 years as the executive chef at 1789 Restaurant in Washington, D.C.

DAVID LEBOVITZ is a pastry chef, cookbook author, and blogger. His latest book is *Ready for Dessert: My Best Recipes*.

RUTH LIVELY trained at La Varenne in France, was the editor of *Cooking from the Garden*, published by The Taunton Press, and was senior editor at *Kitchen Gardener*.

LORI LONGBOTHAM is a recipe developer and cookbook author whose books include *Luscious Coconut Desserts* and *Luscious Creamy Desserts*.

ELISA MALOBERTI is the consumer information coordinator for the American Egg Board.

IVY MANNING is a cooking teacher, food writer, and cookbook author; her most recent book is *The Farm to Table Cookbook*.

KIMBERLY Y. MASIBAY is a *Fine Cooking* contributing editor.

JENNIFER MCLAGAN is a chef, food stylist, and cookbook author; her most recent book, *Fat: An Appreciation of a Misunderstood Ingredient, with Recipes*, was named the 2009 James Beard Cookbook of the Year.

ALICE MEDRICH has influenced home cooks, chefs, and chocolate makers since the 1976 opening of her renowned former dessert shop, Cocolat. Alice's most recent book, *Pure Dessert: True Flavors, Inspiring Ingredients, and Simple Recipes*, was named one of the top cookbooks of 2007 by *Gourmet*, *Bon Appetit*, and *Food & Wine* magazines and was a James Beard Award nominee.

SUSIE MIDDLETON, the former editor and current editor-at-large for *Fine Cooking* magazine, is a chef, food writer, and recipe developer. She is the author of the cookbook *Fast, Fresh & Green*, a collection of vegetable side dishes.

MELISSA PELLEGRINO is an assistant food editor at *Fine Cooking* and author of *The Italian Farmer's Table*.

NICOLE REES, author of *Baking Unplugged* and co-author of *The Baker's Manual* and *Understanding Baking*, is a food scientist and professional baker.

PETER REINHART is the author of eight books on bread baking, including his most recent, *Peter Reinhart's Artisan Breads Every Day*. He is the Chef on Assignment at Johnson & Wales University in Charlotte, North Carolina.

ADAM RIED is a cooking columnist, cookbook author, recipe developer, and tester of all things kitchen-related. His latest book, *Thoroughly Modern Milkshakes*, came out in the summer of 2009.

TONY ROSENFELD, a *Fine Cooking* contributing editor, is also a food writer and restaurant owner based in the Boston area. His second cookbook, *Sear, Sauce, and Serve*, on high-heat cooking, will be out next spring.

ERIC RUPERT is formerly executive chef at Sub-Zero and Wolf in Madison, Wisconsin.

LYNNE SAMPSON, formerly a chef at The Herbfarm restaurant near Seattle, is a food writer and cooking teacher.

SAMANTHA SENEVIRATNE is associate food editor and food stylist at *Fine Cooking*.

RENEE SHEPHERD is a longtime gardener and cook. Her packet seed company, Renee's Garden, offers gourmet varieties at garden centers nationwide, or on the Web at www.reneesgarden.com.

MARIE SIMMONS is the author of over 20 cookbooks, including the award-winning *The Good Egg*.

MARIA HELM SINSKEY is a noted chef, cookbook author, and culinary director at her family's winery, Robert Sinskey Vineyards, in Napa Valley, California, where she works closely with her husband, Rob. Her most recent cookbook, *Family Meals: Creating Traditions in the Kitchen*, was a 2010 IACP Cookbook Award Winner.

JOANNE MCALLISTER SMART has co-authored two Italian cookbooks with Scott Conant and *Bistro Cooking at Home* with Gordon Hamersley.

MOLLY STEVENS is a contributing editor to *Fine Cooking*. She won the IACP Cooking Teacher of the Year award in 2006; her book *All about Braising* won James Beard and International Association of Culinary Professionals awards.

BILL TELEPAN is chef-owner of Telepan in New York City and the author of *Inspired by Ingredients*.

ERIC TUCKER is the co-owner and executive chef at the vegetarian Millennium restaurant in San Francisco, author of *The Millennium Cookbook*, and co-author of the cookbook *The Artful Vegan*.

ROBB WALSH formerly worked as an editor of *Chile Pepper* magazine and a restaurant critic for the Houston Press. He's the author of several cookbooks, including *The Tex-Mex Cookbook* and *The Tex-Mex Grill*.

CAROLE WALTER is a master baker, baking instructor, and award-winning cookbook author whose books include *Great Cakes*, *Great Pies & Tarts*, *Great Cookies*, and *Great Coffee Cakes, Sticky Buns Muffins & More*. *Great Pies & Tarts* was recently sited by the James Beard Foundation as one of The Baker's Dozen 13 Essential Baking Books of the past 40 years.

ANNIE WAYTE is formerly the executive chef of Nicole's and 202 in New York City. Her first cookbook is *Keep It Seasonal: Soups, Salads, and Sandwiches*.

CAROLYN WEIL, a former pastry chef, is a food writer and teacher.

JAY WEINSTEIN is a New York City–based food writer and former chef. His latest book is *The Ethical Gourmet*.

JOANNE WEIR is a cooking teacher, cookbook author, and host of the public television show *Joanne Weir's Cooking Class*.

LAURA WERLIN is one of the country's foremost cheese experts, whose specialty and passion is American cheese. She is the James Beard Award–winning author of four books on the topic including *Laura Werlin's Cheese Essentials*.

ROBERT L. WOLKE, is professor emeritus of chemistry at the University of Pittsburgh and former syndicated food columnist for the *Washington Post*. He is the author of seven books, most recently *What Einstein Told His Cook 2*.

SU-MEI YU is the chef-owner of Saffron restaurant in San Diego, California. She is also an award-winning cookbook author. Her latest book is *The Elements of Life: A Contemporary Guide to Thai Recipes and Traditions for Healthier Living*. She is the founder of a cooking school in Mae Rim, Thailand, called The Organic Cooking Academy by Su-Mei Yu.

INDEX